Stroke A Slain Warrior

Stroke A Slain Warrior

Frank Michael Cortina

Columbia University Press

1970 New York and London

Copyright © 1970 Columbia University Press
ISBN: 0-231-03481-4
Library of Congress Catalog Card Number: 70-133197
Printed in the United States of America

To

Lawrence W. Pierce

First Chairman New York State Narcotic Addiction Control Commission, with profound admiration

Preface

Some time ago a friend of mine, a former heroin addict, and I were talking about the drug scene. He felt the big difference today was the tremendous national preoccupation with drugs. I thought that this was a good thing. He wasn't so sure. He wondered if such enormous exposure didn't affect the public adversely. It seemed to him that the public was repulsed and frightened rather than involved and concerned. For all the publicity, what do we really know about the drug abuser? "Cortina," he said, "you've been talking with drug takers for years. Why don't you get out some of these interviews? Give the public a chance to know the kinds of people who are drug abusers."

Stroke A Slain Warrior *is the response to my friend's demand.*

St. Croix, The Virgin Islands

Contents

Stroke A Slain Warrior

1 *To make things other than they are—through some kind of magic—that is the way of the drug addict. To wave a wand and efface the broken home, the nagging restlessness, the alienation, the neglect, omission and deprivation; to wave a wand and efface the terrible sense of personal incompleteness. Drug addicts refer to themselves as "lames." The Pusher was a "lame."*

The Pusher

You couldn't miss the tattoo marks on his arms. "You're pretty heavily decorated. Do the tattoos hide something on your arms? Or do you want people to notice your arms? Or is it that you just like that kind of decoration?

John looked at his arms and said: "I don't know. Most of them I had put on when I was real young. Seventeen or eighteen I guess. When I was young . . . like my friends."

"Like your friends. You mean a sort of badge of kinship . . . status symbol?"

"Yeah, you know, to be accepted in the crowd."

"John, ever think what might have happened if you hadn't had the tattoos on your arms, if you hadn't been accepted by the crowd?"

"I don't think it made any difference." He smiled. "Well, now I don't think it made any difference. At that time, though, I guess I had to be one of the guys and I figured this was the way to do it."

"This crowd, what was there about it that you found so attractive?"

"The guys were pretty rowdy, always on the move, always something going." John looked at his arms again. "These showed something. Something I suppose like braveness or strength to take pain. They hurt. Sort of like manhood, to have them put on. . . ."

"Almost like an initiation ceremony."

"That's about it."

"How old are you, John?"

"Thirty-four."

"And where do you come from?"

"West Coast." He laughed as he said: "You know, the land of sun 'n surf."

"How much sun and surf did you have?"

"Over the years? Not a helluva lot. I was in and out of the joint too many times."

"What were you busted for?"

John had a characteristic little laugh that made the upper part of his body move up and down. "For everything, everything, but mostly stuff. This time I got arrested in L. A. for a sale."

"You were pushing?"

"Yeah. Heroin. I sold to an agent."

"Narcotic agent? Were you set up . . .?"

"Hell, no. I shoulda smelled him. They're getting very clever. Yeah, they're pretty cute nowadays. They gave me five years without possibility of parole."

"Five years in a rehabilitation program or in a regular prison?"

"In prison, the joint. . . ."

"So actually it was just keeping you off the streets for five years."

John gave that shrugging laugh again. "That's it."

"You know, John, there's a fairly widespread belief that if we could arrest every pusher in the U.S. and put him away for a long time we'd somehow be taking care of the problem of drug use and addiction. Do you agree with that?"

"I don't think so. I don't know, it's like the old saying about the police. You knock one down and ten more sprout up. See, the way I look at sales . . . you know, drug sales, I mean . . . it's like nine out of ten times it's an addict trying to provide for his habit. That's the way it was with me. And that's the way it is with every other guy I talk to, you know. Like they started out just using stuff and then after the habit gets so expensive that they can't afford it by working or stealing or hustling or borrowing money . . . then they got to do something where they can make the money they got to have for their stuff. Usually you start selling a piece for somebody else. You know, you act like a salesman for a dealer. Then maybe you buy a piece for yourself and you're in business. You can make big money . . . the kind you got to have."

"Are the profits so enormous selling heroin, John?"

John looked at me to see if I was serious. "There wasn't a day where I didn't see my money triple or quadruple. Look, if you don't use and you sell, you can make five or six hundred a day, or more even . . . you can make a bundle, I'm telling you."

"But that's the hooker, isn't it, just what you said, 'If you don't use?' "

"Man, that's it. That's the real hooker. Because when you're using yourself you have to associate with people who you got to turn on. . . . Like every time you turn somebody on that's ten bucks in your pocket, and like every time you stick a needle in your own arm that's ten bucks gone. But in the circles it's nothing for one of your partners to come over to you and say: 'You gotta straighten me. You know, I ain't got no bread right now.' So I say: 'Sure, here.' So I give him a gram. That's twenty dollars. But I don't look at it like twenty dollars. I look at it . . . he's a friend . . . while I'm trying. . . ." John shook his head. "I don't even look at it that way. I just look at it like I might be out of stuff pretty soon. It happens, it happens more times. . . ."

"So what you're saying is it's a purely selfish consideration, you're buying a future favor."

"That's all. If I can straighten him out now, I might be able to get straightened myself later."

"Isn't it a fact, John, that the addicted pusher sometimes gets greedy? I mean when he has a large supply, he begins to shoot like mad?"

"Well, you get more relaxed with it, that's for sure. If you just got a little stuff, it's different, then you're always with your hand on your throat. Cause when you're on the stuff you're not a banker. You hear a lot of talk about I'll save a cap for the morning. That's malarky. If you got it you shoot it. You can always remember one thing . . . when you use, you know you're gonna be sick if you can't shoot. And you sometimes will think you're feeling sick just to use. To hell with the morning and everything else. You fix for right now . . . you live for the moment."

"Yes, I've heard many users say how they dreaded the next morning without stuff."

John lighted a cigarette. "That's the worst part of it. Waking up . . . waking up if you haven't got anything."

"What was your habit costing you a day, John?"

"Oh, I was on for two years straight, you know, just one run. It was costing me about one hundred and seventy dollars a day."

"And you were pushing in order to get that one hundred and seventy a day?"

"At the end I was."

"What were you doing before that? Let's face it, you didn't have any kind of a job that was going to give you a hundred and seventy dollars a day clear."

"I started out working. I was a mechanic and I was making pretty good money and I was engaged to get married." John dusted off the cigarette ash. "I had it made . . . I did. I was using drugs, other drugs, not heroin."

"What other drugs were you using, John?"

"I was using marijuana and LSD and peyote. Stuff like that."

"Peyote?"

"Well, I'm an artist and a poet so I tried to dabble . . . I liked it. You know, it kind of gave me an extra drive or something. Like seeing things differently, you know."

"Did you see things differently? I mean, now as you look back on these experiences, did these drugs deepen your perception?"

"Well . . ." John sighed. "I think what I was seeing was just hallucinations. It wasn't real. But then when I'd write something, it appeared to mean like it was really something way out, you know."

"You mean like the drunk walking the straight line?"

John laughed. "Yeah . . . he thinks he's doing it. Like these walls, or the trees, or the way the high buildings go straight up. They hit you, like you take them in for the first time. They're there you think." He shook his head, obviously considering what he said. "I been off everything for a year now. The walls, the trees, them high buildings, they're there. They were always there. Same things . . . more real now if I look at it. Really more real now, you know. . . ."

"John, you've mentioned being a pusher, a mechanic, a drug user . . . you said you were engaged. All of this you've been looking back on. Let's talk a little bit about the young John. What was he like, what kind of a background did he come from? Was your life very different from most kids?"

"I don't know. I think it was probably, from some kids . . . though I imagine there were quite a few kids like me involved in doing the things I was. First of all my father was in the service. And when I was four or five, because of a divorce, my brother and I were by ourselves. So we ended up in a boys' home. And we stayed there seven or eight years. When I come out of there I was fifteen. You see, my father in order to get us out . . . you see, it was one of those situations . . . he was concerned, maybe even he felt guilty about us being away so long. In any case, he had to have a home to get us released. So it seems as if he'd marry anybody just to get us out. He married a woman who was eighteen years younger than he was. They

were fighting and arguing all the time. She was running around.
We moved into southern California with beaches, and like at that
time it was dope and beatniks and prostitutes and everything.
Up and down them beaches was really, you know . . . out of
hand. I was fifteen and I was just turned loose right there."

"Did you live it up?"

"Yeah, well, you know, my father had to work and my stepmother, she was running around with every guy that walked by
the door, so you know, in general me and my brother just went
our way. We was down on the beach stealing stuff for something
to do."

"Did your brother go to stuff, too?"

"Yeah. Followed right along in my footsteps. He was two
years younger than me."

"He went to heroin, too?"

"Same as me . . . same thing."

"How did it start, John? Did somebody come up to you and
begin singing the praises of marijuana or acid . . . and urge you
to try it?"

"No, I'd seen it happening all around me, you know. People
were using weed and pills, and I was in the same crowd. I was
drinking wine, then pot, and you know. And then one day I was
at a party where everybody was going into the bathroom and
coming out and sitting down, nodding, you know. Well, then I
thought, boy, those guys are really feeling good. Really feeling
good, they're just loose, loose, feeling good. . . ."

"They were shooting in the bathroom? Heroin?"

"Uh huh. So I walked into the bathroom and when I seen
what they were doing, you know, the works and all, I got
scared right away because, you know, the needles and everything, they're frightening anyway. So I stood there looking, and
the girl who was dealing out the fixes told me, 'Come on,' you
know. I said, 'No.' I told her 'no.' "

"She was going to give you your wings, huh?"

"No, see, she thought I was a regular, like. I was in the

bathroom and she figured I was a junkie, too. She was real nice about it. She told me to go back into the other room. But I said 'no' that first time. When I got back into the other room, people were all sitting around smoking weed. It was just like a natural thing that I was there. Everybody was together, you know what I mean, together. . . . So when a guy came over and offered me a joint, I just took it. I guess I wanted to . . . I didn't want to seem different. I didn't want to be the one that was there without using, you know, so that they'd say: 'Well, he sat during the whole party and didn't even get loaded with it . . . free, too.' "

"That group meant a great deal to you, didn't it?"

"Yeah, it was kind of like my father and mother and brothers and sisters." John laughed. "Like all of them put together, and it was cold outside. Yeah . . . like it was cold outside. . . ."

"Let me ask you, was your brother with you on this occasion?"

"Well, no it was . . . kinda hard to explain. He was in the same group but he was with . . . you know, I was sixteen and he was fourteen, and at that age two years is like ten now. You know, he'd always want to be with me, tag along. I'd tell him: 'Split.' 'You're little.' 'You cramp my style.' " John laughed at the memory. "I'd tell him he was in my way, that I couldn't rap with broads with him hanging on my heels. You know, me, Big John, acting like all of twenty."

"So you smoked your first reefer during that party. What kind of reaction did you have?"

"The reefer burned my throat and I got dizzy. It was just like my first cigarette smoke, you know."

"Did you pretend that it was doing something for you?"

"You mean to impress my bunch? Not right then because we cleared out right after that and went down to a place we used near the beach. We sat up that whole night smoking and rapping. I don't know if the weed made me feel dizzy or I was just trying to go along with everybody else . . . but that was the first time, remember. After that I sailed, sailed."

"Did you ever deal in pot?"

"That's funny. . . . One time I got lucky. A guy asked me if I wanted to move some . . . you know, weed, for him because I was . . . see, this is part of that acceptance, you know, like the guys that do have a lot of dope, well, they'll shop around for a guy that's real popular in a crowd, that everybody trusts. And I'd been arrested with this crowd, you know, on suspicion. The cops'd see us up all night or out on the road driving around or rapping at five in the morning, so they'd roust us and then I'd live up to the code. I was real belligerent with the cops. You know, when they'd ask for my name, I'd give 'em a real crust. Sometimes they'd slap me around on account of the lip I'd given. But I didn't say anything. So that's how come I got accepted like a real solid citizen. I could be trusted. It wasn't long before I was approached by this older guy. He said something like he didn't want to get out on the block and get popped. 'Why don't you take these five keys and get rid of them for me and I'll cut you a nice piece of bread.' "

"Do keys mean kilos, John?"

"Right."

"Did you know anything about the quality of the marijuana you were selling?"

"No. Only thing I know was what the connection said."

"Maybe you weren't conscious that weed can be adulterated. . . ."

"I heard. I found out after I started." John gave that shrugging laugh. "I was doing it myself after a while. See, later, I picked up a lot of solid know-how about weed. You know, like it depends on where it comes from, how it's cured, things like that. This stuff I was moving come from Mexico and it was pretty good stuff."

"Did you have any difficulty getting rid of it?"

"I could have sold fifty times more than I was selling if I'd had it. I run into a kid . . . surprisingly he was a rich kid . . . had a rich family. I don't know what his father did or too much about the family, but they had a fancy house at the Springs . . . beautiful sport car . . . one of those foreign ones. He became my regular connection. After tying up with him, I never used another guy. He'd bring the weed in army duffle bags. Sometimes twenty or thirty kilos. He asked me if I could move it all. I told him I had no problem. He told me he could get me all I could sell. Just to let him know when my supply was getting low. So the first couple of weeks everybody was just finding out that I had weed, but once the word got around I could sell twenty-five kilos every three days."

"A kilo is just a little over two pounds, isn't it, John?"

"Two point two pounds."

"What did you pay for a kilo?"

"Forty-five dollars a key. . . ."

"And you'd sell it for . . .?"

"Whatever you wanted to, really. That was your hook. I had a kind of system. If you bought by the pound, I'd charge sixty-five dollars."

"So you were clearing . . .?"

I tried to do the mental arithmetic, but John grinned and said: "Let me do it, it's easier, it was my business. I was clearing a hundred and five dollars on a kilo. See, I'd sell it in cans. A can is a one-ounce package. That'd go for ten dollars. There was money in it . . . no two ways about that. . . ."

"This rich kid who was your supplier . . . was he a middleman? You know what I mean . . . was he getting . . .?"

John interrupted. "No, he was direct. This bird had a plane. He'd make the trips to Mexico himself and fly it back. He was rich, this kid." He enjoyed emphasizing this point about the boy's wealth; it seemed to delight him. "He really was a bird. He was a rich kid!"

"With that kind of mark-up you could have gotten rich, too. . . ."

"Nah, I was always a slob . . . no businessman. I couldn't hold onto it. Now, this rich kid, he smoked weed, that's all. . . ."

"Incidentally, before I forget, did this rich kid distribute any other drugs?"

"He moved everything but junk. That he didn't have. Acid, pills, peyote, bush, but no heroin. That's a different league. . . ."

"Before I interrupted you, you were saying that this rich kid just used weed, implying that you didn't content yourself with that."

"I went full circle, I sold everything he had and I used it all myself. Pills, acid, the works."

"But not heroin."

"Not right away, but it was just a matter of time. Remember that bathroom bit when I was sixteen? That's kind of like a symbol . . . you can't get around any kind of stuff without running into all the other stuff. I sold everything that ever was put out and then when I got hooked I sold everything, I mean everything. Guns, hot cars, I was boosting . . . I did everything but push broads, and the only reason I didn't do that was because I had no chance. Once I got hooked I lost the business and I had to get reckless. I had to have stuff. I had to have money. Then they check you real close, they don't trust you . . . your connection'll give you some string but you gotta come up with the dough or you got a dried-up connection."

"How many times were you busted in these years?"

John laughed and shook his head. "Whew . . . quite a few times. I can't even hardly remember. At least twenty times on various charges, at least that. . . ."

"How many years have you spent, all told, in the joint?"

There was a deep sigh. "Jesus. . . ." He began to count the various imprisonments. "Over all about eighteen years. Yeah, give or take a year."

"That's a lot of time. . . . You might say time was your one great luxury . . . did you ever think about John and what had happened to him?"

John laughed. "Time a luxury . . . that's different. But it's so. You think back, it surprises you, the way the pieces fall together." He looked at me slyly. "How you make them fit together the way you want. . . ."

"Did you ever ask yourself the sixty-four-thousand-dollar question—why you used drugs?"

"Yeah. Not only me but every joker who meets me asks the same question. It used to bother me. Because I could ask you why you smoke that cigarette, why you have a drink, why you chase a broad . . . but then I'd be copping out. I don't know why. I could say curiosity, but that wouldn't hold water after the second or third time I used. I don't know why I went to stuff, though I think and think about it. Sometimes I think the crowd I was with. . . ."

"But there were other crowds you could have been with."

"Yeah, that's so."

"There must have been something special about the crowd you gravitated to . . . something that attracted you."

"It was what they were doing. The drugs, the boosting, the parties, gangster-type people . . . it was exciting."

"But what was there about John that he needed this kind of excitement?"

John stared at me. "I felt at home with those people. I could bring up all kinds of things, you know, about the boys' home and my father and my brother . . . but I don't know . . . and I'm not copping out that way."

"I don't think it takes too much imagination to understand where your early years might have made you feel uncomfortable with youngsters whose home life had been more stable."

He looked at me sadly. "A few years ago I would have jumped at that bone and told you a beautiful story, but it's a cop-out. I don't know why. I don't know why. Sure, I was uncomfortable in school, at home, but I'm not sure I wouldn't have been the same way even if home had been different. I'm being honest with myself now. You see, when you've used junk you got to work to be honest with yourself . . . with yourself. On account of it's so easy to spin off. That's all you ever do is spin off on yourself and everybody else. I don't know why I went to junk." John appeared to be talking to himself more than to me. "And that's got to be a beginning, for me. I been rounding for years. Every junkie does. In some of these drug programs now they have group sessions. You know what they are for . . . to make the hype stop lying, stop rounding . . . pulling covers. . . . You know, to kick the lie back in a guy's teeth every time he brings it out . . . so I don't know."

"I would think, though, that questions from different angles would be essential, John, in this kind of self-examination. Perhaps not so much to discover a precise reason for the use of drugs but to uncover aspects of your life, revealing failures, real or imagined, that prodded you, made you keep running . . . or am I way off base?"

John looked at his tattoos. "What you just said . . . that's money. Why did I always have to be excited . . . to keep on the move? I do a lot of reading now . . . I'm working on that. Running is restlessness, restlessness is insecurity, insecurity, inside pain . . . and on and on . . . what you said is money." John seemed pleased with his own eloquence.

"John, let me go back for a moment to your drug-using days. . . ."

He interrupted me and smiled. "Thanks for the delicacy."

"I meant that. Of all the substances you used, which one did you enjoy most?"

"Peyote. I felt that everything was brighter. I read up on it. It was used by certain Indian tribes in their rituals. Yeah, peyote . . . but for me I wasn't satisfied . . . I went on to junk."

"What was the worst?"

"Cocaine. Jesus."

"Did you mix it?"

"No, I shot it straight. One time I robbed a drugstore and got ten 30-CC bottles. I shot so much of it my system had a chemical reaction to it. You know, my face shriveled up . . . I had such a tremendous load. My face went all contorted and scared half the people in the house to death. When they seen me come out of the bathroom my face was all pinched up and everything. Boy, it panicked me." John laughed wryly. "I didn't use it for almost two months after that. But I went back to it because speed is like another world. See, I even catch myself now. I'm thinking of the words I use. Another world. See that? I was running. . . ."

"You probably were pretty much alone even though you were in a crowd. Using drugs, at least certain drugs, kind of completely insulates you from others."

"True. Now that I look back at it and talk to other guys who've used I realize that the word 'friend' has no real meaning for a junkie. It can't have because everything's got to give way before you'll let yourself get sick. So a friend is somebody you work on, and you know you'll be worked on when your turn comes. You're a touch. If I got to be straightened I'll do anything. . . . Trust don't exist . . . real trust. Say you and I are addicts and you know where I've got some stuff hidden and you get busted. Well, I trust you that I know you're not going to say anything about my stuff to the cops. I know this . . . that other world is not going to get to you. But . . . and this is it . . . I trust you that way. But if you were going to leave that room, I'd pick up my stuff from where it was hidden and take it out of there because I wouldn't trust you knowing where I'd stashed it. I'd know that you'd have to come back to try and beat me out of it. See what I mean? Trust, no trust . . . that's the hype."

"Does it ever strike you as curious that the addict, who is so terribly adept at sizing up people, who is so adept at manipulating them and playing on their weakness, is almost totally naive about himself?"

John lighted a cigarette. "I can tell with a person after the first couple words he says if I can trust him or not. I can tell how sure they are of themselves, how they'd like, handle themselves in a situation."

"This is exactly what I mean, John. But you're never at the same time wondering how you're striking the person that you're sizing up. . . ."

John leaned forward and smiled. "But I am . . . because I'm flying something by him. You see, I'm putting something on. I'm a poor poet . . . or maybe I've just gotten into town and I've been robbed by a drug fiend." John laughed. "See?"

"But still, you manage to keep yourself separated from anybody else. What I'm trying to say is that the real you is never allowed to slip out. It is as if you were an actor, always presenting a specific role . . . even to yourself. In other words, all you're doing is deepening this naivete about yourself, the very thing that contributes toward the covers you mentioned before."

John shook his head. "Right, right, I get you now. That's so. What you're saying is every time I con, I con myself, too." He nodded his head emphatically. "I believe that. That's so."

"You become a totally hidden person, hidden even from yourself, John."

"Well, you know, you develop this, it's like an instinct. You got to hustle to get your stuff. You got to learn to beat people out of things, you got to learn to breeze the cop . . . you learn these things, it's like survival. . . ."

"All the times you were arrested, the times you were in prison, did it ever do anything in the way of making you wonder what you were doing to yourself, your life?"

"You know, for quite some time I didn't have a habit. I was chippying. That means I was dabbling. Or I was snorting the stuff. Then I'd lay off for four or five days. Meet somebody who had a bag. You know, I was dibbing and dabbing. I didn't have a habit. Then I got picked up for a joint and thrown in the county jail. I was seventeen. And there was hypes all over that place. They talked junk morning, noon, and night. Man, I had an appetite for stuff like I never believed I could. I ate it, slept it, dreamt it. Broads, you could have them . . . me, I wanted that bag. . . . I got a suspended sentence. Five years probation.

Soon as I got out I found me a connection and I copped. I was hooked inside of a month after I got out. That threw my probation out the window and I went up for thirty-eight months. Yeah, prison's no answer . . . prison's no answer. Don't get me wrong, I'm not going to cop out on that or anything else with you. I don't know what the answer is, but prison ain't. The answer has got to come somewhere like . . . why people smoke, why they drink, why they chase broads, why they got to cop out . . . you know, why do people cop out?"

2 *Meeting "simple" people in this sophisticated age sometimes leaves one with a sense of incredulity. This was my experience when I first began meeting drug users like Pablo. I found myself very skeptical, distrusting their responses. Now, after countless interviews with other Pablos, I realize my lack of perception, my failure to understand the tremendous importance of those small attentions—a smile, a nod, a touch—that the human being must have in order to cope with life. Not long ago, I talked with a drug user on the Texas border. He told me: "My father he is no good man. He is a very bad man. He go to stay in my sister's bedroom. He is a very bad man. But he is my father, and for that I have respect." It was Pablo all over again.*

The Epileptic

From the summerhouse on the hospital grounds our eyes followed the four-engine jet as it tore across the sky, leaving behind wispy trails. Pablo turned toward me. "There is no doubt we are living in frustration and anger. The cities, Vietnam. No doubt about all the trouble. Like myself I was in the service and to tell you the truth I would give everything to be back in the service."

"I have spoken to some young men who have tracked up their arms in order to stay out of the service. . . ."

"I have heard of that, too, sir. But I really don't actually know the reason we are fighting in Asia and I don't know why we have most of the problems we have here in the States but, I really think I would have accomplished something if I would have been in the service."

16

"Why didn't you remain?"

"A physical problem, a big block in my life, since I am myself an epileptic. And I have had epilepsy since the age of fourteen. And maybe you can see more or less why I started using drugs under those conditions and under which I wanted to accomplish a lot of things, one of them which I just told you, to be in the service." There was something very courtly and musical about Pablo's speech. "I had many jobs before the service and I haven't been able to keep them so, you might say, like many other people, I just took the easy way out."

"How old are you, Pablo?"

"Twenty-two, sir."

"And you were mustered out because of epilepsy? I don't understand how they accepted you in the first place."

Pablo wore a grave expression and sat very quietly considering his answer. "Well, I wanted to be in the service very much. Right there that explains much. I didn't tell them."

"How long were you in the army before your condition became known?"

"Six months. Even then I tried anything to keep it away from them, anything to keep them from knowing because I had already passed all of my training. I was just waiting for my orders to go to Hawaii and from there to Vietnam."

"Would you say it was inevitable that they find out, Pablo?"

He was looking at the grass. "Yes, sir. An attack you can't hide. You can't fool the doctors. A lot of people have told me that I was crazy or something for wanting to stay in there. They congratulate me for getting discharged. I don't know actually why I wanted to stay in the service but I just wanted to stay."

"There was a kind of desperation about it, do you think?"

"That is true, sir. I have been wondering how to put it myself. Desperation. You see, I had already smoked marijuana ever since I was in junior high school and well, everybody in my neighborhood up until the present, everybody that I know have used or is using heroin. Was just like my brother-in-law and my sister whom I was living with; my brother-in-law has sold heroin for a number of years. Every day I would just be sitting there with a bottle of beer or with a cigarette or marijuana and I would just see guys come in and go out and everybody would tell me the same thing: 'Well, Pablo, do you want a few drops of it? Do you want some of it?' And I would tell them 'no,' until one day I just said to myself: 'What's the use, I've tried everything else, go ahead, use your health problem as an excuse.' I just turned to my brother-in-law and I told him: 'José, will you give me a few drops of heroin?' He just looked at me for a few seconds and he just told me: 'Pablo, do you really know what you are getting into?' I told him, 'Well, you are using it.' He say, 'Yes, but look at my way of living now.' I say to him: 'Let me have it.' And I tell you, sir, from there on it started."

"How old were you at that time?"

"Well, that was four years ago. I was eighteen."

"And this happened after you came out of the army?"

"Yes, sir. In fact, it was actually three months after I was out of the service."

"Had you been doing anything in those three months since you'd come out of the army?"

"Just odd jobs here and there."

"Was that because you couldn't find a steady job?"

"Tell you true, sir. It was because I had that thing on my mind and I could not shake it off. I wanted to be in the service. You see, I went back to Selective Service and explained again. They tell me even though I was in the army I am only eighteen and I didn't have a job before I went into the service, so that the best they can do to help me was to get me put in the Job Corps and well, I tried it. In fact I was in the Job Corps Camp in New Mexico. I stayed there for only one month and a half and I said to myself: 'What's the use of it?' and I got out."

"Was it so unsatisfactory?"

"As far as work training and things like that are concerned

I wasn't actually learning a thing because, you might say, it was not a training center. It was just something like a halfway house or something."

"Halfway house?"

"Yes, sir, because in that camp are young people that haven't graduated from high school. They have to be there for a time so that they are prepared to be sent to a vocational center. You see, sir, so that they are able to do the work at the vocational camp. . . ."

"You had graduated from high school and felt you didn't need this elementary orientation, is that it?"

"Oh, no, sir, I had just gone as far as the tenth grade and stopped. But you see, sir, I had been in the army for six months and got my equivalency diploma. I was prepared to go right ahead. I could not make them understand. They said I had to. . . . What was the use? I wanted actually, sir, you see, to go back to the service. Ever since I turned the age of seventeen I tried to get into any kind of armed forces: navy, marines, army, anything. . . ."

"Have you ever been curious about this intense desire you had to get into the armed services, Pablo?"

"Yes, sir, I have wondered about that. I think it is important to wonder about it. . . . You know?"

I offered him a smoke. "Did the army seem glamorous? Was it the regularity of the life?"

Pablo let the smoke trickle from his nose. "Well, the main thing that I have thought was just getting away from my home and going out there and finding my own world."

"Actually you would have been interested in anything that would have allowed you to get away from home and be on your own?"

"Yes, sir, that is so. But at that time I did not see it so, you understand. . . ."

"Was home such a terrible place?"

"Well, it was and it wasn't. My mother died when I was at

the age of one year and seven months old, and from there on my father had to look after my two sisters and myself. He didn't get married again until I was around the age of eleven years old so by that time I had already, you might say, learned everything I had to know: cooking, washing, housekeeping, working outside of the home. I can remember when I was selling fruit on the street, shining shoes downtown, and washing dishes in restaurants. Everything, so you may say, as far as working was concerned, I knew about. I could have found a job right there in my hometown, but I just wanted to get away from that kind of living and maybe on the other side of the hill maybe find a brighter light or a better opportunity."

"You weren't discouraged by your experiences?"

"Well, sir, I always wanted something for Pablo."

"What about you and your father? Did he ever seem concerned about your having to work so hard at your age?"

"Well, sir, as far as my father is concerned, like I just said a minute ago, there were three in my family, my two sisters and myself, the youngest one, and ever since I can remember all three of us went one way and my father he went another."

"Not too much going among you? Was that because he was too busy trying to provide for his family or outside interests?"

Pablo was a handsome young man, quietly but very carefully groomed, and there was something aristocratic about his gravity. He nodded his head. "You might say he had interests outside of the home more than just providing for the family, because even though he worked all his life I began to understand that he had actually turned into an alcoholic. Every day and night, even though he continued to work he drank, and every weekend . . ." Pablo's voice dropped suddenly, "different women would come into our home. So, you know, I would just get myself out of the house and find some place where I could be away."

"Your father must have had problems, too?"

"Certainly, sir. Everybody's got problems. . . ."

"In this case, it meant that Pablo and his sisters were neglected children. Was it around this time that you became aware of your epilepsy?"

"It was later, sir . . . I had a seizure at fourteen."

"Did your father know that you had this seizure?"

"The first thing that comes out of his mouth: 'Well, you are suffering from the same thing that your mother died from and that your two older sisters died from. More than likely you are developing a nervous problem. . . .' "

In the silence a single-engine plane droned overhead. "And that's the way he left it? Frightening the life out of you, he just washed his hands of it?"

"It is true, sir. I was I tell you scared. It was the first time I heard of my mother's death, the cause, you know, and of the other two sisters who had died long before I was born. I was scared. I remember sitting on the side of an arroyo wondering what to do. Then I turned to the one person who would tell me, my godmother. Even today when I go to see her, I don't call her godmother, I call her mother. In that house it was a different kind of family life. The children, the husband. Different. So I turned to her and they took me to a hospital. I got medicine and checkups. I still use the same medicine. But in those days I am a teen-ager, and you know more or less how a teen-ager reacts to taking medicine . . . so I wouldn't always take it. When I would get back in my neighborhood I would just go and buy marijuana."

"Did marijuana have any effect upon the epilepsy, do you think?"

"When I would smoke two or three sticks, whatever it was, I would feel fine and everything but the next day I would wake up feeling very nervous. Then I would get scared, thinking about another attack. On this one time, I went out and got something to drink. And so in this manner I began to drink. And I have drank everything from beer to wine to whiskey. I would keep a job just to buy my drink and my joints."

"You were becoming like your father, copping out the way he copped out? Did that ever cross your mind at that time?"

"No, sir. I was only fifteen at this time, you understand. But I had learned about the short-cut drink."

"Didn't your father say anything to you?"

"Never. He had a new family coming on. And his wife, my stepmother, she took me like he took me, to work around the house. A funny thing, sir. I leave that house five or six times, one time for almost two months I stay away, but I always go back. And when I go back all the old jobs come back, watching my new brothers and sisters, cleaning up. . . ."

"Where would you run away to on those occasions?"

"Once to my godmother, once to my brother-in-law and sister, once to my other sister, and two times I try to live on my own but I got scared by the questions people would ask about me. I did not want to be in trouble with the police!"

"Is it possible that you really didn't want to get away from your father?"

"Oh, I wanted to get away from him."

"How far away did you go actually?"

Pablo hesitated and frowned. "I have never think about that. . . ." He thought back. "I never left the neighborhood. . . ."

"Why? You ran away but you really didn't run away. Were you, perhaps, hoping that your father would find you?"

"Oh, no sir. . . ."

"Then why didn't you really cut out?"

"That is funny thing you say . . . I must think about it."

"You talked of your godmother. Did you ever discuss your father and your situation with her?"

"In a manner of speaking, but to tell you the truth, sir, it was not something I like to talk about, and another thing, I feel I am alone. And I am alone so much that I have no wish to talk to people. There were some kids I hang around with. . . ."

"Schoolmates . . . ?"

"Some, but by now they all drop out of school. These kids

I know all of my life. We had been in church together. You know. . . ."

"Were they on marijuana?"

"Oh, yes. . . ."

"Did you know any kids who didn't use marijuana in your area?"

"Who did not? I have to think . . . perhaps a few, but I do not know them so good . . . most of the kids, we smoke weed. See, the kids I know and hang out with, they have trouble at home, too, sir." He extended his arms, revealing tattoos on them. "There were nine of us and we had these put on. Kid stuff. But we had a gang, we belonged together."

"This was a fighting gang?"

"Well, I don't like to fight. We mess around a little. See, sir, my neighborhood it is on the other side of the tracks, so you might say. There are always gangs of kids and there is always marijuana . . . you see, sir, marijuana it is not special in my neighborhood. It is all through it. It is near the border and until I come to the hospital I never consider it a drug really. That is true."

"But you would always return home sooner or later after these runaways?"

"Yes, and I do the work around the house and work in the neighborhood and give my money to my father, but I am drinking, like I say, and smoking weed."

"What about heroin and pills?"

"No, sir. Like I tell you, I don't use heroin until long after . . . when I come out of the army and I am living with my brother-in-law and sister. Pills they are not used much, very little where I come from. . . ."

"This gang, were any members using heroin . . . or anything else beside weed?"

"At that time, no, sir. . . ."

"How come, with your ambition to find opportunity for yourself, you dropped out of school?"

"Well, these kids, they are out of school, and weed make it very hard for me to keep up with the work and I say to myself: 'What's the use? I have epilepsy. I am going to die. What's the use?' "

"Did you ever tell your friends about your affliction?"

"No, but I don't need to, they know . . . they have seen me in a fit. . . ."

"Did you return to the hospital for help?"

"Oh, not regularly. These years between fourteen and seventeen they are like years in a dream, I tell you, sir. Pablo, he stopped going to church. I am a religious man, if you can believe that, sir. I stopped going to church, I stopped school, I think I stopped living, really . . . I have a stick of weed and drink. . . ."

"Did you still do the chores at home?"

"That is the one thing I still do . . . I hate it. They are using me but I still do it. They depend on my work. . . . But I tell you truly, I am in a bad way. I got no pride left, I don't see no future, at that time I have died. Then, when I am about sixteen and a half, I suddenly think: 'Pablo, six months and you will be seventeen.' Believe me, sir, that is like a miracle. Like a shade pulled up on a window. My old feeling about the service comes back. Now I can't wait for my birthday. My friends they don't believe I am going into the army. I get scared about my condition . . . they won't take me . . . but in my neighborhood those kids get taken without many questions. But I am scared at the medical, but they take me . . . they take. Now would you believe, sir . . . I am a good soldier. Would you believe, sir, that I change? No more marijuana or drink. Would you believe, sir, I got my high school equivalency diploma in five months in the army? Would you believe that of me, sir? The service did that to Pablo. . . . And then the crash. Boom!"

"Did you go home while you were in the service?"

"No, sir, but I send them money. I once got a letter from

my sister, the one who is married to the heroin seller. She told me that my father had just gotten another son . . . there were now six new children in that second family . . . no, I did not go home. I looked on the army as my home."

"And after the crash you went to live with that brother-in-law and sister?"

"It was worse then than before. . . . After that first fix it was all over, I tell you. I had found the answer to all my problems. Heroin."

"How did you pay for your stuff?"

"I worked. . . ."

"Can you work when you're on heroin?"

"Oh, yes, sir. I always work, but you see I have special break . . . my brother-in-law is selling. But that bunch of kids I had been with before . . . nine of them . . . three of them are dead from robberies, four of them are in the penitentiary, and two are pushers. For four straight years I am on the stuff. No, excuse me, sir, for three years and ten months, and I have a bad attack on the street and I am taken to the hospital. They see my arms, they see me with pain . . . cold turkey . . . for I was badly addicted."

"And during this time, what about your father?"

"Well, sir, he has a new family, responsibilities. The authorities have him brought once to see me. He told me that he was disappointed with what he saw. Because my two sisters had run away and got married and left him and I had run away and left him, he was disappointed in me. He had hoped I would never do that to him. . . ." Pablo lighted a cigarette and turned to me. "You see, sir, he wasn't disappointed with me. He was disappointed in himself. That I tell you truly . . . he was disappointed in himself. Because now I know he doesn't admit it but he is really hiding his own self, his pride. This is true. All right, I am a drug addict, sir, but my father at that moment was thinking only about himself, not about me, his youngest son. He never said that I looked good, that he hoped

I was through with drugs. All he wanted was for me to hurry and get fit so that I could come home again and help around the house. . . ."

"Well, Pablo, you'll be leaving here sometime. Will you take his offer?"

He sighed. "No, sir, I will not go home again. I will not live with my sisters. I will live alone until I get a home of my own. You see, sir, if I am ever going to do something for this person who is myself, I must start now a new life. I am going to have to start a new life, in a new place, without heroin. That has to be. Without heroin. Because it will only get me no place but the penitentiary. Before, I used it as an excuse for my physical problem, my father, my sister and brother-in-law, this, that, and the other things, all cop-outs. But it ain't that, none of it. I used heroin for some reason. . . . They keep asking me why. I truly don't know, sir. Maybe because I was a baby. Because I was sorry for myself, but I don't know. . . ."

"Isn't that pretty easy to say while you're here in the hospital . . .?"

"True, sir. But it was not easy for me to talk with you . . . to tell you what I have told." Pablo rose from his chair and took a few steps on the grass. He turned to me, his face suddenly pale, his voice trembling with emotion. "I will do it. I tell you I am a religious man. I go to church every Sunday and with God's help I will do as I say. But that is not enough. I am going to have to do my own asking, my own thinking, my own living. Here there are people who have had advantage, who have had opportunity and family and no physical condition to drag them down and they still went to heroin. So, like they always say, it is up to the individual. And I tell you, sir, before. Pablo was a soldier. He was a good soldier."

3 *The female addict almost inevitably has to go on the street. She has got to turn "tricks" to get her money. She will have the use of a room for which she'll pay a few dollars and will spend the hours from dusk to dawn shooting heroin and selling her favors. If she doesn't succumb to the early hazards of heroin use, sooner or later she will succumb to the ravages of age. Then she is out there unwanted, hideous in her own eyes, dreading her days, a totally displaced person. The Call Girl, and there are a number like her, enjoys a summer vogue, but her fate and the street-walker's are the same—ultimate displacement.*

The Call Girl

Sally looked as if she had escaped from a Victorian locket: the gray dress, the demure air, her slightness. She was saying: "I don't like the cold. I don't have enough on my bones. I like the sun. I could lay on a beach and be roasted like an ear of corn."

The voice had a husky quality, a distinctive shading I'd encountered before with abusers. "What makes you stay?"

"Oh, I could skip . . . I have before . . . but not this time." She smiled. "Not yet anyway. . . ."

"On probation, is that it?"

She lighted a cigarette and crossed her legs. "It's like probation in the sense that I have to report every week to show that I'm clean, but it's very different from probation in other ways. You see, I've been on both kinds of probation, so I can show my discrimination in the differences." She sized me up, watching how I responded to her use of words.

"How long have you got to go before they release you from the after-care?"

"About a year this time."

"This time?"

"There have been others." She sighed. "Many others." And again she sighed.

"Am I making you uncomfortable?"

She looked me full in the face. "I'm not very comfortable but it's not you. I just wasn't born comfortable." Quickly she stepped on her own remark. "Let me take that back. That's the hype line, the 'I am special' garbage we cop out with. No, I'm not comfortable, but it's not you, it's me. . . ."

"But it's important for us to feel comfortable, isn't it?"

"Yes, but for us it's something else. You don't make it in the square world but you make it in this other world . . . a world with its own speech, values, attitudes. A subculture." She laughed. "You can see now that I've been in and out of drug programs. I've picked up all the lingo."

"This subculture, Sally. To some it looks glamorous. . . ."

The smoke eased from her mouth. "Well, to some, shit in a basket would seem a bouquet. . . . You see, stuff was there . . . and I used it. I was so young that I didn't have anything but feelings. Maybe it was the language of it all or the comfort as you said, or something . . . one thing for sure, I did come to use the language and have the outlook. It became natural . . . but I was only twelve when I had my first fix."

"Skin-popping?"

"Not Sally. She was too much of a big-time girl at twelve. I went the whole route. I mainlined. I got so sick that first shot I thought all my insides were coming out."

"Did you fix yourself that first time?"

"Oh, no, I wasn't that hep. Somebody fixed me. I turned my head away. I couldn't watch when they popped the vein. . . . Somebody gave me my wings. That's the special language I was talking about before: give somebody their wings . . . jab a needle in their arm."

"How old are you, Sally?"

"Twenty-seven."

"And you started using at twelve? How come? Did some pusher force you?"

"That's garbage, that bit about pushers preying on poor, innocent kids. Nobody forced me. I asked for that shot."

"Had you any idea what you were getting into?"

She seemed to address the question to her cigarette. "Had I any idea of what I was getting into? Yes and no. Yes, I was trying to be accepted by this bunch and right at that time I was going through a lot of traumatic changes . . . I was looking for a place. And the other part of the answer, the 'no' part . . . no, I didn't know what particular kind of hell I was letting myself in for."

"You were looking for a place at twelve? How come you were looking where there was heroin going?"

She sighed. "Well, I don't . . . think. . . . Chronologically I was twelve, but I think I was probably far beyond my years . . . and I'd left my home." Sally crushed out the cigarette. "I was kicked out of home a little before I took my first shot. I was shook out. I was told to leave. You know . . . you know, where most children would probably wander around until it got dark and then head for home, Sally just kept on wandering. To be fair, I was already pretty wild by then. I was beyond my years as I said before. I had no home life to speak of, so there was no grief in splitting. I'm thinking back now. . . ." A frown crossed her face. "It's hard emotionally for me now to think what it was like then. Now I'm scared for that twelve-year-old trying to fend for herself. You know what I mean?"

"There was no grief in splitting?"

"Must sound like a soap opera. Er . . . I'd better explain. Maybe there was grief, maybe I wanted somebody to come and get me and bring me back . . . there was just my mother. It was a broken home and I wanted my mother to be a mother and this wasn't part of her make-up. In fact I'm still seeking that a little bit, although I've come to accept it much better

now. She was just not really ready to be a mother. You know
. . . she was very attractive, sexually promiscuous . . . and
home life, being a mother, you know, just didn't appeal to her
in any way."

"Were you a love child?"

"Er . . . that's a different way to put it . . . I don't think
so. I was born on a reservation. My father was a full-blooded
Indian and my mother was Irish. I lived on the reservation until
I was about four, and from what I understand there was some
kind of trouble my father got into and he was sent to prison.
My mother brought me to Chicago. Between the time I was
four and twelve I kept alternating between my mother in
Chicago and my grandmother, my mother's mother, who lived
on a farm outside of St. Paul. I was just shipped back and
forth. I must hold the record as the half-fare champion of the
world." She lighted a cigarette. "My grandmother would have
kept me with her all the time . . . but my mother would have
these periodic bouts with guilt and then the half-fare ticket
would arrive. My mother and her hangups! She had a conscience, and when it got to her, Sally'd be traveling."

"What was life like when you were with your mother?"

"Well, it wasn't a bad life when I was with her . . . physically,
I mean. My mother was a business woman, she made a hell
of a good living, but emotionally . . . like it was . . . well, it
was from one extreme to another." She was taking quick drags
from the cigarette. "My grandmother was very overbearing and
very overprotective and she had a bad hangup. And this hangup
was my mother." Sally laughed suddenly. "Hairy, huh? See,
my grandmother had guilt feelings about my mother and my
mother had guilt feelings about me. Kind of like some kind of
female penitenté ritual with me as the scourge."

"You've done a lot of probing. . . ."

"Well, when you've been busted, you've got a lot of time to
think, and within the last eight years I've had a lot of time to
chew at Sally and have others chew at her." She shifted her

position. "I think I've gotten through most of the stuff about my mother and grandmother and father. . . ."

"What about the stuff about Sally?"

She sighed. "That's the toughie . . . the critical one . . . huh . . . like . . . right now, I'm so damned aware, and I'm looking for . . . channeling . . . er . . . direction. I have all of this self-awareness. I'm all opened up, every part of me is raw. Sure, it's Sally I've got to be concerned with now. And it's Sally I'm having my troubles with. Let's face it, it's always been Sally that I've had my trouble with. The part with my mother and grandmother, you know, that was hairy enough, but with me, knowing what I'm like, the ugliness and . . .," she added defensively, "and the good. My attributes and everything else, I don't seem to have any channeling for it. I'm still trying to make this adjustment to society. You see, I've been out of circulation for almost six years. Ever try to fill out an application for work and explain a six-year blank . . .? Like it's so complicated, and here's where the addict gets really hung up . . . I never really was part of the square world . . . most of my memories and things are back in the addict world . . . then I'm in the joint—that's the garbage heap of the square world . . . then I'm in a hospital, where they try to make me ready for a world I was never in. . . . It's a real keyhole squeeze."

"Your prison experiences were all on narcotics charges?"

"Narcotics and what goes with it. Prossing, robbery, everything that goes with junk. So I've been removed from society most of my life. I'm a real greenhorn. . . . And this accepting oneself, accepting oneself for what the hell . . . you know, the good with the bad. . . ."

"Don't we all go through it?"

"God, I hope so," she snapped back. "I'd hate to think I'm the only one. No . . . listen to me . . . that's the addict talking. What I'm really thinking is: You don't . . . people don't go through this kind of thing about themselves at twenty-seven. . . . But addicts, they don't grow up. They're stunted. See, right now . . . I'm hung on choices. Let me see if I can explain that. Something happens at work, something that wouldn't bother anybody else . . . but it depresses Sally, makes her go tumbling back through all those memories . . . and she begins to wonder and brood and pretty soon she's got herself to where she's laying the groundwork for a fix . . . that's the way you cope . . . a fix . . . that takes care of it . . . a fix. See what I'm saying . . . you have to learn choices . . . there are better ways. With an addict, there's only one way—the spike."

"Sally, is your mother out of your life now?"

She had to consider a moment. "Actually I didn't see my mother from the time I left home at twelve until I was almost seventeen. One day I called her and congratulated her because she was going to be a grandmother. You see, I was pregnant. I must be honest . . . she took it very well. We reached some kind of understanding. But it was all on the surface, and this patched-up kind of relationship was all right until after my daughter was born. . . ."

"Did she know that you were a user?"

"Er . . . not right away . . . but she did eventually. She had to know . . . a few weeks after the baby came I got picked up with a set of works." Sally shifted in her chair. "Yes, she found out."

"Pretty bad time?"

She lighted another cigarette. She stared at it. "No, it was all of a piece. She was concerned about what people were going to say about her. You know, the conscience bit: 'She had not been a good mother, otherwise her daughter wouldn't have used junk.' She reasoned just like an addict would reason, really: 'The world is too cruel for me, it's unfair, I never had a chance. How have I failed, where did I go wrong?' All that 'I' garbage . . . just like an addict. I just see that now while I'm talking to you . . . the hangup with having married an Indian . . . her mother . . . all screwed up and lying to herself every inch of the way. Screwed up like me, just like me. . . ."

"Do you mean she used stuff, too?"

"No, she didn't use, but I'm saying her falling back on all the excuses, making herself out a victim, like she had no choice, that's typical drug-addict thinking. My mother drank. I think actually she was kind of a periodic alcoholic . . . she couldn't even give herself to alcohol completely. So my getting picked up . . . she used this like she used me, like she always used me when I commuted back and forth between St. Paul and Chicago . . . and she still tries to use me to this day."

"Were you sentenced?"

"No, they sent me to a hospital. They were trying to help me. They really were, but I wasn't ready. And during this time this patched-up relationship I spoke of . . . I really tried to build on it. I tried to make it into something real. What I really wanted was a mother. I wanted to change her. I wanted her to understand herself, make her aware of herself, make her face herself." She glanced at me. "I was pretty naive and I clung to this relationship. I was paroled out to her and I honest-to-God tried, but this relationship was a stone. . . . And my solution was always the same . . . you stuff it and run for the spike. . . ." Sally felt along the fingers of her hand. "And I was trying to make her face herself . . . like, how blind can you be? It really was my hangup, my cop-out. Trying to make her over and do nothing about myself. This double thing . . . you see, I was copping out right there. You can't make people over to your blueprint. The truth is, even if she had been made over, I would not have been made over. She was my cop-out. . . ."

"You're pretty savage with yourself."

She snapped, "Don't use a word like that. That's an addict's garbage word. There's nothing savage about being honest with yourself." Then calmly she went on. "I think the last time I saw her it was better because I knew that she could never be what I wanted her to be because what I wanted wasn't real, because I myself was hardly real. My feelings by this time were so chewed up, so stomped down. A mother for me was a stolen kind of thing from listening to other addicts fantasizing about things that never happened, my own nice little box of cop-outs. It was all heroin garbage." Almost apologetically she said: "See what I mean about being too self-aware?"

"Doesn't this give you something solid, though?"

"Well, I've stopped fighting it. . . ."

"Maybe you've come of age."

"It's about time . . . I'm twenty-seven."

"What happened to your daughter?"

"I have two children, a boy and a girl. They're with their father."

"So when you went back to your mother you were married?"

"That's another story." She laughed. "You really can't touch me without soap opera. I was married at sixteen . . . I lived with him for a few months and then went to my mother. . . ."

"Was he a heroin user, too?"

"No, he wasn't. But he had his hangup too. See, I was addicted. I had about a fifty dollar a day habit and I was making my money prossing. He was a lot older than me and he used to talk to me. You know how it is, the way a guy will make up to you. He's going to help you . . . he's going to make you over. It's the God-damndest world for making over people. You find out, as I did with my mother, that you make somebody else over because you won't do anything about yourself. In any case, this guy was going through a conflict about his manhood. So I turned a trick with him and I got pregnant, though I didn't know it for a while. Maybe a few weeks later, the cops were cleaning up the streets and I got caught in the drag. They had no charge on me but they'd seen me around as a pross and user. They had me examined, they found I was pregnant and I was under age. They threatened me with reformatory unless I could produce a husband and a license. . . . It was a kind of legal shotgun wedding set-up. So this guy went along with it. He had a little business of his own and I guess he figured having a wife and a child would straighten him out. We went through some pretty traumatic years, I tell you. What with his hangup and mine . . . I'm divorced now, but we would have been married twelve years if I'd stuck it out."

"You say you started on heroin at twelve, Sally. How soon did you become addicted?"

"Well, that group meant a lot to me. I mentioned how I wanted to be accepted. I guess I must have figured that the only way I could be accepted was to blend right into the group and do what they did. I used for about four months and then one morning—I was staying with this girl who was six years older than me—I woke up with a Jones . . . you know, I felt achy and my stomach was upset, my nose was running and my eyes . . . I thought I'd caught a cold. My friend said: 'Sal, that ain't a cold. Honey, you got a Jones.' I couldn't believe her . . . so she said she'd prove it to me. She got some stuff and I fixed and all the symptoms disappeared. So I knew I was hooked."

"Did it mean anything to you to learn that you were addicted?"

Sally rummaged inside of her purse and brought out a fresh pack of cigarettes. "You bet it meant something. If nothing else it meant if I wasn't going to get sick I'd have to have junk. But your question didn't mean that . . . what you meant was whether I felt my life had come to a crossroads or something, right?"

"Something like that. . . ." I couldn't help smiling at her. "You're very sharp."

"I've had to be. Let me show you something . . . it's not in answer to your question at all, but I want to illustrate something. Just what you said to me shows a sympathy. Now if I were on the stuff, right now, and I wanted to take you for some money, I'd play you like a fish . . . just you revealing that little bit of interest . . . I'd make up a story that would just fit you. See, the addict gets to be sharp even if he's not really sharp . . . like they say hunger makes you sharp . . . well, heroin gets to be the worst kind of hunger you can feel and you get as sharp as a razor. But to get back to your question, I don't know if I felt anything at all when I discovered I was hooked. Sure, later on, after I'd been on stuff, after I had my face pushed down, then I could see what being hooked meant. Now, see, like it's all of a piece . . . I can see it from the beginning like a string of beads. I was born on a reservation, a blue-eyed Indian with black, straight hair. My grandmother would look shocked when I mentioned my father. My mother, who couldn't stand the life with an Indian, who split just as soon as she could, who hated everything about a reservation . . . what the hell does she do just as soon as she puts me in school in Chicago? She puts those thin Indian bands on my hair . . . and my hair she braids . . . to make me look like an Indian kid. Figure that one out. Those damned braids and head bands made my life hell in school. Besides, I could hardly speak English. Oh, I was different all right . . . I felt more foreign than the kids who came from Puerto Rico. School was just plain hell for me . . . and it continued that way until I found an older bunch of kids who felt the same way. They hung around a drugstore, they were older than me. They kind of made a mascot of me because I was small, but I tried to act older and I pulled so many stunts that after a while I convinced them I was older. See, these were the so-called bad kids, the outcasts. Each of them had their own hangups, mostly family, and they all clung together. Here's this subculture . . . special language, a special kind of loyalty. It's a world where you fit, or feel you fit . . . that's the important word . . . feel . . . feel. . . . You know, it was a crowd that skipped school, that drank, smoked weed, made love in the back seat of cars, shop-lifted . . . brushed with the cops. But I fitted in there . . . at least I thought so. Now I know that's not so. Now I realize I don't fit anywhere. You remember those people who went sailing all over the ocean looking for a country where they could land and start a life . . . what were they called?"

"You mean displaced persons?"

"That's Sally—she's a displaced person."

"But other kids have felt different and inferior or had problems with family and somehow they've made it. Did you ever wonder what there was about Sally that made her . . .?"

She interrupted me. "You're saying I was weak or a follower . . . or maybe even that I set myself up for this? That I use this displaced person bit as a cop-out for myself?" She shook her head gravely. "It's all a matter of how you cope with things. You know, you think and think about things. When you're an ex-addict, you've got to . . . it's a kind of salvation. It's a kind of hair shirt you wear. Like this bunch I threw in with . . . we had a kind of collective cop-out, if you know what I mean . . . this is where attitudes and values come in. We all believed in the attitude of putting our fingers to our noses at society. . . ."

"There's something I don't understand, Sally. How come the authorities never looked for you? You had run away from home, left school . . . and you were only thirteen. How come?"

"It's a good question. Now, I think it must have been my mother. You know, sooner than reveal to anybody that her daughter had slipped out on her, she probably spun them a story about my going back to my grandmother in St. Paul. That would have been like her."

"But that doesn't explain it all. You must have been picked up other times by the police if you were running around with that fast crowd."

"You know, I never was but once when I was that young . . . and then I got out of it. We were trying to help a guy who'd gotten shot in a robbery. And somehow the cops got wind of it and they collared the guy, but I managed to just drift away. . . ."

"You were just helping?"

Sally smiled. "I used to be the decoy on jobs . . . I looked like such a skinny little kid . . . I could stand on a corner or in an alley or across the street and nobody looked at me twice."

"But you must have thought about the closeness of this call."

"Oh, sure. It just made me realize I had to be more careful. But I was hooked . . . I had to have money. It was later when I came to prossing that I stopped the robberies and things like that. . . ." She paused. "When I had a bustline and something like hips, I could pross . . . I couldn't at twelve or thirteen. . . ."

"This man you later married. . . ."

She chuckled. "He really liked me. He was an Albanian. When we got married he was twelve years older than me. He had a violent nature but he could be charming and suave. I was enchanted with him really. I think I fell in love with him. . . ."

"You seem surprised, Sally."

"I am, because I think I've just discovered it . . . but it was a weird marriage."

"You make it sound very dramatic."

"Oh . . . addicts are always dramatizing, you know. He wasn't home very much . . . this business he had kept him traveling . . . besides, I was using stuff. You really can't have any kind of sexual relationship when you use heroin, you know. . . . Heroin is your bed. Now, he knew I used and maybe that bothered me, too . . . I mean, that he knew it and didn't do anything about it. . . . But if he'd tried I would have split." She looked at me intently. "Do I sound all mixed up? Well, I'm thinking back now on those days when I wasn't raw like I am today . . . I mean raw with self-awareness. I used to feel that he used me, like my mother used me . . . he had this hangup about his manhood, he used me . . . but then I used him. . . . Now . . . I think maybe he loved me as much as he could in his way. If it were now . . . it might be different."

"Could it have been different if you were using heroin?"

"No. That's right." She sighed. "There's always that . . . that makes the difference."

"So you left him. What happened? You went back on the street?"

"Well, no, not really . . . I got lucky. I got a job as a model. Believe it or not that Indian-Irish mixture was a help for once. I had a break and hit the big magazines as a model."

"You stopped using heroin?"

She snorted. "Stopped? I was shooting a hundred and forty to two hundred dollars worth of junk a day."

"Between one hundred and forty and two hundred dollars a day? You mean it? Take the smaller figure—that's almost a thousand a week."

"I was making money. It just rolled in . . . and it rolled out just as fast. You see, not only was I one of the highest paid models around, but I was also one of the highest priced call girls in the city. Oh, man, did I rake in the dough. When I look back on it now . . . money. . . ."

"What happened?"

"You won't believe it. One night I was coming through the Loop, late, real late. It was cold and slushy. I was loaded on junk and I was dressed to the eyeballs. You know, by then, I had a wardrobe enough to make your eyes pop. And I was jumped. Two guys jumped me and roughed me up and took everything I had. . . ."

"Two addicts? Ironic. . . ."

"They weren't junkies . . . it would have been better if they had been. No, they cleaned me out of everything but four bags of heroin. If they'd been hypes they would have taken that right off. . . . No, these were a couple of kids. In any case, the cops came, I went to a hospital, and I was charged with possession."

"It's still ironic."

"I suppose so . . . but everybody gets taken. I wasn't complaining. God knows, I'd done my share of beating others out . . . though the rough stuff I could do without. So I was busted, but this time instead of going to the joint, they sent me to a program for criminal addicts . . . and I came out last December. When I think about it now, I'm glad it happened, because everybody who uses stuff gets tired. If you had to ask me about the one thing that gets to every hype sooner or later, I'd have to say weariness. You get so tired. . . ."

"Did the program help you?"

She laughed nervously. "Ask me a couple of years from now. It brought certain things out in the open for me. For instance, even though I've lived with Sally for twenty-seven years, there's a lot I had to learn about her. Did it help me? It should be the other way around. Did it help me to help myself? That's where it's at . . . it's where it's always been at. Not my mother or grandmother or father or the reservation or anything really. . . . But Sally. . . ."

"What's it like now?"

She lighted a cigarette and said apologetically: "Not to sound too like a hype . . . I'm scared . . . I'm raw and scared. I've got a job in a dress store. Nobody knows about me. Each day is a full day . . . Sally has to beat through each one. There's no other way. . . ."

"Are you going back to heroin?"

For the first time in our exchange, there was a barrier between us. Her voice dropped. "You remember that bit about the people on the ocean looking for some place they could land . . .? I'm still on the ocean and I'm looking . . . I'm looking."

4 *It is disquieting to interview drug users like the Musician. There is no taint of the ghetto, no great neglect or deprivation—seemingly at least. They show signs of passivity, immaturity, dependence; but then so do many of us, and we don't go to heroin. Why not some other crutch? Why heroin? After extensive conversations with middle-class users, many of them professional people —the kind who never get into trouble because their means allow them to support their habits without criminal activity—I'm struck by their extraordinary insights about drug addiction; at the same time I'm baffled by their inability to explain why they chose heroin. Recently I discussed this with an acknowledged expert in the field of drug abuse. He said he was convinced that certain people were fated to use heroin, like star-crossed lovers. I looked at the doctor—surely he was kidding me—but his expression was perfectly serious.*

The Musician

Our meeting had been arranged through an intermediary, and Russell accepted my assurances about protecting his identity.

"I'm not all that fastidious and I'm not trying to appear to be better than my neighbor, it's just not in the nature of my job as a teacher to broadcast the fact that I'm an ex-addict." He had a wonderfully soft voice and easy smile. "You know, you can be ever so respectable and take tranquilizers, stimulants, hallucinogens, depressants . . . but you can't have anything to do with heroin and escape the charge of being just a little fiendish."

"The hypocrisy of our age . . .?"

"No, just a lack of perception, I think. . . . And let's be honest

41

about it, heroin use is kind of fiendish. Although I'll never understand why a community doesn't get up in arms over the legal
addicts . . . their plight is in some ways worse than that of the
street junkie. Sure, you know, the prescription drug user; the
barbiturates, the amphetamines, the mood-altering drugs, alcohol . . . the housewife, the harrassed businessman, teacher, the
professional man. All these people who really hover on the
brink . . . they can't function without their particular prescription. The community should be genuinely concerned about them.
Lots of times they hold important jobs in the community, too.
. . ." He offered me a cigarette.

"This is called the pill society, Russell."

"But, you know, you've got to be on stuff yourself to recognize
other drug users. I tell you, it was one of the most startling dis-
coveries of my life to see the number of people who use all kinds
of drugs who are not heroin addicts. Man, it was like the scales
fell from my eyes. The most respectable, upstanding members of
the community using pills, and all blithely oblivious of the fact
that they were drug dependent. I'm not trying to alibi, or justify
the use of heroin, but at least the junkie on the street has a kind
of harsh reality. He knows he's an outcast, he knows that he's
incomplete, he knows he's always on the brink of arrest or sud-
den death or disease. And believe me, the junkie knows he's on
the bottom of the heap. . . . Did you know, that even in prison,
there's a kind of hierarchy . . . status? Do you know what place
the criminal heroin addict occupies on the ladder? He's placed
below the child molester. And the addict agrees with this, for
this is his own opinion as well."

"Russell, how long have you been off stuff?"

"One thousand, eight hundred and forty days."

"That's, let's see, a little more than five years. . . ."

"I prefer to calculate my way by days, with twenty-four
hours in them . . . life is a pretty frail thing and for the ex-user,
hours are significant."

"Does it disturb you to talk with me?"

"I don't think so. . . . In any case, it shouldn't. It was a part
of my life, and you can't obliterate part of your life. I could
have ducked this meeting, you know." He smiled. Russell was
slender and slight, his hair just starting to turn grey. "You know,
really, I wouldn't mind telling anybody what happened to me.
It's one of the few ways in which the ex-addict can make a
genuine contribution to society. But for me, a teacher, I dread
that lack of perception I mentioned before. The public is frightened half out of their lives when you mention heroin. But I find
that the public is frightened of heroin for all the wrong reasons.
And they're not frightened enough about other drugs which our
society will tolerate. . . ."

"There's terrific publicity about drugs. . . ."

"Yes, and terrific ignorance. That reminds me of something
that happened the other day in school. . . ." Russell laughed and
his laughter had that soft musical cadence I had noticed before.
"I really shouldn't laugh because it's not funny. I was in the principal's office for something when a kid was brought in accused
of having a reefer. Well, just before that kid came in the principal
had popped a tranquilizer in his mouth and swoshed it down
with a gulp of water. He mentioned that it was his nerve medicine. Man, it's a climate that pervades the country . . . a drug
climate . . . how to avoid pain. . . ."

"You breathe the same air as everyone else. You said you
couldn't obliterate a part of your life . . . don't you get a han-
kering to avoid pain, too?"

"You bet your life I do. But do you remember what I said
before about the legal addict and the street junkie? How the
street junkie has a certain kind of reality? That's what I mean.
I've been there. At the bottom of the heap. I'm not boasting,
there's no pride involved. But I've been there. . . . Seeing drugs
around me, their widespread abuse, acts as a reinforcement . . .
it keeps me off them."

"Do you ever want a shot?"

"That's the inevitable question. That and the other one: 'Why

did you start using in the first place?' You see, it's not just taking
a shot. It's a state of mind, it's really taking on a way of life.
It's joining another culture, a special culture with its own language and mores . . . if you use heroin, you're part of this, you've
got no choice. Sooner or later you've got to throw in with it. You
can't have one without the other. I don't want any part of it . . .
I've had . . . I've had it. . . . You know the square world, your
world and mine." He smiled as he included himself. "The way
it's taking on about marijuana is really sinister. We use all of
the old saws which reveal our ignorance to the kids, an ignorance
which the kid suspected anyway, and the kid is strengthened in
his use. Marijuana is being pushed into the same bag as heroin.
. . . Don't misunderstand me, I'm not talking of the kid who just
tries a joint a few times. . . . I mean the kid who goes to it in
order to cope, just like the principal popping his tranquilizer, or
the housewife popping hers to prepare for her mother-in-law . . .
but since marijuana use is verboten . . . its users develop a subculture . . . the pot user gets forced into the same limbo as the
junk-user. Though marijuana is not physically addictive like
heroin . . . you can become psychologically dependent . . . and
this is the big hangup for heroin users as well as pot users."

"Should we legalize marijuana?"

"Oh, Lord, that's no answer. Don't we have enough legal
drugs now? Again, that's begging the issue. The real thing here
is: why do people have to have crutches in the first place . . .?
No, I think the problem is more difficult and . . . er, simpler at
the same time. . . . I think we have to re-examine everything . . .
all our social institutions . . . marriage, the home, the school, the
community, law, church. . . ."

"What a job!"

"Yes . . . but that's where drug use grows . . . in these social
institutions. See, Russell broke down, ran out of gas, didn't have
it, and ran to the spike. I just wasn't where it was at with myself. . . ." Russell lighted another cigarette. "But I had none of
this awareness when I was using junk, believe me."

"Did you use pills?"

"Yes, I did . . . ups and downs . . . the amphetamines and barbiturates . . . depending on how I felt. I usually kept both on hand."

"Were you using pills while you were on heroin?"

"No, when I was on heroin, I didn't have any desire for pills . . . though there are some who do use pills while they're on junk. But I'll tell you a strange thing—after I became addicted to heroin, I looked back on pills, especially the barbiturates, as very dangerous things." Russell laughed. "Kind of like the man over his head in the water relieved to see that he's escaped the fire, huh? But I could see around me people who were hooked on pills. They're ten times worse than junk . . . and God knows, junk is hell."

"You used pot too?"

"Yes, I smoked weed."

"Do you think there's a progression . . .?"

"Do you mean that if you smoke pot that you'll sooner or later become a heroin user? No, absolutely not. However, in my case it turned out to be exactly that. But the significant thing here is that I was looking for a cop-out . . . I was looking for the better high. And even of greater significance, in my crowd, everything was going, so in my case there was this progression you mentioned. They do relate, but not in the way that the news media make it out to be, you know, directly . . . or that it's inevitable. See, I've known weed smokers very well who never used anything else, it was simply not in their mental make-up to use heroin, you know. It would be the furthest thing from their minds. You'd have to tie them down and forcibly administer the shot and at that they'd probably burst their bonds. Cigarette smoking is a far greater hangup in some ways, damned sight more dangerous . . . but cigarette smoking is one of those socially tolerated evils. . . . Not that I'm for legalizing pot, because I'm not . . . there's too much not known about it. But it's in the area of motivation. . . ."

"Since you introduce the word, Russell . . . what was your motivation in smoking pot?"

"Well, let's see . . . I first smoked weed in my freshman year in college. I was introduced to it by some of my acquaintances. You see, as a guy, I was a great putter-offer." He smiled. "Now with that kind of temperament, I'd somewhere along the line have to make up for lost time. I'd have to hit the books real hard. Pot seemed to make me concentrate more. . . ." He said quickly: "Now, I know you're going to ask me why I needed this spur to concentration."

I had to laugh. "You're way ahead of me."

"I didn't see the point of going to college. Really I didn't. I was a musician. I could have made a living that way. But my parents wanted me to go to college. I didn't have the gumption to go against them. This being a procrastinator was just a very bland kind of resistance. . . ." Russell became very intent. "This is the danger with pot, right here. I didn't know why I went to it. See, actually, I used it to cope. Because I lacked the balls to tell my parents that it was my life, I . . . I forced myself into this, well, this improvisation . . . and after a while I went to the pills in the same way. My . . . er . . . bag of propellents, you might say. . . ."

"But what about heroin? You said before that in your crowd everything was going."

"Yes. I had a good idea of what it was and what it did because I'd been around users. This was after college, I should say. I had fixed addicts. I had held heroin in my hand and I had gone through the whole thing—the cooking, and drawing up, and shooting people. And I never had any illusions . . . never . . . no, no illusions." His voice was very soft. "And then I had a crisis in my life where it just didn't really . . . I knew full well what I was doing but it just didn't matter at the time. It didn't matter, and when it did matter I thought it was too late. I had created a real problem for myself by using heroin."

"You mean you'd become addicted."

"That led to so many, many problems. So much degrada-tion. Heroin has a way of taking all your problems and blending them into one gigantic problem which is the substance itself. . . . But I'd like to say that I had known about heroin as an onlooker. I'd seen what it did to people . . . I thought I knew it pretty well. . . . But I didn't really grit into it until I started to use. To really know what it's like."

"What's it like, Russell?"

He sighed deeply. "It's the worst thing that can happen to a human being. I think it's worse than cancer or being maimed for life or losing your eyesight. I think it's the worst that can happen to a human being . . . and one of the most difficult things to get out of. As a matter of fact, most junkies I've run into feel the same way when they're high."

"When they're high?"

"Yes, and they . . . and we make up all sorts of promises. You know, this is it. I'm going to pull up, I'm going to do this and that . . . what I like to call heroin resolutions. . . ."

"It's a warped perception, isn't it?"

"Yes. Actually, it's just like what I felt about marijuana allowing me to concentrate better . . . that's a warped perception, too. But you see, the conclusion is inevitable. Russell just wasn't really very perceptive. You see, even though I've come back and this represents years of digging into myself and having others dig as well, I can't put my finger on the reason why I went to junk, the real, ringing reason. I think I know some of the aspects. . . ."

"There was a reason?"

"Yes, there had to be, conscious or not . . . there had to be."

"You said before that there had been a crisis in your life. . . ."

"But there must have been particles floating around within me that were crystallized by this crisis . . . it just doesn't happen like that . . . there are seeds. . . ."

"What about your background, Russell?"

"Pure establishment. Good, middle-class upbringing. Father a professional man, my mother a college woman . . . advantages, expectations. . . . My mother, I suspect, had not had an easy time when she was growing up. She was pretty forceful, good manager. . . . No, don't misunderstand, she wasn't a man-eater, or anything like that, but she did like to direct things. . . . And I didn't find it in myself to oppose her plans for me. But all things considered, I think the main thing was my frustrations in late youth and early adulthood. You see, I overcame these frustrations by adapting myself to the situation and then that situation was snatched from under me. And I found myself . . . I found myself . . . at another place. Let me try to bring this into focus. I'm a musician. I've always been interested in music. All through grammar school and high school I'd studied music, and there was no doubt in my mind that I was going that path. My life was going to be playing and writing music. In my senior year in college . . . I got married . . . my wife got pregnant, we'd been going together ever since my freshman year . . . er . . . my wife got pregnant and we got married. . . ."

"This is the crisis you mentioned?"

He looked puzzled. "Oh, no . . . this wasn't it . . . but it put a different light on things. I didn't want to get married," he sighed, "but at the same time I did have this responsibility, so when I took my degree I got a job teaching music and direct-ing the band in a high school. I felt cheated, you know. I was doing something I really didn't want to do and I felt that I'd never have the opportunity to do what I'd always dreamed of doing. This went on for a couple of years . . . this feeling of frus-tration that I had. . . ."

"Did you share any of this with your wife?"

"Yes, yes I did. My wife is . . . was the only woman I ever met, you know, that I could have married. She understood and she was sympathetic. So after this, we figured out a way that when the school year ended, I'd go out on the road playing with different organizations. Occasionally I got to New York for a recording date. I made some connections, I got to be pretty well known, and things went along fine. As the years passed, I began to enjoy my family life and my work as band director and music teacher. . . . And after about five years I used to regret having to leave in the summer for my road work. . . ."

"Curious twist."

"Yes . . . I guess I just didn't need to escape any more. . . ."

"Were you using anything?"

"I was smoking weed. It relaxed me."

"Were you still using pills?"

"No, I'd stopped the pills."

"You hadn't started on heroin?"

"No, but I was surely surrounded by it during the summer when I was out on the road with these professional bands. In one particular organization I was with the band leader who was himself an addict. But he couldn't shoot himself and I used to fix him."

"Did that mean anything to you?"

"Then it didn't. It was just like giving somebody a shot of insulin. . . . But I didn't use, had no desire to use. . . . Except for weed, I was clean. I really felt that I was enjoying life. I made good money, I had a new home, couple of cars, two lovely little daughters . . . I enjoyed my winters teaching in school. . . ."

"Why didn't you give up weed if you were so satisfied . . .?"

"I enjoyed it."

"Were you psychologically dependent on it?"

"Yes, I think so, now . . . I didn't think about it then. As a matter of fact, I should have been curious as to why I needed to be relaxed by marijuana with everything else I had going for me. . . ."

"I'm sorry I interrupted you before. . . ."

"Oh. . . . I had a lot going for me. On the weekends I had a little band in one of the supper-clubs in my hometown. . . . One Saturday night, a neighbor called. My wife had passed out and been taken to the hospital." Russell rubbed his hands together slowly. "She had an incurable disease. The doctors told me it was hopeless. It could be weeks or months . . . in six weeks

she was dead. This was . . . you know, I was the kind of fellow
. . . I never paid any attention to bills, or what I owed, or what
had to be shopped for, or income tax. . . . She was my business
manager . . . yes, she was my business manager. It comes back
in snatches, that time . . . I recall one afternoon, I had just gotten
finished teaching and picked up my two small daughters from
their school. I was trying to get something for their supper. I was
fiddling around trying to open some cans, and I was trying to get
some of their dresses together to take them to be laundered . . .
the house was a mess, I never got the dishes washed up . . . it
was chaos. . . . And then, right then . . . a fellow I played with,
another musician, dropped by the house. He was a heroin user
and he asked me if he could fix at my house because he couldn't
fix at his house because his wife was giving a cocktail party. I
said okay . . . and I don't know . . . I asked him for a bag. . . .
Just like that, in a flash, I asked him for a bag. I can see everything just as clearly in that room . . . a Utrillo on the wall, one
of my daughter's sneakers, their dresses on the sofa. . . . That
first fix was almost too much . . . it hit my stomach like a fire-
ball. . . . I got sick, so sick . . . but it had started."

"What about the next day?"

"I fixed the next and the day after. . . . Once I started I never
looked behind."

"And your children?"

"I took them to my parents. You know, I was going to bring
them back each weekend so that we could be together. But
that was just a fiction . . . I realize that now. Man, I was on stuff.
If it had been a woman I couldn't have been more infatuated.
. . . It was as if I had been waiting for heroin all my life. . . ."
Russell lifted a finger in emphasis. "And I must have been. Why
else did I hang around it, have friends who used it stop at my
house . . . ?"

"What happened to your teaching?"

"I continued. I figured I'd finish out the school year and then
move to another town."

"Were you hooked?"

"I never gave myself a chance to find out. I'd psyched myself into becoming an addict. You see, I built up such a dread about withdrawal sickness that I kept using to fend it off . . . and in so doing addicted myself. It's all in your head. . . ."

"And how old were you when you took your first shot?"

"I was thirty years old. Can you imagine, thirty years old." Russell shook his head. "I had money. This is different from most heroin addicts. So that was no problem. I could keep my habit real private. But I still had to find a supplier, or a connection as he's called. Most times that posed no problem at all, but occasionally the source would dry up and then I'd have my troubles. Man, I'd sneak out of the school in my off periods to score and then come back and teach. I could see where I was at. It couldn't go on. I knew it couldn't go on. . . ."

"Were you aware of a change in yourself?"

"Change? It was a transformation. But not outwardly. It's very hard, as I said earlier, unless you're on the stuff yourself, to tell when somebody is using. . . . But Russell was a different man. My colleagues sensed something, no question about it, but they attributed it to my wife's death. But things that I used to look forward to doing lost all meaning. . . . My duties as a teacher could only be performed with difficulty. I was furtive and suspicious, I became isolated . . . I tell you it was like dropping from the living room of life to the lowest, darkest, dirtiest cellar. . . . For instance, when I sent in my resignation, everybody was genuinely shocked. I was esteemed . . . I had a place, a function. Really, I am astonished now to think how highly they respected me as a teacher and a musician. They gave me a banquet, an expensive new instrument, a purse of money . . . and all the while I was practicing the most vicious kind of hypocrisy. . . ."

"You were hung between two worlds."

"Right. That's a good way to put it. I was really stretched between the square world and the world of the junkie. And in the junkie world you don't have friends, you have people you know. There's a kinship of dependence . . . you never know when you're going to need to be straightened out . . . so you're forced to cling to one another. In any case, I resigned and left town. I slipped out. I used to think when I was high that I'd slipped out of the world. How could I abandon my children, my career, everything? Look what I'd traded all that for . . . a lousy room, a group of foggy characters. . . . You see, I felt I was superior, I was better than they . . . I wasn't going to sink to their level. . . . But, man, I was there. I was using shit the same as they. . . . And then I'd make a vow. I was going to stop. . . ."

"Did you?"

"Of course not . . . I never intended to . . . those were heroin resolutions. Oh, I'd delay shooting, delay maybe an hour and then get so strung out with fear that I'd race to the connection and fix. I'd watch myself as if I were somebody else. I'd watch myself with loathing and contempt. Have you ever gotten to the place where you viewed yourself split into different people? I wasn't crazy . . . I didn't know it then but that perception was accurate. I was really several people . . . I was this primitive, instinctive . . . this frightened, slinking, totally selfish creature . . . this cunning, reasoning, adroit criminal, and the spectator who was appalled by his other parts. Honest to God, the animal part of me drove me crazy. . . ."

"Sounds like a breakdown. . . ."

"Oh, I crashed all right . . . but I was a pretty rickety guy at best. . . . You know this thing of holding yourself together, this personal identity, is a frail thing. . . ."

"Were you working?"

"No. I was a supplier. Now see if you can follow this. My craft was so great that when I resigned and split, I knew that I'd have to have money and stuff. So by instinct I bought a piece of junk wholesale, cut it up, put it in bags, and sold it. This way I could supply my own needs and make enough money to continually renew my supply. I was out on the street every night selling. . . . And all the while Russell, the spectator, watched himself contemptuously. . . ."

"How much were you using?"

"Well, I couldn't get by on less than a hundred and twenty dollars a day, and most days I was shooting a hundred and seventy-five. . . ."

"Did your appearance change?"

"Funny thing about that . . . that's one thing I watched. I saw junkies change from well-dressed individuals to the sloppiest, crudest-looking bums, and in order to make myself think that I really hadn't lost control, I kept myself immaculate. But inside I was worse off than the crudest junkie. It was this capacity for sinking to the lowest dregs that reinforced my use . . . as if heroin itself sought out my weakness and played to it to keep me an addict. . . . This is just fantasizing, you realize . . . I used because it allowed me to escape . . . that's for real. . . ."

"Did you ever bump into anybody you knew from the square world?"

Russell hesitated. "No, I was in a different town. But you know, that wouldn't have fazed me any. I would have taken that in stride. It would have been a challenge that I would have used to prove to myself that I was still in control. Every instinct for gaming, deceiving, manipulating would have come to the fore . . . and I would have been watching myself perform with loathing. . . . I wish I could explain and make it understood how this mirror game of addiction works. How you use and abuse yourself. How you hate and protect yourself at the same time. How you grow so weary that you want to be caught and busted and how you take the most ridiculous precaution to elude the police. You truly are alone with the hell of yourself. Heroin is as close as you can get to suicide. . . . I think it's a self-destructive prompting for those of us who can't stand the real thing. . . ."

"What happened finally?"

Russell lighted another cigarette. "What always happens. I got picked up and busted. . . ."

"And all the parts that were Russell came together?"

He smiled. "Yes, in a way . . . in a very raw, painful way. I took cold turkey in a cell with a couple of alcoholics and a pickpocket for an audience."

"Terrible?"

"No, not as bad as I always imagined it would be. I was sick and miserable, but nothing like what I thought it would be. . . ."

"Did you get sentenced?"

He puffed slowly on the cigarette. "No . . . I got a lawyer. The legal proceedings went on for weeks. . . . It cost a bushel of money. I had to go to my parents and confess everything. . . . I got off and got a year's probation."

"Did you go back to heroin?"

"I signed myself into a hospital where they had a narcotics rehabilitation program. I stayed there for eighteen months. . . ."

"They helped you?"

"They helped me to help myself. Nobody can help you until you want to help yourself. . . . But Russell was torn down, stripped right down to the raw grain until I could see the immature, passive, irresponsible, selfish, resentful, undisciplined escapist. And not only could I see myself but all the others who were in the program could see me as I could see them with their hangups. I relived my life, saw my mother and father, my wife and myself, my use of weed, pills, heroin, my hanging around with junk users . . . the whole bag. . . . I tell you I never wanted to leave that hospital I was so scared, so helpless. . . . But I did . . . I did. . . ." He licked his lips. His hands were shaking. He looked at them and at me.

"I'm sorry that I put you. . . ."

Quickly, sharply he interrupted me. "If I can't go back over it, I can't make it. . . ."

"Heroin addiction can be cured."

"Cured? I don't know. I don't think I quite know what cure is.... If it means everything is wiped out and you become somehow reborn differently, I don't believe it is curable. If you mean stopped, arrested . . . well, I'll buy that. But it's living every day, every hour, so that tomorrow for me it will be one thousand eight hundred and forty one days. . . ."

5 *Some drug users are people with money and impressive back-grounds, but these abusers rarely come to the attention of the police or appear in the press. Myra was one of these. Of the many drug users I have interviewed over the years she stands out fresh in my mind. I showed this chapter to a former heroin-user and asked for his reaction. His comments are interesting: "Most people understand themselves pretty well. They know when they are out of 'sync'. Myra knew this. She had to curb that fearful destructiveness of herself. Raw power like raw heroin kills."*

The Rich Girl

"There's a reality to everything. Whether we're up to it . . . well, that's something else again."

The reality of Myra was palpable: artistocratic, chic, statuesque, poised, dusky-voiced. The reality of the setting was also impressive: the velvet elegance of a sitting room in a posh sanitarium. The combined image of person and place struck me as being anything but real, but then my doctor friend had intimated that this would be a "special" insight into the drug world.

"I find this reality different . . .," I ventured. "I don't think the general public would think of the drug addict in these surroundings.

"Perhaps not," she said, obviously studying me.

"But then the public is pretty well bewildered by the drug abuser. They don't know what to think. . . ."

"Nor does the addict himself know. . . . The addict shares the same kind of misconceptions about addiction as the man in the street. It's a continuum of falsehood. The reality of drug addiction is unreality."

"There's nothing unreal about the public's fear of the drug addict. . . . That's very real."

"Is it?" She lighted a cigarette. "What are you hoping to get from me, Mr. Cortina?"

"I really don't know . . . at best another fragment . . . another view of drug abuse . . . always hoping to clear away some of the falsehood you mentioned."

"The alcoholic, the child molester, the compulsive gambler, the glutton, the reckless driver, the murderer . . . the public may not like them, won't embrace them, but considers them human. The 'dope fiend' is inhuman . . . the public denies our humanity. This is the unreality I'm talking about. Not very much is known about drug abuse, perhaps that's why we have so many experts."

I was surprised by my own defensiveness. "I'm not an expert."

"You are writing a book, though."

"Again, just to perhaps lay a few of the ghosts. Who knows more about the problem than the abuser? That's why I'm talking with former users." I found her disconcerting.

"How temporary you make that 'former' sound. . . . However, I think, it's a safe way to put it . . . a phase . . . addicts are always between phases. How else could you describe me? I'm not a cured addict because I don't know of a hundred percent cure . . . I'm not a rehabilitated addict because I don't know if the values I have to rebuild into my life were ever there in the first place. . . . So I am a 'temporary,' like most heroin users when they're clean."

"You know drug addiction firsthand. Perhaps you can help the public to understand better. . . ."

She crushed her cigarette. "I'm perfectly willing to talk about myself, but I doubt if anyone will ever get the public to accept the heroin user as a human being. It's like trying to stroke a slain warrior, he's beyond response. Look at it this way, the simplistic way the public views it: 'Anybody could stop if they wanted to. Heroin use is just weakness. People don't stop because they're just no good, worthless. They want to be animals. Don't indulge them. Hire more police, stiffen sentences, find some remote place and exile them.' This harsh judgment is made by the same public, incidentally, that uses all the palliatives of the pill and alcohol, the same public that cannot give up the cigarette, the same public that deplores and promotes the use of every pain killer that is marketed."

"It's a paradox."

"Now if you're thinking that I'm attempting to rationalize my use of heroin by pointing out the public's soiled garments . . . that's possible . . . though it doesn't detract from what I've said. The reality is simply that heroin is in the same bag as all other human escape devices. . . . But my world, the world of the junkie, is an extension of escape that makes people shudder." She crossed her legs. "Did you ever wonder why the addict is regarded with such unconscionable fear, contempt, abhorrence, why the distortions, why the inexorable desire to punish the 'dope fiend'?" That cultured, dusky voice had a magic about it. "Do you know why the public wants us destroyed? Because we are the gross realization of themselves. We are all of those traits in themselves they most fear, loathe, and conceal."

"Curious . . . you mean the addict being the crystallization of our personal horrors . . .?"

"That's the reality . . . we have completely copped out . . . we've crashed . . . while the public is in torment about their daily near-misses . . . their averted crashes."

Myra was like no addict I had ever met. I was puzzled and uncomfortable. Something eluded me. I asked bluntly: "How come you became a heroin addict?"

"I'm thirty-three years of age. This is my fifth time here. I've been back three weeks now. I was outside for twenty-two months and went back on stuff . . . crashed." She looked at her polished nails, her immaculate fingers. "How could Myra with all of her advantages, her perception, her seeming ability to cope . . . how could Myra shoot heroin into her veins? You know, in a way it's like ragpicking. You examine every shred of your life: impulse, action, frustration, hurt, failure, lie, school, family . . . you hold each of these rags, you shake it out. . . . We are immature, passive, irresponsible, unmotivated . . . compulsive escapists. No question about it." Myra sighed. "But having said that. So what?" she rested her head against the chair.

"I can't help but wonder what other addicts thought about you. . . . You obviously have enjoyed advantages. . . . Frankly, it's hard for me to see you as an addict. . . ."

"Why? Why shouldn't Myra go to heroin like Mary or Sally or Joanne? You've been spooked out, Mr. Cortina . . . spooked out by the press, TV, books, magazines, the experts. Addicts run the whole spectrum like every other cultural group. We wear many guises." She glanced at me. "Some addicts I know are prostitutes, some thieves, some are engravers, some are doctors, some are lawyers, some are bums, some are housewives, and some are policemen. Yes, you'd be surprised at the range. . . . All addicts have fronts, like everyone else. . . . for the addict the front is essential, heroin is an expensive habit. . . ."

"Weren't you repulsed by the seaminess?"

"You sound Victorian. We started by talking about reality. . . . Every addict knows that without heroin he gets sick . . . sick. . . . Anything that has to be done to avoid that is the reality of addiction . . . Myra's reality . . . simple, compelling, direct."

"Somewhere I read that the average drug habit runs to a little more than thirty dollars a day. And to get that money most addicts have to steal three times that amount."

"Yes, New York State developed that statistic. Personally, I don't know any addicts whose habit is that small. My own ran up to two hundred a day."

"Two hundred a day . . . fourteen hundred dollars a week?"

"Yes . . . it's just money, Mr. Cortina. . . . Isolating it that way doesn't motivate anything."

Her manner stung me. Unlike most drug users I had talked

to over the years, this woman, her aloofness, her arrogance got under my skin. "It seems to motivate a good many robberies, assaults, thefts, muggings . . . crimes of all descriptions. . . ."

She gazed out of the window. "Addicts steal and game, they con and manipulate, they prostitute, they pimp, they pander. . . . But heroin is a depressant . . . sex crimes are out for them . . . crimes of violence also are out of their bag . . . that is one of the outrageous distortions. Heroin addicts are rarely violent. Now of course if you see a young child nailing a bird to a board and dismembering its wings . . . if this child goes to heroin later . . . that would be something else. Ninety out of a hundred addicts are passive, bland, ingrown people living by their wits."

"Then, a person who feels destructive, or feels sexually atypical, or feels urges he dreads, or who has difficulty relating, might this person go to heroin?" Something in what I had just said seemed to prick Myra. I sensed the difference in her—she seemed not so equable—she was studying my face, though not really seeing me. I asked: "Before, you said that your habit cost about two hundred dollars a day. I wonder if you'd tell me how you could afford that."

The voice was the same but something had changed. "I'm rich and I had husbands who could provide me with stuff. One was a seaman and one was a doctor." She lighted a cigarette. "You asked me a question a moment ago, one I didn't have a chance to answer . . . about people going to heroin for relief. . . . I think that's part of the heroin bag . . . escape, crutch, compensation, emotional suicide."

"What was it with you?"

"Curiosity, alienation, a need for acceptance. . . . That, I think was it in the beginning. You know, addicts are social animals of a kind, too; we have a world of our own, where we communicate our incompleteness . . . it's always a kind of shadow play—any real action on our part would be a disclosure of our failure. Do you understand that?"

"Do you mean fantasizing?"

"Right . . . our only reality is what must be done in order to get stuff."

"What was home like?"

"Upper class, advantages. Great big house . . . one of those 'relativey' families . . . you know, uncles and aunts and cousins always parading in and out from all over the state. My father was a successful professional, my mother was a committee woman . . . a committee woman. . . . I went through school, graduated from a prestige college. . . ."

"Sounds pretty carefree."

"It wasn't a carefree time for me. In fact, there were many things . . . problems I guess, that struck me when I was a child as being insoluble. I think that there were many things that I couldn't handle—emotionally, I mean. I think that being an only child for almost ten years and then getting twin sisters was part of it." She was speaking quietly, deliberately now, weighing every word. "I think the family background—the fact that my mother was overly religious and my father a nonbeliever—was part of it . . . and I had a cousin who was a heroin addict—that was directly responsible for a lot that happened to me. . . ."

"Did he live with the family?"

"No, he was just one of those eternally visiting relatives that came and went. He was a lot older than I was. He was an officer in the merchant marine. Harve always seemed to be having fun. I watched him . . . he was nice to me . . . gentle . . . he seemed to have time for me. He seemed to do the things I wanted to do and couldn't."

"What was he doing that seemed so attractive to you?"

She looked out the window; the afternoon sun had dropped. "Oh, he'd come into port from some marvelous place and he'd stay with us for a few weeks. His friends would come to our house to pick him up. They'd talk about Java and Singapore and Murmansk. . . . They'd laugh and kid around. I was a brat kid . . . always in everybody's way. I was too old to be young and too young to be old. . . ."

"How old were you at this time?"

"Twelve and a half or so. May I have a cigarette, please? Thank you." I lighted it for her. "I was a precocious kid . . . a brat. Some of my relatives used to treat me as if I were some kind of wunderkind. They'd indulge me for a while, then they'd laugh and go off on their adult way . . . I was never included . . . my sisters were babies . . . my mother was off committeeing, my father, you know, was immersed in his business . . . and my cousin, the seaman, he seemed . . . well, wonderful."

"You had no school chums or friends?"

"I was a fat bookworm. A fat bookworm. Most of the kids were way below me . . . they were playing with the things that good, healthy kids played with, they were attractive to boys, they got around, they were popular, they were in demand. Myra was a brain . . . but my cousin. . . ."

"How did you know that he was a drug addict?"

"I didn't at first. It took me about a year. You know how a kid can keep studying something, pondering it, trying to make sense out of it . . . that's what I was doing. This cousin and his friends would come in. They'd kid around with me for a while and then they'd get restless, irritable at my hanging around all the time. They'd start telling me to do my homework or go fly a kite. Didn't I have some dishes to dry or something? They'd go into my cousin's bedroom and when they came out they'd be laughing, they'd make a fuss over me, give me money, even take me out with them and buy me things. They were changeable, these people, very moody, I thought. I brooded over this, trying to figure out what it was that would alter their mood. I kept thinking and thinking about it . . . something about that bedroom. . . . There was a large rosebush just outside of my cousin's room. I took up a regular station there and peered through a crack in the shade. I did this for days, spying on them, always hoping to see what it was they were doing. And then one afternoon I saw what it was. I'll never forget that moment

. . . the sunlight on the wall paper, the blood red thorns of the rosebush, and four men, their arms bound up—fixing."

"Were you frightened?"

"I don't think so. You see, it had taken weeks before I actually saw what they were doing. It came as a kind of triumph for me . . . I had learned the secret, I felt important. I must have felt that what they were doing, I should be doing, too. I wanted to be like them. . . ."

"You were about thirteen and the prospect of a needle in your arm didn't faze you?"

"I didn't consider that . . . but I knew they must be doing something wrong . . . I knew it because it was always so secret . . . they kept it from my family. But this added to the allure for me. It struck me that this was a ritual you went through in order to become a happy . . . a very nice person. They were so different from my mother and father and the others I knew. It was so attractive. They were nice to me when they came out of that bedroom. You know, kids like rituals, secret societies, codes, invisible ink, that sort of thing."

"It never occurred to you to ask your mother or father about what you'd witnessed?"

"Not at all. My mother would be too busy with her committee work and my father would be preoccupied with his profession. Besides, I liked my cousin and his friends after they emerged from his bedroom. Before they went in they were cross and when they came out they were wonderful, so there was really nothing to tell my mother about. You see, it didn't seem weird or sinister to me . . . it pleased me to be liked by them, they seemed to welcome me when they came out of Harve's room."

"Had you ever heard about drugs and addicts?"

"Yes, but I didn't connect what I'd heard with this, with my experience with my cousin and his friends. They weren't fiends or child molesters . . . or killers. I didn't find any of these things so at all. Why should I accept what I'd heard about drugs as the truth . . . when my experience was just the opposite? A fat bookworm, pushed aside by everybody, found herself wanted. Now, of course, I realize a lot of things. For example, I always wanted to be with adults and they pushed me off . . . I resented my sisters, I resented the lack of attention from my parents. I resented the constant bickering over religion that went on between my parents." Myra went over to the window, her back to me. "There was something else, too. A few years before, I had had a very serious bout of rheumatic fever . . . I overheard my mother and father arguing about whether I should be told that I might die . . . my mother feeling that I should have a chance to cleanse myself before I met my Maker, my father saying that was primitive nonsense. You see, it wasn't the critically ill kid so much . . . the main thing involved here was their conflict. And I think, in all fairness to them, there was something else, as I look back on it now. I had tried to act so much older all those years that I think they were taken in by it and thought perhaps that I was old enough to be told the truth. I don't think they meant to hurt me. . . . I can remember my father creeping into my room, tears in his eyes, staring down at me, touching my hand, or my mother bringing in religious practitioners to hover over me . . . I think that they were very much frightened. . . ." She came back and sat down. The long rays of the sun slanted into the room. "But as you can see, I lived. I lived inside a body cast for nine months. I lived very painfully and uncomfortably. The great, bright spot for me would be when cousin Harve would come back from a voyage. . . ."

"It was after this, then, that you spied on him and his friends?"

"Yes. It was after I recovered and the attention slipped away again and I became the fat bookworm."

"Did you ever see your cousin on the nod?"

"Yes, I saw him on the nod and his friends, too . . . coasting, some addicts call it. I saw them burn holes in their clothes. . . ."

"This wasn't upsetting for you?"

"Yes, it was . . . but they were quiet and subdued and very nice to me. Actually, 'upsetting' is not the right word for my feeling. It was more comfort, acceptance . . . there was really no horror."

"How long did this continue?"

"By the time I was fourteen years old I was hooked. One afternoon when my cousin came back from being at sea for several weeks . . . he was very irascible with me . . . and I was my brat self again. I came out and told him what I had seen from the window. His face turned white and he stared at me. I told him I wanted some of what he was using. I told him bluntly that I was going to tell my mother if he didn't give it to me . . . I backed him into an absolute corner. Poor Harve, he tried so hard to explain to me what it was all about. He was stuttering, he was so distressed. He explained about the police and over-doses and the constant struggle to get stuff . . . he fell back on every device of the square world to discourage me . . . my arms and legs would be tracked up and I might die. I saw then, for the first time, how weak and confused Harve was. . . . He finally pacified me with a few pills. I liked them. I was magnified by them. I learned freedom and release. But Harve was shaken badly. He kept telling me what would happen, trying somehow to put me off. But you know, I realized my power, I was con-trolling him . . . I used his weakness . . . I knew he wouldn't inform my parents. He would tell me about women selling their bodies, about stealing, how men used women because of drugs, the world you had to live in. . . ." Myra got up suddenly and went back to the window. "And then . . . I'll never forget it . . . he gave me a shot . . . with tears running down his face, shaking his head, muttering: 'My God, my God, my God. . . .' It was like something out of Dante . . . but it had started."

"Did you get sick?"

"No, I didn't . . . he must have cooked a very small amount. It was good stuff, too . . . most people get sick their first time, but I didn't. That was the start. So each time he'd come back from a trip, I'd be on stuff . . . I hadn't developed a habit. . . ."

"You mean your parents didn't notice anything?"

"Yes, they thought I had become easier to live with, they thought I was less of a brat. I stayed away from them and didn't bother them . . . see, Harve had taught me how to fix and he would parcel out enough stuff to see me through until he returned. One time he went back to sea and a few weeks later, when my heroin supply was exhausted, I woke up in the middle of the night with awful cramps, my joints were aching, my back gave me such pain . . . I cried out for my mother. She came into my room and I was rushed to a hospital for an emergency appendectomy. It wasn't appendicitis at all. Harve explained it all when he got back. I'd been strung out . . . I'd been taking cold turkey and didn't know it."

"You mean the doctor didn't recognize it?"

"Apparently not. It's almost comical."

"Your parents never suspected? You must have had a set of works. . . ."

"Yes, they were hidden in my cousin's trenchcoat in his room. But they never suspected. It was only much later that they learned . . . very much later. So I had kicked my first time. Harve tried again to discourage me . . . asking me if I hadn't learned what a terrible thing dope was. Poor Harve, what he went through with me. . . . He showed me where you find stuff on the street, the junkies, the squalid neighborhood. He explained that I was a lady, that I should never sell myself. . . . It's amusing now . . . he was so straight-laced and prim. You see, he never bought on the street . . . he never had to . . . he always brought it back on his voyages. He said that next time there would be no appendectomy as a cover-up . . . I had to stop. I told him I would stop if he would . . . oh, I was a brat. But you see, I had learned something . . . I had learned a way of coping. I didn't need friends, I didn't need parents, I didn't need acceptance. Harve was in an impossible position. Here I was fourteen

years of age. He was twenty-nine. He had been addicted for
years. He couldn't stop. And yet, I believe now that he would
have done anything short of kicking heroin to have kept me off
the stuff. He knew that if it ever got out that he had introduced
a kid of fourteen to heroin he would have been killed, literally.
I told him I liked it. I told him it was too late to worry . . .
I didn't care. I told him that he would have to keep me supplied. . . ."

"Incredible."

"Not really. He had no choice. This went on until I was out
of high school. I just became one of Harve's group of friends
. . . all of them users."

"You never got into the subculture itself? You never had to
look for a connection?"

"Never. I never knew about pushers or copmen or bagmen.
I had a supply from Harve."

"What about school, didn't your work suffer?"

"It must have, but I still graduated from high school at sixteen and went on to college. I had changed, though. I was a
user . . . I was suspicious of everyone . . . I thought everyone
was a hypocrite . . . I watched the pot smokers and the martini drinkers and the acid users and the cheats. You see, this
allowed me some room in which to justify my own habit. And
I'd grown coarse and selfish . . . or maybe I'd always been that
way at bottom. It was in my junior year in college, one of
Harve's friends that I knew came up to school . . . Harve had
died . . . he'd sent a note to me: 'Please, please, Myra, give it up.'
I realized the spot I was in. When my supply ran out, I'd be sick.
No more Harve to supply me. Larry, the friend who brought
the news, of course knew all about me. He'd been one of the
friends who came to my parents' house with Harve. He was
about thirty-five, a seaman, and a heroin user, too. He was a
timid, passive sort of fellow. He stood there passing his tongue
across his lips. He wondered if he could do anything. I asked
him if he had any stuff. He said that Harve had told him to tell

me to go to a hospital. As I looked at Larry I could see Harve all over again, cut from the same cloth. I decided how I would handle the situation. Larry was going to supply me . . . he hadn't a chance. I decided that he was going to marry me."

"Just like that. . . . Didn't he . . .?"

"It really was quite plausible. He didn't have too much choice . . . I knew too much about him. He was like Harve . . . weak, ineffectual. We were married."

"And your family?"

"I sent them a note, telling them. It really worked out very well for Larry. He had a place to come back to. We got an apartment just off the campus, I continued with school . . . everything was going along well. . . . Then I became pregnant . . . ironic . . . it was something unexpected, for our sex life was meager. Larry was at sea then. I got sick. A doctor examined me . . . I was sent home. The family doctor told my parents I was a drug user."

"What happened to your husband?"

"My family insisted that Larry was to blame. He had introduced me to heroin . . . he had seduced me. They swore out a warrant for his arrest and the marriage was annulled. Then my child was born . . . and I came here for the first of my stays."

"And your child?"

"My daughter is thirteen years old. My mother and father have raised her. I've seen her occasionally but they used coercion to keep her from me. My father recalled the time so many years before when I lay in my cast, when he had crept in to see me with the tears in his eyes. He said to me: 'You'll destroy your child, Myra. Leave her with us . . . you have no feelings . . . you have no feelings . . . you'll just destroy her. . . .' I think I've explained to you that my mother and father for all their advantages were not terribly perceptive. . . ."

"Did you take your daughter?"

"No. I always planned to when I got out of the hospital, but it didn't quite work out. The second time I came in here I met

a young doctor . . . he thought he could help me. I explained
to him that heroin had done things to me . . . but he was convinced that his love would help me to stop using. . . ." Slowly
she slipped a cigarette from the package and lighted it; the
smoke trickled from her nose. "He supported my habit for three
years, until he lost his license . . . and I came back here again."

"What happened to him?"

"I'd warned him. He joined some religious group, went to
South America where he could practice. . . ."

It was dark outside by now, just a red glow on the horizon
where the sun had gone down.

"My father said I was a menace to my daughter. He said
that I destroyed lives around me. I've been in and out of
hospitals, in and out of psychiatric bags. He said I was a dangerous woman. . . ."

"Are you?"

"I'm still rag-picking, still rag-picking. I want to find out. . . ."
She looked at me suddenly, her features strained, her dusky
voice still filled with magic, a magic she was unaware of. "I
think I want to find out, Mr. Cortina. . . . I think I want to find
out."

A few months later I was talking with my friend, the doctor
who had arranged my meeting with Myra. He said: "Your account is pretty accurate from what I knew about Myra. The prog-
nosis was all summed up by what she said at the end . . . about
thinking she wanted to find out."

"How did she die?"

"An overdose."

"Incredible."

"No, Frank . . . I think in some ways it was the most credible
thing about her. . . ."

6 *The mortality rate for hard drug users is appallingly high. The stories that reach the press of their deaths usually concern overdoses, rarely do you read of the enormous toll taken by hepatitis, septicemia, and other infections. The addict usually knows what to do in the case of an overdose; in fact, talking to them you might get the impression that they are amateur chemists. But the real irony and pathos is that the heroin addict wouldn't ever think of sterilizing his needle! Again, when the addict is strung out he is capable of the most vicious acts. He'll steal from his mother, father, wife, children. He'll scheme and connive with brilliance, he'll spin the most convincing tales, all to get his fix. Yet, the same individual can rarely motivate himself to attain even the most elementary goals. This "Badly Made Doll" is a pathetic representative of many that I have talked to, usually in a prison setting. Often I feel that maybe we are lucky that they go to heroin and not to guns. Often I am astonished that they endure at all.*

A Badly Made Doll

"It's jest a bunch of mixed up people, you know. They's kinda bustin' out at the seams because they's jest not with it."

Perce was a slight, fair man, his hospital garb set off the pallor of his skin.

"Though I don't think much about the world," he stroked his white pants leg, "Got enough on my own. . . . I'm pretty busy with my own life. . . ."

"You mean you have to concentrate on your own life?"

"You only got jest so much en-er-gy. . . . Time I got. . . .

70

Yes, suh, time I got . . . but I gotta put it all into little ol'
Perce."

Perce's face was seamed and appeared out of shape, but his
blond hair obviously was a source of pride to him, for it
was carefully groomed. "This need to concentrate on your own
life, Perce?"

"I'm twenty-nine years old and I got a wife and children and
I got a mother and I got a bag of busts behind me. . . . I'm a . . .
lemme tell you, Mister. . . ." He pointed to a scar below his
temple. "This is from a Texas pen, this knob over here is from
a Louisiana pen . . . and my teeth, which pushes out my lips,
they come from a kindly warden in a Mississippi joint. So you
see, Mister, I ain't got but so much time for anythin' but Perce
and his family." He said it simply, without emphasis, as if he
were giving me street directions. "Somehow, I gotta git through
Perce so as Perce kin git around to the supportin' his wife and
children. I'm thinkin' of that all the time. You see, it's Perce,
who's got . . . he's got to come up with the git to do it. . . ." He
gave me a sideways look. "Be awright, Mister, if I smoke?"

"Go ahead . . . I'm imposing on you, Perce. I'm obliged to
you for seeing me. You didn't have to."

His words came out wreathed in smoke. "Believe me, it's time
that Perce he got with it. He kinda brung himself together. He's
all parts like a badly made doll. A part from this prison, another
part from the parish jail, another part this reformatory. . . . Yes,
suh, Perce, he wanted to talk to you, to tell you about shootin'
dope. I think it even surprised the doctor after he tol' us about
your comin' that I offered up to talk. . . ." Perce grinned,
almost to himself. "They wuz surprised that Ol' Perce he spoke
up and ast to go and talk. . . . See, they's other guys here who
talks better . . . but I got my story, too, and it's good for Perce."
He smoked his cigarette in that husbanding way, a mannerism I
had come to associate with the prisons. "Not that I wuz ever
too much interested in the world . . . not really, you might

say. . . . On the outside it jest seems like I wuz always on the go, runnin' around with a bunch of people I shouldn't have rightly been with and windin' up shootin' drugs, and then when I got hung up on drugs I didn't care about nothin' . . . I didn't care about nothin'."

"So your preoccupation was really with Perce. Not with your family—with yourself."

"That's the way it wuz. Perce feedin' his habit."

"Where did you come from?"

"Louisiana, way down." Perce looked at me, a momentary suspicion on his face. He shook his head. "Damn, but it's hard to talk."

"Were you using drugs before you got married?"

"Er, I wuz chippyin', like you might say I wuz dabblin'."

"What drug were you dabbling with?"

"Well, I started out with dilaudid. . . ."

"That's morphine, isn't it?"

"It's what we usta call drugstore medicine. That's what I got turned out on. . . . Well, though, that ain't so either, from a kid I usta fool around with other things too . . . barbies . . . barbiturates."

"I didn't think anybody could fool with the barbiturates."

"Well, you know now, Mister, that's true, you don't fool with them. I meant I wuz dabblin' with them. . . . See, Perce he always wanted somethin' bigger . . . he went from tobacca, to booze, to weed, to pills, to dilaudid, to heroin. No kit wuz ever big enough fer Perce until he hit heroin. I always wanted somethin' bigger."

"You've had a fairly long experience using drugs."

"I have."

"And all kinds, hard and soft." I watched him carefully, neatly, shred his dead cigarette into the ash tray. "How long were you addicted?"

"More'n eight years . . . you know, on and off . . . cause sometimes you can't git horse and so you can't shoot so you just take what you kin git. But before I wuz ever addicted I wuz usin'."

"How old were you when you started to use anything?"

Perce leaned over, rested his elbows on his knees. "I musta been twelve or thereabouts. . . . It wuz weed I smoked. Then I started on redbirds, they called them. . . ."

"Secobarbital?"

"Yeah. It kinda gives you a mella feelin'. It didn't make you wanna git up and push around. It jest sorta set you down and let you be real free and easy . . . coastin' . . . long . . . slow . . . coast. . . ."

"Were you that kind of kid, who needed quiet and to be by himself? Were these redbirds just made for your temperament? You see what I mean, Perce?"

"I do . . . it's an interestin' point you made there, Mister. I'm gonna think about that . . . I can't answer it. . . . At that time it wuz jest the kinda bag I wanted to be in. But you got a point . . . an' they's another thing, too—they wuz the things runnin' jest then, too."

"You mean they were available in your area?"

"Right. The other kids wuz usin' 'em. And they wuz cheap. . . . Be all right if I smoke, Mister?"

I saw that he would ask me the same question right on through the exchange; it was second nature. "Sure. Perce, you just followed these other kids?"

"I wanted to be accepted, you know. I thought this wuz what I wanted to be, accepted by them . . . and to be accepted I had to be one of them."

"Have you ever thought back on that now? Have you ever considered that you had another choice, that perhaps you might have gone with another crowd?"

"Oh, yeah . . . I've seen and heard of several others of my school buddies who didn't run with the crowd, they's quite successful now . . . yes, they's made it good." He said it very equably, almost with respect.

"Does that fill you with regret, or is that a stupid question?"

"No need to apologize, Mister, my feelin's ain't all that tender, though I thank you. Besides, it ain't a stupid question because questions like that gotta be asked junk users, because nine times outa ten them is the very questions the junk user has been runnin' away from answerin'. Does it fill me with regret? It makes me stop and look at myself . . . see what I coulda accomplished. . . . And I think I could a made it, too. . . . But I wuz always one of them hard-headed types, nobody could tell me nothin'. And I wind up all the time in a bunch of trouble."

"Nobody could tell you anything, Perce . . . or could it be the other way around? Nobody who meant anything to you ever bothered?"

"Well, yes and no . . . I never knew my father . . . I can't remember him none at all. As I git it he jest kinda faded away when I wuz just an idda biddy kid. . . . My mother, now. . . ."

"Your mother came down real hard on you?"

"No, my mother was real lenient, very lenient . . . too lenient. . . . Anything I wanted I got. . . . Well, I thought I wuz gittin' everythin' I wanted. . . . Now that I've stopped shootin' and you know what these doctors dig outa you . . . they really dig up stuff about you that you never even thought of . . . seems like I never had the right kind of parents. My mother wuz too lenient, and not havin' a father . . . I just kinda misused her, jest took advantage of her . . . like a kid he's gotta have a framework around him. . . . When things is too loose, like you might say . . . he's got too much room to walla around . . . take advantage of. . . ." Perce cowled his cigarette.

"Do you think the doctors are right in their suggestion?"

"I think they got a bead on it, Mister. Of course, I didn't realize any of this when I was doin' it as a kid."

"You had trouble in school?"

"I wuz always a clown. . . . In other words, I always had to git. . . . I mean I always had to be the center of attraction. When

Perce he wuz there everybody laughed, you know. I wuz always
a joke cracker."

"You say clown, Perce. Interesting description."

"It's the right way, Mister, to put it. When you're a clown,
you gotta turn on the jokes no matter what."

"What did you think would happen if you didn't?"

"I keepa image . . . I keepa image. . . ."

"Were you scared that if you didn't clown they'd pass you
by . . . is that it?"

"You're right. They woulda passed me by . . . not give a damn.
. . . I see that now."

"How far did you get in school, Perce?"

Again he went through the cigarette-shredding ritual. "I finished the sixth grade and I quit . . . I jest up and quit. . . . My
age wuz against me."

"Your age was against you?"

"At sixteen, you shouldn't be in the sixth grade . . . no, suh,
accordin' to the way of things, you shouldn't ought to be in the
sixth grade at sixteen. . . ."

"Were you truanting so much, or sick, or unable to do the
work. . . ?"

"I did everythin'. Hookey . . . I wuz smokin' weed . . . I
couldn't really read good . . . I still can't though I'm gittin' better . . . and the teachers they had a real hard time with me on
accounta my bein' the clown like I told you. See, they kept me
in the fourth grade for three years. . . ."

"A clown. . . ."

"I wuz jest a comedian, you know. My thoughts weren't all
that happy, I expect. But, see, I never really got down on myself.
If I hada done that, got down on myself, things mighta been
different. I jest put in the time . . . I don't know why things were
like they were or I did the things I did, I jest wuz always tryin'
to pass the time I imagine. Cause like I say, I come from a good
family, what little family I have. I'm the oldest of my brothers

and sisters. And I got a younger brother; my younger brother he carries hisself better than me. And when I got addicted to drugs, man, I jest lost my family . . . they jest put me down . . . my brothers and my sisters, they put me down."

"Would you have done the same to them?"

"No, I don't think so . . . but it's hard to say. I'm thinkin' all this at the present time. Hard to say what you do in the past with your present thinkin'. See, this younger brother he never had no drug experience. The first time I heard he wuz tryin' pills, I like to beat him half to death, you know, because I wuz already hooked on them myself. Them damned things . . . Jesus!"

"Barbiturates can really hook you badly. . . ."

"They can be jest plain hell, Mister, jest plain hell. . . . You don't never know when you is really off the damned things . . . they's worse than horse, a dozen times over. But my brother he wuzn't usin' redbirds . . . he wuz tryin' goof balls . . . them is the amphetamines. I usta take them and go half crazy behind them . . . half crazy behind them jest like a steer who drinks water with a chemical in it . . . I usta jest go crazy behind them."

"And yet, you stopped your brother, and continued to use them yourself?" He frowned. "You weren't addicted to the amphetamines . . .?"

"In those days I didn't know nothin' about bein' hooked . . . all I knew wuz that they made me go off my head. I took them because you jest want to do something, you want to be out, to git high or whatever you want to call it. . . . But these amphetamines, I wuz turned against them finally, finally . . . one night I went out and I had a handful of these pills . . . they didn't seem to do nothin' first. I went with about six of them and I jest got a little sting like but I kep' eatin' them like candy. And it wuz three days and three nights before I come to. They found me on the wharf and figgered I wuz dead. They thought I wuz dead. . . . It turned me away from them goof balls."

"What about the barbiturates, did you give those up?"

"No, I didn't, they give me grief, too. It's a different trip, though . . . but they's hell those damned things, they really is. I used redbirds lots of times when I'd be sick from heroin, so sick I couldn't git to hustlin' to git myself straightened out. . . . Then I'd eat about eight of these barbiturates. Now, they wouldn't take my heroin sickness all away, but they made it easier. But I seen people who tried to kick from the barbies . . . Mister, they is bad. . . . Now, me, I took cold turkey with heroin all by myself on the street, I took it three times. Each trip worse than the last. It gits worse . . . man, I wuz so sick like I wanted to die. . . ."

"What made you kick?"

"I wuz busted . . . I couldn't git heroin. The last time I wuz in the parish jail . . . took twenty-one days fer me to git over it. . . ."

"Twenty-one days. . . ."

"Yes, suh, Mister . . . about nine straight days of cramps that tore my gut . . . twenty-one days before I come back. . . ."

"How long has it been since you've had a shot of heroin, Perce?"

"About eleven months. I been here in this hospital fer eight months, before that I wuz three months in the county jail. . . ."

"What were you in for?"

"I wuz on several charges, like . . . I wuz out on bond already fer simple burglary and possession of narcotics . . . and then I got picked up fer armed robbery. I wuz innocent to the charge and they knowed it, too . . . but I understood I wuz gittin' too much in their hair I imagine. Every time they'd see me they'd try to shake you down or put a vagrancy charge against you or somethin' . . . git you offa the street. . . ."

"I suppose if you have a reputation and there's no law to specifically cover. . . ."

"Absolutely right, Mister. They's no law to cover it and they gotta clean up the street, so they git you . . . they git you. They stay on you till they git you. It's their job."

"How much have you stolen over the years, Perce?"

"Well, I wuz shootin' up over one hundred and thirty a day. And I wuz supportin' my wife and three kids as well. So what with one plus and another plus. . . ."

"How much did you have to swipe in a day?"

"At least three hundred, at least three hundred. And on that I'd be sick on accounta I couldn't shoot enough to keep me well. I'd be all right if I could git about four hundred and twenty-five a day. . . ."

"What were your types of crimes?"

"Burglary . . . I'd steal anythin', anythin' . . . anythin' I could get my hands on. Colored television sets, stereos. . . ."

I stared at him, his slightness of physique. "How could you manage . . .?"

"When you're sick, Mister, you kin carry a mountain. I'd git in and outa those homes with big sets in my arms. I'd lug the stuff out the back onto the grass, or I'd bust a winda; I wuz reckless, I wouldn't check whether anybody wuz home, er . . . I wouldn't try to disguise the fac' that I wuz a burglar . . . I didn't care, Mister, I jest didn't care."

"And the stuff you stole . . . would you have it fenced?"

"I had three, four fences, different fence for different things."

"Did you haggle over the prices they offered you?"

"Well, you know, jest bein' a drug addict . . . jest bein' a drug addict they kinda think they could misuse you, too . . . you git beaten out on all sides. . . . And the people look at you as if you're a mangy dog. . . ."

"I suspect part of that is maybe because you feel like a dog yourself."

"Well, you don't have much respect. See that wind out there pushin' them leaves . . .? That's what a hype's like . . . the heroin pushin' him. He ain't got no respect. Ever fish, ever catch a fish, and look at that hook in his mouth . . . that hook that's got a barb on it? That's where it's all at, Mister . . .

hooked . . . that steel thing in your mouth . . . you ain't wrigglin' off. . . ."

"You were able to provide for your family in this way. . . ."

"Well, I jest kep' 'em with somethin' to eat, a roof over their heads, it wuzn't nothin' extraordinary. You couldn't even call it a home, you know, because of the attitude I'd be in. You know, I ain't never seen my third boy, my youngest one . . . my other children . . . Mister, I don't know . . . maybe you're a doctor, maybe you know . . . you don't . . . you take your last penny, and you don't worry about it. You don't worry that your wife and kids ain't gonna eat, you don't worry about nothin' exceptin' you're gonna git straightened. I mean I wuz really gittin' down rank you know . . . rank, rank. . . . I said before that my family put me down . . . but my mother and my wife, they stood by me, they never cut me loose like the rest of the family. My mother had heart attacks and everythin' behind what I did. . . . Lord, man, Lord, she'd get a call from the police . . . 'Here's your son down here with dope.' I had a '66 new Chevrolet, I lost that, I lost my family, I like to have lost my wife and kids. . . . I had all my own furniture . . . I wuz doin' good at first . . . real good . . . I had money saved . . . I wuz a tile setter. I learned the trade in prison. I washed everythin' out . . . I went down, down . . . you kin only go one way with the heroin . . . down, Mister, down."

His Louisiana patois was like music, soft and lulling. He was staring at the ground, his hands clasped together, the nails showing white from the pressure he exerted. "I been in prisons all over the Southwest, I been in jails, in reformatories, and now this hospital, my last resort . . . this hospital. . . ."

"And most of your charges?"

"Burglary and narcotics. . . ."

"No crimes of violence?"

"That wuzn't my bag . . . I never touched nobody . . . I always been scared of guns . . . I never could use a gun or a knife. . . ."

Perce pointed his finger at me: "I spent most of my life in the joint."

"Did any of your lock-ups help you?"

"No, I jest got worse. . . ."

"That's a pretty devastating comment. . . ."

"It's true, cause my problem wuz dope and in the joint I kept shootin' in there."

"You mean, you could get drugs inside the prison . . .?"

"Jest the same like in the street. Lemme explain, Mister. When you're in the joint you're clean so you don't need to git so much to take off. . . . Your body it ain't built up this need fer a big jolt . . . you jest kin coast with a smaller shot. . . . But there ain't been a joint I been in where I couldn't score. They's a connection anywhere you go and you got the money fer a fix. So the joint wuz no answer. . . . It's jest been in the eight months that I been here that I kin say I really begin to see some help fer myself . . . and I come here to beat another rap . . . I come here to miss a charge. . . . It's all a accident, Mister, a accident. . . ."

"Why is this place so different?"

"They kinda put me to myself. They put me in a predicament where I gotta cope with my problems better and problems I never knew I had. See, they make me somehow see that I done things with dope because of problems. . . ."

"Do you believe that, Perce?"

"Yes, I do. Don't nobody act like me except fer a reason. . . . See, I got hangups . . . other people caught their hangups at a younger age than Perce . . . I got hangups, Mister."

"Do you know what they are?"

"Sure, biggest one is my mother. I wuz always a kinda mamma's boy . . . I never knowed that, Mister . . . but it is true. I see that now . . . my mother, to this present time, she don't want to cut loose of me. Like you got a wife and kids but she still thinks you need her to clean up after you. You see, when I axed her about this. . . ."

"You mean you actually confronted your mother. . . ?"

"Mister, I'm talkin' about my life now. Don't you see, if I ain't honest now . . . now . . . I'm through. I axed my mother, I confronted her with it. She don't want to accept it . . . it hurt her, Mister, it hurt her . . . she gived so much fer me . . . it killed me to do it. But I saw jest at that time she never had talked with me as to a grown-up. It hurt, Mister . . . I tol' her though. She stopped writin' three months ago . . . I lay down in my bed some nights, I sweat, fearin' that she's a dyin', that I druv her to somethin' cause she don't understand how all this got turned around, but it has. . . ."

"That really takes guts."

"It don't take no more fuckin' guts, than it takes to game yourself. I've been gamin' all my life. I'm twenty-nine years old. You gotta admit to yourself the truth. I mean you gotta want to do something yourself . . . otherwise you go right out there and start all over again. I'm twenty-nine years old . . . I'm old. See, Mister, there is so much about this dope that's all in the head. The kickin', like I was gonna say before . . . if you could remember the pain you had kickin', if you could remember it like it wuz, maybe you wouldn't shoot any more. You know . . . the cold sweats, and cramps, and backache. Like a woman who could remember the pain of the childbirth she might never git pregnant again. . . . But at least she's got the baby. . . . See, here, I learn heroin has got a life of its own . . . got a world of its own. You don't chippy with it. It takes you, cause you wanna be taken. See, I can't ever fergit the high . . . never as long as I live . . . I can't ever fergit the gutter that I throwed myself into. The pain has no meaning . . . once you're addicted to heroin, you're always addicted even through you git cured. . . . That's true, Mister . . . like an alcoholic . . . he's gotta stay off, he can't chippy. Look, I ain't no brave or strong man . . . sometimes I usta wonder whether I wuz even a man . . . but I'm gonna know why I went to use heroin and all the rest of the stuff I took."

"Perce, you're in a unique position to help. You have children of your own, you've been through the drug bag, you say you're through it. . . . What are you going to do to prevent your children starting . . .?"

He fingered the scar below his temple. "I haven't really thought about it like you jest put it to me. See, I ain't really been a father . . . but I will admit that it's somethin' I'll have to think about . . . because drugs is goin' be around, it's here to stay, it's goin' be like this fer some time. I think my little boy who's six, he's seen some of what his Poppa's been through. You know, my wife usta give this same boy lunch money and maybe she'd have a coupla pennies to give him to buy hisself somethin' extra . . . like candy or like that . . . and he say to my wife: 'You keep that, Momma, and save it for Poppa on accounta Poppa's gonna need medicine because Poppa gits sick." Perce straightened up in his chair and searched my face. "I told that little boy about my bein' sick. One day he bust right into the bathroom when I had the outfit in my arm . . . I see his face wonderin'. Yes, Mister, I put that story to him about his Poppa bein' sick and takin' medicine . . . to make him better. . . . That little boy, he saves his pennies . . . I mean, Mister, how do you think that makes me feel? I git all twisted up inside when I think of that . . . what kinda man could?" Perce couldn't find the answer and let the remark dangle. "See, I had no father. Lord only knows if it woulda been different if he'da stayed . . . but that ain't no reason to start the whole mess all over again with my kids because their old man is a hype. I'm gonna tell my kids . . . I'm gonna tell 'em the God's honest truth about their father. I ain't gonna scare 'em. I'm gonna tell 'em as honest as I can what about pills and weed and junk . . . I'm gonna tell 'em much as I know as to why their Poppa used. Scarin' don't work with a kid . . . and bein' away in the joint as much as I been don't help your kids to know you or listen to you. But this is over and done, Mister . . . the hype he's always cryin' and moanin' and runnin' . . . all for hisself . . . he's only sorry for hisself. . . . Me too . . . but Perce, God he wuz so ignorant . . . ignorant. But I ain't anymore . . . maybe I don't know exactly all the way where Perce is comin' but I know enough. I thank

the Lord that I come here to this hospital . . . I thank the Lord.
I don't know how long I gotta stay . . . but I got a goal. . . .
You know, like people got goals to be big businessmen, or successful somethin' or other . . . I got a goal . . . to go back with
my family . . . rightly they don't need me but I need them and
maybe some time it'll be that they will need me, when I show
them . . . when I show them I'm worth needin'."

"So it's over, Perce."

"No, Mister, it ain't over. . . . It'll never be over until Perce
is dead. Heroin is there . . . I respect it . . . I don't know how
much it's gonna take . . . how much I'm gonna have my face
rubbed in shit . . . but I hung it up . . . Mister, I hung it up . . .
Perce, he's hung it up."

7 *I looked down on that cold pallet, viewing what thirty-six hours earlier had been a strident bird of prey, swinging her hips, uttering her raucous cries, seeking her quarry—did I know her? To look down and see her so waxen, so shrunken, so frail, so dead—did I know her? Gone was the fierce compulsion for that white powder, that fever of survival, the pounding, harrying burden of heroin; gone was the mumbled phrase, the nodding, the fog, the filth, the half-memory—of husband, of child, of parents; gone was the stupendous weariness, the despair, the self-destruction. I stared at that puny creature, her ribs like welts, occupying so small a space, so still now that life was gone, and read on those frozen features all of the unutterable ravages of the heroin union. Did I know her? Yes, I knew her. I knew her and dozens like her: Rosa-Rosey.*

Rosa-Rosey

Whenever I am in New York City, there is a certain street that I walk through. It is on this street that I can occasionally spot my special acquaintances, drug abusers. When I see one of them on this beat, then I know I must pass them by, for they are at work, poised like birds of prey awaiting a victim. But it was a cold October rain that splashed down and I hadn't recognized anyone in the passing faces. I turned the corner and quickly moved back from a spray of gutter water raised by a speeding taxi.

"You dirty son of a bitch . . .," she muttered. She was very close to me. "Selfish bastards. . . ." I turned and looked at her trying to shake off some of the water from her skirt. She had

84

gotten thinner, but I recognized her immediately and waited to see if she remembered. I followed her to where she had taken cover under an awning. She said, still preoccupied by her sodden clothing, "I was following you, Jack . . . when that bastard sprayed me. It's a wet night, Jack. I thought you might be looking for some fun."

"Rosa-Rosey."

She became motionless, then turned and looked at me with surprise. "Oh, my God, it's the Professor. . . ."

"Rosa-Rosey . . . I'm glad to see you."

Something like a smile hovered on her face. "Likewise. . . ." She quickly looked away. "I can't talk now, I'm very busy."

"I realize that. But you can't go on working with those wet clothes on."

"The hell I can't," she said grimly. I could tell by the color of the voice what I suppose I already knew—she was back on stuff. "Can't talk to you, Professor." She shook herself like a hen, lifted her head scarf, and prepared to step back out into the rain.

"Are you back on stuff, Rosa-Rosey?"

"I'm much too busy now, Professor . . . some other time?"

"Can't I buy you a drink, let you get in out of the rain for a couple of minutes . . .?"

"I swear I can't, Professor."

"Rosa, you can't game me with that. . . ."

"How much would you go for a drink? Would you go for seven-fifty?"

"Sure."

"Okay, gimme the seven-fifty and I'll be right back." Quickly she palmed the ten-dollar bill. "Christ, good thing I know you . . . they'd take you skin and all. Be right back. Don't go 'way . . . and don't wink at any pretty girls like me."

She was back in ten minutes, a cigarette dangling from her mouth, her head erect, her clothes still wet. "Okay, let's have that drink."

We found a bar around the corner, got a booth and ordered our drinks. She sat there smiling at me. "For Chris'sakes. I hardly recognized you."

"But I recognized you right away."

"You ain't gonna write me up tonight though, Professor."

"I'm flattered by the Professor, Rosa."

"You don't know but half of it . . . I only took enough to keep me from sickness just now, so's I would want to talk with you."

"The last time I saw you. . . ."

She reached over and put a finger across my lips. "No last times, Charley . . . no last times."

When an addict feels the let-down of heroin he doesn't like to be disturbed; it interferes with the high. I said quietly: "How long have you been back on, Rosa-Rosey?"

"I nearly wet my pants when I heard that 'Rosa-Rosey' out there in the street . . . 'Rosa-Rosey' said to me in the rain . . . I nearly wet my pants . . . I was that surprised."

"How long have you been back on?"

"For days, weeks, years . . . who knows, Professor?" It was like watching someone in slow-motion, to see her movements. She hunched forward on the table so she could look up at me. "Were you frolicin' tonight . . . were you out shoppin' for a little bit of chicken?"

"I was just walking. . . ."

"Lookin' for me . . . weren't you . . . lookin' for me?"

"No . . . I wasn't . . . I'm glad and sorry at the same time that I saw you."

"Please, none of that shit . . . it's so nice and quiet in here."

A juke box was blaring, a couple of sailors were singing out of tune, the bar was packed with customers, and the miniskirted bar girls had to thread their way through the crowded aisles; but for Rosa-Rosey it was quiet. "Rosa, come back to my hotel with me?"

An arch expression on her face, she said: "You wanna turn a trick? Or you wanna talk? No gaming Rosa-Rosey."

"I'll pay regular rates, Rosa . . . regular rates. . . ."

"You'll pay . . .? Gimbel's basement rates . . . twenty-five dollars a trick."

"I'll pay, Rosa."

She downed her drink, slowly got herself together, and rose. She took the arm I offered her. As she pulled it close I could feel her rib casing—what a far cry from the twenty-four-year-old I had spoken to in an institution ten months before. Then she had complained about getting fat, that institution food was mostly starch, a fact, she said, that came home to her every time she sat down.

"I'll get a cab . . . my hotel's on the East Side uptown."

"Blow the cab, Professor. You come with Rosa-Rosey. You're so cute, you are . . . you come with Rosa-Rosey. You're comin' to my place. . . ." We started down the block toward Ninth Avenue, a series of brown stooped houses stained by the rain. I was impressed by Rosa-Rosey's walk; apart from her saunter-ing pace, she seemed to walk naturally. We passed a policeman who paid no attention to us. I waited to see if Rosa reacted to him. She made no sign and continued to talk in that faint murmur. "I never got to read your book, Professor. You was writin' a book . . . you wasn't a cop. Some of the girls said you was a cop tryin' to shake us down . . . but I knew you wasn't a cop. I knew you was lookin' for information. Up here . . . watch the top step . . . some God-damned kid broke the stone . . . you could trip."

It was fascinating to watch her open her purse, take out the key, open the door; everything was natural except for the pace. Inside there was a dimly glowing globe hanging from the ceiling, a bank of mailboxes, and a flight of stairs that curved up near the landing. She preceded me and said: "No pinchin' now. You guys are terrible these days, you pinch . . . especially these God-damned foreigners. . . . I'm black and blue from this pinchin' bag. What the hell is it with the pinchin'?"

When we got to the first floor she led the way into a narrow corridor with doors on either side. We stopped at the last one in the rear. I could hear voices inside, and music. Again in that slow, let-down way she opened the door. "Welcome home, Professor. Grab yourself some chair." The voices and the music were coming from the television set in the corner of the room. She pointed toward it. "My company . . . I'm gonna change."

The room must have been the back parlor of the brownstone at one time. It had a high ceiling with a plaster frieze, wainscotted walls, and a pair of narrow Victorian windows. There was a small rug, a studio couch, a rocker, and one stuffed chair covered with chintz. In a corner I spied a hot-plate partially hidden by a bedsheet hanging on a line; a smell of lemon oil hung in the air. There were no books, no pictures, no magazines, no papers. I removed my coat as she came out in a chenille bathrobe.

"Professor . . . how did I come out in the book, huh? Did I go back to my husband and kid? Did I go back to California and live happily ever after?"

"No, Rosa-Rosey." I found myself speaking slowly, very distinctly, quietly. "I ended the story with you still in the hospital, with you saying to me that your future was chancy."

" 'Chancy,' is that what I said? Very good for me. You made me smart . . . talking to me, you made me smart. Rosa-Rosey said 'chancy.' That sounds good. . . ."

"How much are you using?"

"As much as I can get."

"You've gotten greedy?"

She took one of my cigarettes. I lighted it for her. "I liked talking to you that day. Tellin' you about my mother with her God-damned religion. Rosalie can't go dancin'. Rosalie can't be with boys . . . made me like an idiot . . . didn't I say that?"

"Yes. . . . You also said, I recall, that your relationships with men were lousy. You said you knew how to please men sexually and how to abuse them sexually but you didn't know how to get

along with them in a regular way. Remember, you told me you
were taking a course in a marriage counseling program?"

"Yes, I did . . . I did, take a course, too. . . . But it didn't
work. He couldn't stick, neither could I . . . Professor, we
couldn't do it . . . we couldn't talk together as much as you and
me can talk. . . . I always figgered what's his percentage. . . ."

"Where's your son?"

She shook her head, shrugged off what appeared to be an
unpleasant reality. I took a guess. "The kid has wound up with
your mother . . . the very thing you said you didn't want to
happen because you feared that the same thing would happen
to him that happened to you. . . ."

"Shush . . . Shush . . . I'll make you leave . . . you're in my
home. You ain't in my business quarters . . . I done you a great
honor, Professor, I brought you to my home."

"This is not where you turn your tricks?"

She was staring at the television picture. "I never turn it off
. . . words come tumblin' out of it . . . words, words. . . ."

I remembered from our interview months before she'd said
that one of her great "hangups" had been to be able to talk with
people. She felt that most of her trouble was in expressing what
she was feeling. She had said that she and her husband continued
to bottle up everything until it became so intense that there was
an explosion. He had been a user, too. "Rosa, has your husband
gone back to stuff?"

She shook her head. "This is my home . . . I didn't take you
to the pad where I do business. . . ."

"Has your husband . . .?"

"Man, I heard you. You don't have to yell . . . speak soft,
man, like speak soft. . . ."

She wasn't going to answer that question. She had said months
ago that addicts learn how to turn aside, learn how to "round"
on a situation that they didn't want to be bothered with. "You've
gotten very thin, Rosa . . . you've lost a lot of weight."

"I'm gonna go on a diet to gain some weight, when I come out of my bust . . . I was a hundred and forty-eight . . . a hundred and forty-eight. . . ."

"What's your weight now?"

"Weight? Who the Christ knows. Bless yourself . . . we have uttered the name of Christ in this house. My mother would look up, her eyes closed, and mumble a prayer . . . Blessed be His wonderful Name. . . ."

I imagined that Rosa had lost fifty pounds. "Rosa, how long did you stay off after you came out?"

"How long?" She shook her head. "Thirty-six days . . . and I blew California . . . I wasn't goin' back to that place . . . three strikes and you're out . . . three strikes and you're out."

"Does anybody know where you are?"

Suddenly, unexpectedly, she straightened up, a study in fear, the television playing a running accompaniment. "You rattin' me out?"

"Of course not, Rosa. You know I've no official connection with any program. I just wondered if anybody knew where you were."

She continued to study me, her pupils dilated, almost as if I had slipped out of focus. She slowly fixed her eyes on the TV screen.

"How much are you using a day, Rosa?"

"Sixteen bags . . . if I can get it."

"How many tricks do you have to turn to support your habit?"

"As many as I can. But not tonight . . . I got my Professor. You sure you don't want to turn a trick with me? I'm real fine . . . real fine. . . ."

"I'm sure you are, Rosa-Rosey."

"But I can't turn a trick with you if you call me Rosa-Rosey. . . . I get all choked up when you call me that . . . don't call me that . . . Rosa-Rosey. . . ."

"What's going to happen to you?"

"I'm gonna kick. I'm stoppin' . . . seein' you . . . I'm gonna squash it. . . ."

"Shall I take you to a hospital then?"

"Shush . . . shush . . . you make so much noise, so much noise. . . . Man, like you jar me, man. . . ."

Twenty-four, what had once been blonde hair, a face gaunt, arms that were like sticks where they stuck out from the chenille robe, her breasts hanging slacky beneath the robe. . . . I couldn't keep the picture of the Rosa-Rosey of ten months earlier from my mind. She hadn't been garrulous then, but she seemed to enjoy the experience. She had said some very interesting things about the problems of age and the female heroin addict—how the female user was really through at forty or perhaps earlier, for her looks would be gone and she couldn't attract men. She said that one of her nightmares was to find herself an aging female addict "trying to pross, repulsive, looking like some sea beast that should have remained on the ocean bottom." It was this fear, since she had always supported her habit through prostitution, that had made her enter the hospital. She had said: "You know, you look in that mirror every day. And every day there's just another faint sign. Then you fix and you look . . . you're high and you say now the mirror is telling the truth . . . now it's telling the truth. Rosa-Rosey looks like a doll . . . I'll always be young . . . I look like a doll."

I wondered now, as I looked at her, if she was conscious of her altered appearance, of her present reality and how different it was from what she had planned when we spoke in the rehabilitation center. I was willing to bet that Rosa-Rosey never forgot a single failure no matter how small it was. Using heroin brought only short-term surcease from the addict's terrifying recall of persistent and nagging failure. She looked so wasted, so weary. She certainly didn't look like a doll now, with her head nodding, her hands folded, her body slouched.

"Rosa-Rosey, why don't you let me take you to the hospital?"

She stirred and pulled up the robe closer around her body. "Aw, why don't you go and let me alone, Charley? For Chris' sakes. You got your story from me . . . what do you want . . .? Come here houndin' me like all the rest of the square sons of bitches with their square Bibles. . . . Blow, man, blow . . . take your cap and shoot, man. . . ."

"Rosa, there's no percentage. . . ."

"You're gonna take me back and put me on that magic carpet so Rosa can be out there with the rest of the faggots . . . cut, cut. . . ."

"I have a friend, Rosa. He's a doctor. They have a methadone program in the city . . . he'll help you. Remember what you said when we talked . . . you said: 'Maybe there's some of us who can never live without some kind of stuff to keep us going . . . some of us who've got to have a special kind of world. . . .' Do you remember that you said that to me?"

She was frowning, her breathing was faster now, she appeared to be less relaxed. I looked at my watch. Two hours or more had passed since she had asked me for the seven-fifty for her shot. "Yeah . . . so what . . .?"

I didn't quite know how to talk to her without her feeling that I was preaching at her, coming over "square" on her. "Rosey, I want to help you. . . ."

She smiled. "You do?"

"Yes, I do. . . ."

"You want to help me? I'm gonna be sick on accounta I only took half a bag so's I could talk with you. Pay me the money you promised me . . . so I can fix. You wanna help me . . .?"

I smelled the lemon oil, the dampness that must have been in the dark wainscotting, the odor of Rosa-Rosey's drying clothes. I pulled some money out of my wallet and passed it to her. Her hand, like a talon, grabbed it. "Never trust a hype . . . you should know that by now, Professor. . . . Now you can blow . . . blow . . . delighted to see you . . . blow. . . ."

"Rosa, won't you try and consider . . .?"

She got up abruptly, her robe hanging open, "Tomorrow . . .
tomorrow . . . don't save me tonight. Tomorrow, you come back
and save me. Now unless you want me to earn my money . . .
I gotta get dressed, man . . . I'm gettin' awful jumpy. You know
. . . I'm pluckin' my nerves and they're tellin' me that I gotta go
look for my connection. No more words, no more words . . .
tomorrow. . . ." She went into the bathroom and closed the door.

I pulled on my coat and sat down. Perry Mason was engaged
in some legal exchange with the prosecuting attorney on the
television set. Rosa came out, dressed for the street.

"Come on, you ain't stayin' here all night. This is my home,
not some flop-house . . . let's go." She carefully locked the door
behind us. "Awful crooks in this neighborhood . . . junkies mostly
. . . I leave the TV on so's they think somebody's inside, otherwise they'd beat me outa all my belongin's."

On the street it was still raining. Here and there someone
passed. We walked toward Eighth Avenue, and I tried once
more. "Rosa . . . I'm glad to have seen you. . . ."

"That's shit and you know it. You think I'da been glad to see
me . . . shit . . . I'm a God-damned tramp . . . which is what I was
before when I saw you in California. . . . Just a God-damned
tramp . . . blamin' my mother and my husband and my kid for
what happened to me. I'm a God-damned tramp. . . ." We were
under a street lamp. She put out a hand and touched my coat.
The rain slanted down. "See, see how I can put you off . . . keep
you away . . . how I can spin out things . . . you don't know
when I'm gamin' you . . . you don't know when I'm lyin'. You
don't know who's the real Rosa-Rosey . . . you don't know,
Professor. . . ." She looked at me, frowning. "I don't know that
I know anymore . . . but I'm gonna get sick . . . I gotta score,
Professor. . . ."

"Rosa . . . what's the percentage?"

"I'm gettin' older . . . that's the percentage. I'm not gonna get
to be some skinny hag that frightens men to death and makes
them run . . . I'm not gonna get to be a sea monster . . . I'm

gonna kick. Oh, yes, Professor, I'm gonna kick . . . but not tonight. . . ." She put out one thin hand. The rain glistened on it as it touched mine. "Next time, I'll give you your money's worth."

And she strode swiftly away. It was terrifying to see the energy in her stride now. She had a purpose, she had a drive— she had to get her bag of heroin. It was the one motivation in her life.

8 *Mr. Trellis stands out in my mind, his fists clenched, his head cocked defiantly, every inch of him breathing forcefulness, wanting desperately to strike out against somebody for what has happened to his son. His strength, his personal energy is powerless against his son's heroin addiction. The Trellises of this world cannot understand how their very strength fosters their child's weaknesses, how their dominating love represses and emasculates.*

The Too-Present Father

"You use different words when you have a son involved. Everything else fades before that. Phrases, ideas, fears, all seem on the outside. It has happened to my son. It has happened to me directly. My son is a heroin addict." Mr. Trellis sat erectly with his hands clasped in front of him.

"How old is your son?"

"Going on eighteen."

I reckoned Mr. Trellis' age to be around forty-five, though judging by his fit appearance he might have been younger. "Well, there's nothing remote about that."

"A whole series of factors come into play. The division in the family, court costs, the effect it has upon my life. . . . It's like a great big spreading blot." His words came out precisely, as if they had been honed.

"That's a curious thing. Lots of times when I talk to drug abusers they'll say that they aren't harming anyone by using drugs but themselves."

He shook his head. "Yes, I'm familiar with that. 'I'm only damaging myself.' Yes, I'm familiar with that. But the truth is that it's not just my son's habit, it's my habit, it's my wife's and my other children . . . its the neighborhood's and the city's. . . . One person on heroin and countless lives are involved. I can't walk down the street the way I used to because of my son's habit. I can't work the way I used to because of my son's habit . . . like a blot. I bear the blame in my neighbor's eyes. How could Trellis allow his son to become a heroin addict, Trellis who has had advantages, Trellis who is a teacher? I can interpret what they're saying. Trellis could do something about it if he really wanted to. You know, Trellis, he could beat it out of his son . . . shake some sense into him. Must be something wrong there, when your son uses heroin, when he becomes a thief, when he's arrested by the police . . . oh, yes, the blot spreads."

"I'm sorry that I've stirred up old wounds, Mr. Trellis."

"Nothing bothers me. Believe me. I'm happy to talk with you. If I can get some action by airing my views I'll talk until I'm blue in the face." He hitched his chair closer to the table. "This is not something you keep quiet. Even if you wanted to, you couldn't. This is something that should be brought out into the open. Children all over the country are being swept up in this drug curse."

"I admire you for this attitude . . . after all, prevention is the best cure for drug abuse."

Mr. Trellis struck me as being a man who would not mince words or flinch from an action. He reminded me of a drill instructor I'd once had.

"The whole subject of drugs is so distorted by emotion, by concealment, by sensationalism . . . to fight it, you have got to be ruthlessly honest."

"How old was your son when he started on heroin?"

"I learned about it when he had turned seventeen, but he admitted to me that he had been using for two years before that."

"And I suppose that means that he had been using a soft drug even before that, since a youngster doesn't usually begin on heroin."

"He used marijuana, sniffed glue, popped pills. Marijuana covers the city. In the school where I teach you need a gas mask to enter the boys washroom the fumes are so thick. Yes, my son must have started on the soft drugs at about thirteen or so."

"What about the neighborhood you live in?"

"It's right in the middle. Let me explain. You remember your history? You remember what a border state was? My neighborhood is a border state, the worst of two worlds. One block south is money, one block north poverty, one avenue east poverty, one avenue west affluence. For me I can see the Park Avenue of the New York Central overhead, I can see the wealth of Fifth Avenue, but for kids the borders are not there, they just feel the currents. The pills are from Fifth Avenue and the marijuana and the heroin from Park Avenue. . . ."

"You're a teacher?"

"American History."

"This border neighborhood . . . you had junkies . . .?"

"The junkies loll through the streets on their way to Central Park. All kinds of crimes are committed. . . . In the block where I live, we still have a certain kind of pride . . . but it's going. Most people there have fairly good jobs. You know, we make too much to live in a project and not enough to afford Fifth Avenue and a doorman." Mr. Trellis talked without hesitation, as if he had memorized the conversation. "The youngsters had discovered that the building I lived in supplied them with a lookout. From the roof they could see the four corners, they could post someone downstairs . . . and they could make their escape over any one of half a dozen roofs. . . ."

"So the police never had a chance."

"There was never any fear of that. The fact is complaints to the police were never looked into. I have supplied the police on numerous occasions with license plate numbers, car models, names, telephone numbers, addresses . . . their reaction was always the same: 'My job is to be a policeman and yours is to be a parent. Now you go do yours and let me do mine.' "

"That was said to you by a policeman?"

"That was said to me by many policemen. I tried to explain that I couldn't very well be a parent in a vacuum . . . I couldn't be a parent unless he was a policeman. I think I came to be regarded as a crank . . . even by neighbors. I'm not saying that every policeman was like this, but a great many were. Occasionally there would be a young cop who might buy the kids ice cream or play ball with them. . . ."

"I talk to a good number of policemen in the course of a year about drugs, and they're just as concerned as the rest of us. After all, they have children, too."

He raised a finger. "Mr. Cortina, the parents on my block went to the precinct house many times, alone and in committee. They shrugged their shoulders. They gave us the telephone number of the Narcotics squad . . . I called and called that number making reports . . . I began getting parking tickets . . . my wheels didn't face into the curb the right way. . . . The message was loud and clear: 'Trellis, don't rock the boat.' Most of us were harassed because of our concern. Listen, on a Saturday I used to take my son and his friends and other kids on the block to the park . . . I used to teach them how to play ball . . . I was trying to compete with those apes who were in the park distributing drugs for nothing. . . ."

"For nothing?"

"Yes, for nothing . . . in the beginning . . . so that they would become hooked. I explained this to my neighbors. Most of them just looked at me . . . their attitude . . . shrugged shoulders. 'What can I do? The police are powerless . . . what is it I can do?' So Trellis, he was a boob . . . he went to the police. . . . One social worker in the welfare department was on the street one day as I talked to a policeman. This social worker didn't know me but he came over to me and he said: 'You seem a terribly threatened man . . . I have a private practice . . . if you'll come see me I might be able to help you with your feelings.' Isn't that incredible?"

"You sound like one man against the mob."

"It was almost that . . . but it wasn't me I was struggling for, it was my son and those other kids in the neighborhood . . . because those apes still were in the park handing out their glassine packages."

"Why did you stay in this neighborhood?"

"I've lived there for more than twenty years. My job is in the city, I'm known on my block . . . the answer isn't abandonment. You start running and you run all your life long. This is border . . . ghetto on one side, abundance on the other. There's a challenge here . . . it's an area that could be used as a jumping off place to roll back the crime machine, it's my area. . . ."

"With your awareness, your concern as a parent, how is it your youngster began to dabble with soft drugs at thirteen years of age?"

"It's hard for me to isolate that, very hard," said Mr. Trellis with a frown.

"But it is the critical question."

"The really critical area is that of idleness. . . ."

"Idleness?"

"Exactly. You see these children in the ghetto, they don't know what to do with their time. They drop out of school, consequently they have even more time in which to be destructive. Now, there are some programs sponsored by various agencies to teach them skills or provide them with part-time jobs . . . but this is at best minimal. What is needed is a "life-training" program. These children are denied individuals, every single one of them. Every kid in this ghetto area . . . is a neglected child."

"I don't understand, Mr. Trellis, you said your block was a border block, wasn't part of the ghetto. . . ."

Pedantically, he said: "What I said was that ghetto doesn't stop at a street sign . . . the spirit of ghetto flows like a current. . . ."

"Are you saying that your son was corrupted by ghetto youth?"

"I am saying my son was influenced by these undisciplined children. I am saying that my son saw the values that I had inculcated in him unworkable with his ghetto companions. My son saw that his father had position, had a fair income, saw that his family was very different from the broken homes, trouble-ridden, impoverished people that his friends came from. . . ."

"You mean your son got so confused that he forgot the, as you put it, the values you taught him?"

"I mean that in order to have friends, in order to be accepted, my son had to forget, my son had to show loyalty to the gang. . . ." Trellis clasped his hands. "Children are subjected to this kind of peer pressure . . . they develop loyalties to the group. . . ."

"Does this extend to heroin, Mr. Trellis, to using heroin?"

"That's exactly the point. It extends to everything and anything. The peer pressure is unceasing . . . you have to be part of the crowd . . . you must not stand out. May I ask if you are a hermit, Mr. Cortina? May I ask if you are obliged to follow in our society?"

I wasn't rising to that bait, I was not there to argue with him. "He was more loyal to the group than to you or the family . . .?"

"Yes. If I asked my son where he was on a particular evening, he'd tell me he was out for a walk. And when I'd press him for more specific information, he'd tell me that he'd walked along Fifth Avenue. Never who he was walking with or why he was walking. . . . You see, he knew that if he mentioned names I might have forbidden him to go around with those fellows . . . I know a good many of those bad apples . . . I had forbidden him to go with many of them. He had developed a false sense of loyalty to these bums. In other words, he would rather honor those who supplied him with drugs than he would his own father."

"But there must have been some time when your son was frank and open with you, Mr. Trellis?"

"Of course, before he fell in with this bad company, when he went around with those kids I approved of. You see, it was nothing for me to take a whole bunch of them swimming or to a baseball game or to Palisades Park across the river. As soon as he met these bums he stopped being honest with me, stopped being frank. I have ways of finding out . . . I knew what was going on in this underground . . . it's an underground."

I lighted a cigarette and watched him. "Mr. Trellis, were there no children in your block who didn't use drugs, children who weren't getting into trouble? Why didn't your son look for that kind of kid?"

"The kind that gets into trouble is exciting, dashing, daring; they don't have to make an effort, they don't have to think. . . . I'm an ordinary man . . . a teacher. I work hard for my money . . . I can't afford to give my son forty-dollar Stacey-Adams shoes or hand-tailored pants or fancy Italian sweaters. These ghetto kids my son was running with had these things. Consider it . . . their fathers, if they knew them, were unemployed or drunk . . . the family was on relief, but they had these fancy clothes. Me, hard working, respectable, upright . . . you see, one weighs things, especially a young person. . . . How much reward is given to the hard-working man who struggles? How much reward to the person who does nothing at all and who garners all kinds of return? The ghetto inverts values, Mr. Cortina . . . topsy-turvey. I don't have an Eldorado, but every dope peddler does . . . I don't have a roll of dollar bills that make my pockets bulge, but every pusher does. . . ."

"And your son wanted these things?"

"My son wanted to belong to his group."

"But why?" I waited a moment. "Why did your son need this kind of company?"

"We need greater narcotics control. The law needs more bite
. . . it needs to be more powerful . . . it needs to be enforced."
Trellis went on—had he even heard my question? "The uni-
formed policeman should be given more training, greater orientation in this area, greater authority. . . . The policeman should
stop and search every one of these kids. Pull the marijuana from
their pockets and arrest them. He should go into the park and
hallways and backyards and arrest these dope peddlers. . . .
Right now they turn their backs . . . we need Federal involvement here. . . ."

"But, Mr. Trellis, doesn't a kid go with a certain group, do
certain things, because he finds a place in that particular culture?
Isn't this something that exists, drugs or no drugs? Why did your
son gravitate. . . ?"

"It's an interesting phenomenon. . . . What we have is an ero-
sion of moral values. How could my son stand up against this
tide?"

"Why couldn't he?" Trellis seemed to ponder what I was
saying. "That is the question, isn't it?"

"Since the time of the Industrial Revolution, when the wife
also entered the labor market, families could bring more money
into the home, could acquire certain of the creature comforts . . .
from that time the family lost something . . . things . . . important family values were neglected . . . there was a breaching of
family solidarity. . . ."

In an attempt to pin him down I asked: "Are you saying that
your wife had to work . . .?"

"I'm not saying that." He said it with finality.

"But your wife has been conspicuously absent in our exchange, isn't that so?"

"My wife is a disorganized woman. I have continually to
organize the home. She's a housewife . . . she lacks direction . . .
I supply that. . . ."

"But Mr. Trellis, children are attracted or repelled the way
we are. . . ."

"Exactly," he interrupted. "Our world has corrupted them. They don't have any standards anymore. I can remember when my son was younger. We'd go everywhere together. What delight he would get when I took him to the zoo, when I took him to a ball game, when I explained to him the need to keep his body strong. What delight when I taught him how to hold a fishing rod. . . ."

"Delight? For whom, Mr. Trellis?"

"For my son. . . . If my father had spent a hundredth of the time with me that I spent with my son . . . my life would have been so much richer. There was nothing I spared myself . . . I gave everything I could to my boy. He has my name, he's the first born. . . ."

"And your wife . . .?"

"She did her best to spoil him. That is and was part of my boy's confusion . . . his mother's lack of strength. But how could my son be proof against the heroics of the street, how could my son, singly, fight against the ways of the street, the professionals handing out their papers of dope out in the open? It's organized . . . they give it to the kids so that they'll get hooked . . . it's a business. When one of these apes is arrested . . . you see him back on the street a couple of hours later, or another one has taken his place. . . . No, Mr. Cortina, we need stricter laws, more training for the police, less lenient judges. . . ."

"Why did your son, with all your training and interest in him, go to drugs, Mr. Trellis?"

"He became involved with other children. Once a child goes to school his horizons broaden, other influences come into play. . . ."

"Did you know of any children in your block who did not go to drugs?"

"Yes . . . but they were fortunate enough to be transferred to different schools. They found different friends . . . their ways took them out of this neighborhood. . . ."

"Cigarette?"

"I don't smoke . . . and neither did my son. . . ."

"Did you ever ask your son why he elected to run around with this group of kids who were in trouble?"

"Hundreds of times. I'd talk to him about it. I'd tell him what he was doing to himself, to his family, to me. . . . My boy . . . well, let me explain. I'd get back in the afternoon from teaching. I'd say 'Hello, Mark. How are you? Come and sit down with me and we'll talk." He'd say a few words. He was not talkative . . . he'd much prefer to listen to me. . . ."

"Was he a very sensitive boy?"

"Sensitive? Very aware . . . intelligent boy. I remember talking with his teachers . . . good student. He reminded me of myself in some ways. Very quiet, really."

"He sounds as if he isolated himself. Did that occur to you?"

"I don't think you're right. We got along together fine until he fell into bad company. I used to tell him how lucky he was. How different things were for me when I grew up. I had ten brothers. I hadn't what he had. . . . Yes, we got along well together. We had mutual interests. I taught him how to row, I taught him how to swim, I taught him how to sail. . . ."

"Did he ever say anything?"

"He was quiet. I first noticed a change in our relationship around the seventh grade. I explained male and female differences to him. I told him about sex, frankly. I began to notice that his appetite was off . . . I smelled marijuana in his hair . . . you can't mistake the odor of marijuana. I attacked it directly. I told him about drugs and how they kill a man in his soul. I walked through Harlem and showed him junkies. . . . I saw the change that came over him. I used to bring books home for him to read . . . we'd look at television together at night. . . . The books gathered dust, and he would be down on the street. He would be too busy to play ball with me or go to the museum. He'd ask his mother while I was away if he could go to a friend's house. She, you know, wouldn't have the sense to say 'no' to him. . . ." He turned in his chair and faced me. "I'd say, 'let's go to Bear Mountain on Saturday . . . let's go visit Grandma's house in Pelham. We'll go sailing. . . .' I could see the change. He said to me one time: 'That's for the birds . . . there's nothing to do there.' My son said that to me! You can't bring up a child alone. Your wife has to make some kind of effort. . . ."

"Why didn't you move?"

"Never . . . that's no answer. . . ."

"So your son went to heroin."

"Yes, they sucked him in, finally. . . . He left school, he left home, the police got him . . . then the police acted, *then* they acted. But the apes are still in the park selling dope or passing it out. . . ."

"Why did your son go to heroin?"

"Bad company, environment . . . perhaps the weakness of his mother. . . ."

"Mr. Trellis . . . did your boy have a choice?"

He looked at me, every inch the teacher. "That's an absurd question. Of course he had a choice. . . ."

"Then why did he go to heroin? What was he escaping from?"

"He wasn't escaping. He was caught by bad company. . . .

"You said before that there were other children in the neighborhood who didn't use heroin, who didn't get into trouble. What was there about your son that made him different?"

"His standards were too high. He couldn't fight against a whole way of life. . . . It's incredible . . . my boy jab a needle in his veins . . . fill his body with that filth, sit on a park bench nodding, oblivious of himself and the world around him . . . a tragedy. . . . There he was in the police line-up. He had broken into an apartment and stolen a television set. My son . . . my son . . . that I had to see this. . . . The police lieutenant told me that he was a drug addict . . . wondered what I could do about it."

"Where is he now?"

"He's awaiting sentence."

"Do you visit him?"

"He's my son . . . he says now that he chose the wrong way. . . ."

"Did you ask him why he went to heroin?"

"Yes. . . . He said he had to find out the hard way that he'd gotten in with the wrong company."

"You're satisfied with that?"

"Oh, he went on about not being understood . . . communications gap . . . parents not understanding children. . . ."

"Your boy said that?"

"Oh, yes, you learn to be very strong, Mr. Cortina. He said that I was too much of a perfectionist . . . I demanded too much undivided loyalty. I was too stern with him. I was 'hipped' — that's his word—on making him useful. He felt that the kids he ran with had learned something by sharing garbage . . . sharing garbage . . . that's my son's expression, Mr. Cortina."

"What your son said . . . could you agree with any of it?"

"Oh, yes. Oh, yes, I could agree. I could see it was largely my error. I had failed to make him understand. I should have made my motives clear to him. I should have explained so that he could realize that I wasn't pushing him for my sake. That was not it at all. . . . I should have made it plainer to him. Any trophy that I urged him to win, any diploma he would get . . . these would have gone up on the wall . . . they would have been placed right next to my own. . . . It really was Trellis and son . . . but I must have failed to make him understand. . . ."

9 *Many of the hard drug users I meet seem to have a distinct artistic flair. They write poetry or paint, act, dance, play an instrument, design clothes. It's open to considerable speculation whether this flair ever turns into a strong and disciplined artistic talent. Much of the poetry and painting has a personality-development ring to it, a kind of therapy tool. But once in a while you meet a person who seems to have not only a gift but the determination to cultivate it. Such discipline and energy are rare among the hard drug addicts. It is even more rare when that art can be so totally consuming that it will separate a man from heroin.*

The Artist

"Everything echoes in prison," he said, his head cocked to the side. I listened with him. I understood, for in that quiet there was no silence; sounds of all kinds reverberated against the bare walls, ceilings, the canyons of corridors, the metal doors, the bars like inflexible strings of strange instruments, the floors humming with the shuffle of many feet. "Everything echoes . . . that's because it's hollow. Prisons are hollow because our treatment of the transgressor is hollow!"

"Transgressor?"

Malcolm smiled disarmingly. His teeth were irregular, his nose had been broken at one time. "Why not indulge me? It's a nice word and it gives me status to use it. It's my little daub of color that makes you put me in relief, to separate me from my background." Again he paused and listened. "Do you hear that?"

It was the rumble of his deep voice echoing in the small cell that had been made available for our meeting. Outside the bars a middle-aged correction officer sat on a stool staring in at us.

107

"You'd use a palette made up mostly of whites to suggest this place . . . whites and reds . . . with the reds well-thinned."

"You're an artist?"

"I'm a painter. See my hands." They were thick and strong. It was apparent that Malcolm accepted the guard's presence as he accepted the walls and bars, but I found the man's quiet surveillance devastating. "But you didn't come to see my hands, you came to see my tracks. Isn't that so? You came to talk to the dope fiend, not the painter."

I smiled uncomfortably. "Aren't they the same man? How long have you been painting?"

"Nine years. Pigments are my phrases, clauses, parts of speech. Paint is my mode of expression. A painting is something you can see, you can hold it away from you and look at it . . . it's lasting. It captures a moment and preserves it. It's a piece of me rendered creatively. Everything I paint is a projection of me, so that when I examine a group of my paintings, I'm really examining me."

The amount of energy Malcolm used seemed just sufficient to activate his voice, to animate his face and body, a kind of metabolic rate peculiar to prisoners. "This preoccupation with yourself . . . you require this scrutiny?"

"Man, do I need it! I'm a vacuum cleaner. I'm sucking up images, feelings, and light. And I'm in that bag, too, man. What kind of a bag am I coming from? That's the quest, man. What kind of a bag am I coming from?"

"How long have you been here?"

"Three years."

"How much time have you got left to serve?"

"Sufficient time for me to fresco up these walls and ceilings if you can get the warden's consent. I might do a minor Sistine."

That flat prison cadence effectively kept Malcolm at a distance from me. His banter was a defense, and having been a heroin user he was already a well-defended individual. "Is this your first time in?"

"Second time."

"Drug-related offense."

"How delicate . . . how delicate, the faintest touch of a thin brush stroke. . . . Possession and sale is what the man said. Possession and sale. A user and a pusher."

"The second time the same thing. . . ."

He hesitated for a moment, and I realized he was weighing his response, sizing me up, deciding whether it was worth his while to be truthful. "The second bust was called possession and sale but it really wasn't. You know, timing is very critical in law and order and the administration of justice, as critical as it is in painting or music or stock broking. My bust came at a bad time. There was a terrific campaign about dope peddlers in the schools. You know, a nickel-and-dime politician had stirred the fire about pushers depraving the toddlers in the schoolyards. The newspapers got on it, the magazines, television crews were out interviewing school principals and parents and into this drama stepped Malcolm, who had a bundle on him and who was selling to a toddler of forty-five with grey hair, and Malcolm he got forty-four months in a California country club. . . . Bad timing, bad timing."

"Were you an addicted pusher?"

"Of course. I was flying when they busted me. They just picked me off like a logy October fly." Malcolm was studying me intently. "I ended up in a cell so fast, I was provided with all the essentials for a good big Jones."

"You mean cold turkey?"

"You dig me, man. Yes, sir, my withdrawal was accomplished in seven savage days . . . I even served as an object lesson. While I was going through my raving maniac stage, some reporters were brought in to see how ruthlessly the city administration took care of these child molesters. I put on a good show, too . . . it impressed . . . incidentally, the guy who raised the stink originally did get elected. He got elected and I got forty-four months. Bad timing undoubtedly."

"How old are you, Malcolm?"

"You mean in years? On account of sometimes I think I was laid down when they first started on the pyramids." This is the kind of response I was accustomed to from dried-out addicts, a blend of fancifulness and subtle evasion. "I'm thirty-four years of age, five feet six inches tall, one hundred and sixty pounds, blood type O, I was born in Los Angeles, I went to art school for two years, I'm not white, I'm not Anglo-Saxon, I'm not Protestant, I'm not middle-class, and I must be pretty damned interestingly flawed because all kinds of people are forever questioning me. It must be my dope experience, because for damned sure nobody was ever interested in me before that time. You note of course that I didn't say vital statistics . . . I'm not sure about their vitality. . . ."

No detectable bitterness in the voice, no nuance broke through that planed-down speech. "I'm sure you've been questioned endlessly."

"Amen, brother, amen. But I'm enjoying myself. I'm exercising, I'm painting my words on you. I'm trying to capture the light that filters through you and me. It's all a matter of timing and cycles. See, when you're in the joint you realize certain things. Prisons go through changes. Right now in my state we're in a rehabilitation bag. So this means I got to make with my feelings and motivations . . . but this will change. We'll have another phase which will be strict custody . . . no trafficking with feelings or rehabilitation. The guy does time. . . ."

"Have any of the questions ever helped you to understand yourself in any way?"

"All of them helped me. All of them were fed into me, swallowed by me. I'm an artist, man. That's my coin, questions. Every guy who ever questioned me left a part of himself for me to use. He thought he got a lot from me but he didn't . . . I got it from him. He held an empty bag . . . mine was full, full of him."

"Too bad. Too bad that you couldn't have been caught unaware. . . ."

He glanced at me quickly, and there was a subtle change in
his voice. It didn't increase in volume, but something had altered
in it. "You're right, man. I've gotten clever. And that works
against me because it means I'm not honest with myself, a real
critical danger with a drug user, because the junkie always fiddles
around with anything on the surface because it keeps him away
from himself. So I really welcome somebody with questions. It
becomes my mechanism for keeping me screened from myself.
Lemme tell you, I've probably sent more social workers to bed
happy at night, secure in the idea that they have helped me to see
the light because I answered their questions. I've served as
therapy for more social workers, psychologists, psychiatrists,
than you could shake a fist at. I've made them feel they were
ninety-seven percent functioning. . . . Now, man, you gotta
admit that is really turning people on. . . ."

"And now I'm about to become the recipient of your therapy,
is that it?"

"Absolutely . . . though I have tipped my hand."

"Well, I must say I'm flattered. I wonder whether you lose or
win each time you succeed in manipulating?"

He stared at his hands, murmuring, "I lose . . . I lose . . . I
lose. . . ."

"Is that why you paint, because you can't game the canvas?"

He nodded. "It used to be hell to use the brush because I saw
each failure dripping in color . . . Malcolm the color-smearer,
Malcolm the smearer."

"What's the next move? Am I supposed to offer you sympathy
now? Am I supposed to attempt to disabuse you of this feeling
of failure . . .? That is the way of the addict, isn't it? Doesn't
he expect a letter of commendation for zipping up his own fly?"

In the pregnant silence Malcolm sat motionlessly, so motionlessly that the guard moved on his stool to see him better. I

wondered if the interview was over. Somewhere a steam pipe clanked. Then I asked: "How did you discover that you wanted to paint?"

"I got in with a bunch of creative people . . . I liked them because they seemed to be doing things that other people never seem to do. Always a lot of chatter, things going on . . . and they lie to themselves so beautifully, always posing, always getting an attitude . . . that meant something to a guy like me. They value their hangups, they dramatize them, they grab sensation like it was precious, everything has a kind of freak value for them. . . ."

"Was that your value for them?"

He grinned. "Yes . . . that was exactly my value. I was a Black, a pusher, an addict, and an ex-con . . . I had freak value."

"When you say creative people, just what do you mean?"

"Well, there were some writers, musicians, designers, people in show business. . . ."

"How did you tie up with that kind of world?"

"Well, for damned sure I wasn't born in it. I was just a junkie who was pushing to support his habit . . . and there was a panic . . . like there was no stuff anywhere. You know, like drugs just dry up and the hype gets flushed out into the street like a cockroach . . . he's trying to get into a hospital or get busted or kicking in the gutter. Now when a panic strikes, even those people who've kept their habit hidden, who lead respectable lives, who keep up appearances, they have trouble getting their supply, too. That's how I met this creative bunch. This time I'm talking about there was a real panic on. Man, L. A. was drier than Arizona. It was so bad that the God-damndest, most white, Anglo-Saxon Protestants were visiting my ghetto looking for stuff. For once I was lucky, I had by accident gotten almost a kilo of first-class stuff from a guy off a Filippino ship. He had his ass in a sling and needed money real bad. I gave him three fifty for it. Almost a kilo. Man, I was the MAN, to have that during a panic with the town's veins popping out. But I played it

real cool. I laid up with my mother. I wasn't going to let on that
I had stuff . . . I wouldn't have lasted an hour. . . . My throat
would have been cut. I put on that I was hurting just as badly
as everybody else. I was sitting on a bench in the sunlight when
this young white chick she comes along. Now, man, she really is
dressed . . . her clothes they don't holler out . . . they just drawl
their class. Right away, I spot her . . . she's strung out, she's got
that same tightness around her mouth as any ghetto junkie. She
sits down next to me, opens her pocketbook to get a cigarette,
doing it in such a way that I've got to see the roll of bills inside.
. . . She says she's got money to invest in a good thing. But I
laid back. How did I know? She could have been fuzz, a syndicate stakeout, she could have been anything. She tells me she's
an actress and a model . . . she tells me she's sick, she needs to
score bad. I'm still having no part of her, and my speech is
getting more and more darkie. But she really needed straighten-
ing . . . I could tell . . . I been that way often enough myself.
After a while I began to feel sorry for her . . . she's sitting on the
bench jumpy as a sand flea. I just keep watching her. . . . Finally
she gives up. . . . I followed her. . . . Finally, after a few blocks,
I catch up with her. Now, you know a young white girl and a
black boy in a ghetto neighborhood, they are conspicuous, man.
I ask her where she lives . . . just in case I happened to run into
somebody who might help her. About an hour later I found myself in Hollywood outside of one of those bungalows that the
creative folks like. I looked over that place real good before I rang
the bell. She let me in. There were four guys inside and they were
all sick . . . man, did they have Joneses. One guy was a writer,
one guy was a commercial artist, one a photographer, and the
other guy a sculptor. God, did they have money . . . they shoved
it at me like it was fruit, man . . . like they wanted to get rid of
it. You know, I was insulted . . . I hadn't planned to sell it . . . I
had just wanted to straighten out the girl because I was sorry for
her on account of she looked like a doll my sister once had.

That bathroom in that bungalow became the most popular room in the house as each one went in to fix. . . . That was my debut into the creative world."

The guard shifted on his stool, obviously intent upon what Malcolm was relating; the latter ignored him and continued. "The panic eased, as they always do. Stuff was available again, and the world settled down to its thing, but things had changed for me." He nodded his head. "Yeah, things had changed for me. I was their supplier . . . I never lost sight of that . . . but it was something else, too." Malcolm looked at me, a simple expression of wonder on his face. "Man, I dug these people . . . I liked to hear them talk . . . I dug where they were coming from . . . I liked the way they came up on something. Sure, they were all junkies, same habit as any junkie in the ghetto, except they didn't have to beat themselves out every day to get their stuff. They all had fine jobs, plenty of money and they took me in . . . like I really felt I belonged there. You know, my freak value. I learned about music and books and plays and painting. I got introduced to all kinds of people. . . . I'd drift into this commercial artist's place and watch him work . . . I really got around. . . . Now I knew I was just their connection . . . but sometimes they almost made me feel like they wanted me around. The girl, Jody . . . we got real tight. She was a nice girl . . . she had the smallest hands. . . . A funny thing happened. For the first time it crossed my mind that drugs were a damper on me . . . a damper."

"Drugs were keeping you down?"

"Right. It was the first time I ever felt that. Oh, I wanted to kick a lot of times just because I was tired of hustling, of being beaten out or being sick, but I never really knew that drugs might be screwing me out. . . ."

"This was because of the girl?"

He frowned. "Partly. . . . Now, see, she was hooked. All she wanted was not to get sick . . . and since she had money, she never had any reason to get dragged down like the street girl. But, see what happened to me, I got it in my head that there really was something to this art stuff . . . I really dug light . . . light, man . . . light. . . . It was just like that great Englishman Turner . . . I got fascinated by light. I'd watch that sunlight hit the palm fronds, collapse around it, and leave a thin purple line . . . or sometimes I'd watch the gold drip from the branches. . . . Man, I tell you, I dug that . . . so Jody, she could see. . . ."

"You were sleeping with her?"

He sighed. "I know you had to ask that. No . . . that was her thing, sex, that was her hangup. An agent had had her when she was just a kid actress . . . he'd hurt her bad. It turned her around. You couldn't go near her, besides, when you're on horse you don't want sex. No, Jody was really turned around . . . she'd practically flip out. . . . That's why she was on stuff. I told her so . . . I told her so . . . I wanted her to go to a hospital."

"Could she see that sex was her problem?"

"Man, no junkie sees his own problem. That's what the out-sider calls it . . . a problem. . . . See, the addict, he's just got reactions to things, he's not some kind of machine that starts to spin a lot of reels that are going to produce his reason for shooting dope. No, the addict he just reacts. That's a laugh, everybody talks about the dope problem . . . as if it were the problem . . . dope use is just the surface aspect of many prob-lems, all kinds of problems . . . that's why the establishment is so hung up over the drug situation. So Jody, she didn't see that sex was her problem. . . . Every time she'd begin to feel some-body was inching up to her she'd just panic, that's all. I tried talking to her, you know, I was trying the same questioning bag that others had tried with me . . . it didn't work no more for her than it did for me, because she'd round on me . . . she'd round on me. But you know, it startled me to realize what was wrong with her, to see it as plain as day, and yet I could realize that there was nothing I could do to make her get down with it. . . ."

He put his elbows on his knees and leaned forward. "It was the first time that I saw somebody actually trying to block out a part of their life with heroin."

"What did she think you were trying to do? Wasn't she suspicious of your motives?"

"Sure . . . she was a junkie . . . suspicion courses through them along with the red corpuscles. With Jody, all her fears started and ended in the same place—sex. She thought I was trying to take her to bed . . . but I couldn't tell her that and make her understand her own captivity."

"And with all this awareness about her, you continued to use heroin yourself?"

Malcolm smiled. "That's the remarkable thing about the junkie. He's most adroit with others, but for himself . . . that's another bag. And that's a real curious thing, man. Real curious, because in a way I appealed to Jody's need to get outside of herself, too. You know what I mean . . . maybe only a hype can understand this . . . but my being around kind of allowed her to use my hangups to keep her own hidden. You dig that at all?"

"She was analyzing what she thought were your reasons for shooting dope as you had analyzed hers?"

"Right . . . right. . . ."

"What had she isolated in your case?"

"Oh, she had a book on me, man . . . she had a book. She was a real bright girl about everything but herself. She called me her half-developed eccentric."

"Half-developed eccentric?"

"I had the drive to get out of the ghetto but none of the discipline or the tools with which to do it. She made me realize that any individual who overcomes major cultural or environmental patterns has got to be an eccentric. In my case I used heroin . . . so I was only a half-developed eccentric . . . existing in limbo."

"So you're saying that it was the desire to get out of the ghetto . . . a desire that was frustrated . . . that led you to heroin?"

"Rendered at its simplest and least revealing, I suppose so. . . ."

"So what was she going to do . . . help you to become a total eccentric?"

"Man, you dig . . . you're bright . . . that's what that little chick wanted to do with me."

"And her reason for doing this was to keep herself blocked out from her own problems?"

"Right. It gave her something to hold on to . . . it gave her some kind of excuse to use so she would be doing something other than just shooting heroin for the high. In other words, the more she could tinker with my life, the less she'd be up tight about her own, the less guilt she'd feel about shooting drugs. She could relate with my sense of inferiority, my continual pulling back from making an effort, my wanting to be a big, important man that people looked up to, my feeling that I really couldn't do anything. . . . I was trapped with feelings I could never realize. . . . Jody could relate to that and work with them because they were *my* feelings. . . ."

"You were using one another . . . kind of gaming each other?"

"That's just it . . . junkie's game all the time, but this was fruitful gaming. She found out about my drawing. She took me and signed me up for night college courses in art. You know, in art history, in anatomy, in design and perspective . . . I got to be her thing. And man, I dug it . . . I dug it . . . like it was sunlight bubbling. . . ."

"But you were still on heroin. How could you concentrate?"

"Listen, there's so much nonsense about heroin, just sheer bullshit about what it does or doesn't do to an individual. Not much is really known about what it does. Believe me, I been off and on it since I was fifteen years old . . . and I'm always learning something new about it. I stuck to that college course for almost two years. I even cut down on my daily dosage so that I could just get by without getting sick . . . but I kept selling heroin. See, I was Jody's connection, and her friends', too . . . besides, I had my own habit I had to feed. . . ."

"These creative people, didn't it bug you that you just had freak value for them?"

"Do you hate the sun because it can burn you up, man? I knew exactly where I fitted in their scheme. I knew they were just artsy-smartsies. They called me their Caliban, their dusky angel . . . that was their lingo . . . but that was all right by me . . . every group has its own argot . . . they were phonies . . . but so was I. But I was getting something of value out of it."

"And Jody?"

He said gravely: "She belonged to the group because it allowed her an environment, she was accepted. Man, I got so involved with that girl. I swear to God I did. She came from back East, Phillie. She graduated from a good eastern college. Her old man was a corporation lawyer. We spent a lot of time together. . . . I painted her over and over again . . . and in her face I found my feelings. In that white, thin skin with its pallor of blue-grey around the cheekbones and mouth I portrayed my own hunger, my own pain, my own loneliness. . . . Sound weirdo to you? We were tied together, that girl and me. We complemented . . . we didn't copulate, we complemented . . . she-me, me-she. . . ."

Way back in the maze of corridors doors trundled, a shuffle rose and grew, a billy club rattled against the bars, our watching guard said: "Chow time for C block." He offered it to us almost as if he were a party to our tête-a-tête.

"Malcolm, did you ever really find why you went to heroin? She was bringing things out for you to consider, but did you ever find out something solid?"

"I cut down on my dosage like I said. The more I painted Jody the more I projected of me, my feelings in her features. She was an alien, she was ingrown, she was incomplete, she was immature, she was unmotivated, she was devious, she was crippled, she was sick . . . so was I. . . . Being a black man was one strike,

being a dope addict was a second strike, and being an ex-con
was a third strike ... all of these, incidentally, were, but they
didn't really have to be, as dramatic as I made them out at that
time. I was using misfortunes to cop-out ... I know that ...
same as I was using her as she used me as a cop-out. But there
were things ... there were things. ... My father walking along
the street, he'd been a gravel handler—when he worked—him
walking along the street dead drunk mumbling to himself and
a couple of white cops goosing him so that he'd jump into the
air, shrieking: 'Oh, good Lord to God.' Watching my mother
using her body trying to sweet-talk the landlord out of evicting
us on account of my old man was off on his own. ... Watching
the welfare worker picking over our plates in the sink to see if
we'd been eating luxuries. ... Like I say, there were things that
scorched my belly when I thought about them. Plenty of things
were there to hang me up. Mostly it was the spirit though, it's
the spirit that kills ... in the ghetto. ... Others have had worse
experiences than me and they made it out, or stayed in the ghetto
and made something of themselves ... but for me that stench
of hopelessness, that feeling that you can't really compete because you don't start from the same place as the MAN ... you
know, the fancy cars, the clothes, the broads, the roll of green
stuff, people looking up to you. ... See, Jody was right ... I was
only a half-developed eccentric, because I really wasn't coming
from that bag, even though I didn't know it at the time. I didn't
know that I didn't want to compete, didn't want all the creature
things. It was only when I came to know Jody and her bunch
that I began to dig myself. Of course by that time I'd been
hooked for years and heroin was the thing. You don't forget
your pain, your failure, your fever ... you just float for a while
and you know through a kind of white saturation that H is always there to cushion you. ... But even so, with Jody and her
friends I really saw where Malcolm came from. Pigment on canvas, and light ... light ... light ... God, it was a bomb that
blew off right in the pit of my stomach ... a speedball. I knew

I was half-developed now for sure. . . . No ghetto, no wealth, no competition . . . none of it. That wasn't where Malcolm was at. No . . . Malcolm was at the purplish-blue that glistens on a raindrop, the aura of a fly's wings . . . that's where Malcolm was at. Now Jody and her friends, they talked about the great talents . . . the great actors, the great composers, the great painters, the great performers . . . but the way they talked they made it seem like the more screwed up you were, the more aberrational, the better creator you'd be. But I could see what they were doing . . . they were blowing themselves, they were copping out, they were justifying what they were doing by saying this. They were just like any God-damned pissed-up junkie. You know, they'd take an acid trip because it would make them see colors brighter or feel emotions more intensely. They'd try anything—pills, glue . . . this made them artists . . . talented . . . they were sacrificing themselves in the service of art. . . . Man, could they shit themselves . . . liars . . . but all junkies are alike, and these junkies I owed a lot to. They opened me up. Especially, Jody . . . we were tight together, real tight. Jody, she listened and swallowed all this stuff. Poor little slob was so turned around. She'd try anything. In her case heroin . . . when she came to use heroin, it was a blessing because it killed her fooling around with acid . . . on account of acid will kill you . . . you can't handle it."

"So will heroin kill you. . . ."

"But it won't drive you off your nut. One time that sculptor in the bunch took a bad trip and broke through a plate glass window because he thought he was in the cabin of a sinking boat and he was trying to escape. No, heroin in Jody's case kept her away from worse stuff. . . ."

"Was she a successful actress?"

"In a way. I saw a couple of her pictures and some of her television shows, but I could tell she wouldn't ever make it big because of her hangup. She never struck you as a woman . . . that sex part of her was crippled and it always came over. Even if she had been gay it would have been better for her, but as it

was she was just crippled . . . and she knew it. That's why she
went on using, why she hung on to me. . . . But really I did dig
that bunch . . . I needed them . . . I was dependent on them . . .
I knew exactly that for them I was the brightest scalp on their
belts . . . my freak value . . . a real live black dope addict-pusher-
ex-con-painter. But that kooky bunch did a lot for me. . . . You
know, I almost kicked the habit . . . I almost kicked the habit
while I was studying and hanging out with them . . . but I got
scared . . . I figured that they wouldn't want me around any
more, that they'd reject me. Maybe that was a cop-out, maybe
I couldn't give up junk, but man, I tell you, I got so hipped on
light . . . light . . . Jesus, I'd sit watching a ribbon of sunlight
ooze across a door or a wall. . . . Light was my thing and I
became a worshipper . . . and I came to realize that all these
people were cripples, they would never be great. Even though
heroin was in my central nervous system I was beginning to get
down with it. I began to see that the real artist is like everybody
else, and he's got to keep himself opened up so he will get hurt
and feel pain and will feel alone and an alien, and not try to
escape from this opening up. That it's really pain that makes
him grow." Abruptly, Malcolm glanced at the guard. He said
almost self-consciously: "You see, I was on the opposite side
from the heroin bag . . . on the opposite side. I was really hung-
up . . . I was really hung-up. Heroin is escape from everything.
Heroin is inaction. Heroin is a way of life. I was an addict but
I could see what I had to do . . . I was hooked and hung-up at
the same time."

"Did Jody know this?"

"I told her. She understood. See, after classes I'd come back
to her place . . . she let me paint there . . . like I said we'd gotten
real tight. Some night she'd come to the university and wait for
me to get out and we'd walk along together . . . especially when
she was down . . . so we'd talk then. I remember one night, I'd
been doing a lot of thinking . . . we'd been studying Rembrandt.
And I let fly at Jody about her sex hangup . . . I leveled with

her. . . . Man, she wasn't ready for that . . . she just dropped behind, dropped behind. . . ."

"Dropped behind?"

"She crumpled. See, I came at her real hard . . . she didn't read
me . . . she thought with that kind of panic she lived with inside
of her that I was trying to get into her. . . . She crumpled . . . it
was the way I came at her. . . ."

"What happened?"

"I didn't see her for about eight or nine weeks."

"But you were her connection, weren't you? You supplied her
and her bunch with drugs. . . ."

"She didn't want any part of me. I went around to her place,
but I wasn't wanted and they let me know it . . . they let me know
that I'd had it with them. There was no panic on so they could
get stuff easy enough from ten other sources. But they let me
know somehow that I had broken the code . . . I'd leveled Jody's
screen and you don't do that. . . ."

"Did you deliberately set out to strip her cover?"

"No, man . . . see, like I said, I was hooked and hung up
at the same time . . . this is where I was coming from . . . I had
to get it out otherwise I'd have had to shoot more to keep it
down. . . ."

"Did you ever see Jody again?"

"Yeah . . . that's how come I'm here. . . ."

"I thought you said earlier that it was on a possession
charge. . . ."

"That's what they called it." He bit a fingernail. "It wasn't
dark yet . . . I was on my way into the art building when she
called. She was inside a cab. I went over and got in . . . I'd never
seen her so chalk white before . . . right away I thought of one
thing only—overdose . . . overdose. . . . I knew what to do but
I panicked . . . I panicked and told the cabbie to take us to a
hospital. She was holding her private parts, her hand over her
private parts and she was bleeding. . . . We got her to the hospital, to the emergency room. The cops were there . . . I still

can't put it all together . . . they figured I raped her, they found a deck on me. Let's face it, here's this white chick and me a Black and a dopetaker, and everybody knows from the newspapers, the movies, and television that all drug addicts are first fiends and then sex maniacs. . . . So it was a perfect set-up . . . but they could only run it out according to the script. I was charged with rape and possession. I was held without bail . . . man, it was rich. . . ."

"But Jody?"

"They brought her out of the O.D. Her old man came out from Phillie, and that was it. . . ."

"But she must have told them you hadn't raped her?"

"That charge was dropped . . . but they slammed me with the possession charge, because they didn't believe Jody about the rape . . . they figured she was covering up.

"What had happened to her, Malcolm?"

"I don't know for sure. . . . I think I was responsible in a way. . . . See, when I leveled with her so hard about her hangup with sex, she cut me off, but it's likely she didn't cut off what I said . . . and I figure maybe she was trying to face into it and she couldn't . . . she couldn't. . . . She probably had a man, and was up tight . . . she had to be hurt. . . ." He bit his lip.

"And you got busted."

"I got my bust . . . I was being wrung . . . I was being wrung anyway . . . man, you can't believe how I was being wrung. . . ." He stared at me and moved his lips. "Do you see what was happening to me . . . do you?"

I hesitated. "You were hung between painting and heroin. One the antithesis of the other. You found yourself coming from two ways at the same time . . . you were being destroyed."

Malcolm rose swiftly and threw his arms around me. "Man you do dig. . . . Oh, you beautiful white brother . . . you understand. . . ." His face was radiant.

Meanwhile the change in Malcolm's voice had disturbed the guard; he quickly entered the cell on the defensive and said sharply: "That's all . . . that's all. It's over . . . it's over. You had your hour."

"Would you give me five minutes more, Officer?" I asked.

"This isn't a country club. My orders were to get you out in an hour."

"It doesn't make any difference, white brother. You'll hear of me . . . YOU'LL HEAR OF ME!"

The door clanged behind me, and the guard escorted me along the corridor. He said defensively: "Five minutes wouldn't have made no difference . . . he'll tell a different story to the next guy that interviews him."

In April I was in Washington, D.C. at a museum that exhibits American art. They were having a special showing of contemporary oils. I was drawn to a large canvas that appeared to me to be a study of sunlight. Perhaps it really was a rendering of light itself. Down in a corner there seemed to be a disproportionately small figure. When I looked at it more closely it turned out to be a doll. I looked at the title plate: "PANIC." I had heard of Malcolm.

10 *Some drug users have a highly developed distrust of people who take notes: social workers, psychologists, researchers. In their experience, the pen and paper means criticism, denigration, failure, and cruelty. The Pickpocket was one of these. Trace much preferred the obvious discipline of a prison to the openness of a treatment facility. For him, as for many old-time drug users, prison was the place you went to "lay up," to put yourself together. Prison required nothing of you but conformity. This Trace and his type could give, for it allowed the privacy essential to him. But when Trace was placed in a rehabiliation program, where the emphasis is on personal effort, involvement, and serious group therapy, he was exposed to everything he dreads most: people who ask questions, people who take notes, people who expect something of him. For Trace this kind of environment is Hell. For him the need is habilitation not re-habilitation.*

The Pickpocket

"The cold bothers me . . . I can't ever get warm here. Sure I wanted to get busted . . . I wanted to be locked up . . . but not here, not where the cold gets inside of me. . . ."

"It doesn't seem like a prison."

"There ain't no bars, no cell blocks, no guards. But did you get a look at them woods, at them swamps, at them seven thousand acres? This is prison like no prison I ever been in and I been in plenty of them. All I can see is them miles and miles of trees, and there ain't no noise . . . ain't no noise . . . and the air it smells cold . . . cold like I never felt air in no city."

"How long have you been here, Trace?"

"Six weeks tomorrow."

"What would you call this place?"

"I wouldn't call it nothin'. Unless I was here I wouldn't drop a dime in a phone to call it. . . ."

"It is an institution of a sort though, isn't it?"

"It's a sneaky kind. You know, the kind that pretends like it ain't . . . and that louses you up. If there's anythin' I can't stand its dishonesty."

"Dishonesty, Trace . . .?"

"Yeah . . . I keep waitin' for the club to fall. . . . Like I know this place just ain't what it seems . . . it ain't."

Trace was short and wiry with sharp features. He was biting his nails as he leaned toward me. "Prisons, I been in. You can relax, you know what's what . . . you got security. Ain't no question but you know what's expected of you. . . . Like here, you never know what these loonies are gonna do . . . you just never know. . . ."

"That disturbs you?"

"Why not . . . if I wanna be all on pins and needles all the time I coulda stayed outside. See, even my language ain't right in a place like this . . . I say outside . . . outside's what's botherin' me." He gestured with his arm toward the window. "Looka that frost . . . ain't that somethin'? Looks like a coatin' of lead. . . ."

"How come you came here?"

"It was a mistake. I thought I was gonna get a bust but they put me here instead. Ain't that the God-damndest thing? There's nothin' in our world you can be sure of no more. . . ."

"How many times have you been put away, Trace?"

He ran his hand nervously through his red hair. "In the real lock-up, five times. Three stretches in the state of New Jersey, one in New York, and one in Pennsylvania. . . . But I was held on juvenile charges before that . . . you know, like hookey and runnin' away from home . . . you know, stuff that's illegal but ain't like a crime."

"So how many years have you spent locked up?"

"About fifteen years. But if I hada been sent to a place like this the first time I woulda straightened out real fast. . . . This is too much . . . I can't relax . . . I'm so jumpy all the time. . . . You go out for a walk and somethin' jumps outa the bushes . . . or suddenly somethin' will scream from a tree. I'm a nervous wreck. This is solitary . . . this is really bein' in solitary. Who ever heard of a guard addressin' you as Mister."

"What did you do your time for, Trace?"

"Armed robbery mostly. I was doing plenty of other things but never got caught . . . I had to have money for my habit."

"So really, yours were all drug-related crimes."

"Sure, you don't think I was just a common burglar. I had a habit."

"You're very precise. Is there a distinction that I'm ignorant of?"

"Well, Jesus, unless I was a junkie, I woulda been a successful burglar . . . I pride myself on doin' a good job. Anythin' I ever turn my hand to, I do the best I can. But when you're on junk you can't do a good job, on accounta you're never sure. . . . Things get mixed up . . . you can't plan too good because you gotta get your fix otherwise you get sick. See, you can't allow no time."

"How did it all start? For instance, how come you were playing hookey and running away from home?"

"I come from a broken home. I'm very nervous . . . I don't like a lotta hasslin'. My parents they just fought the First World War right up till the Second World War . . . and like I was no man's land in between. . . ."

"Did you have brothers and sisters?"

"I was the only kid . . . so, see, I had enough of their battlin' and some left over . . . so I'd cut out. . . ."

"Did they separate?"

"Yeah, when I was about ten they had a fight, the cops came, the old man had to go to the hospital to have his head stitched up . . . real sordid stuff . . . so they separated. . . ."

"With whom did you go?"

"They even fought over that. . . . I'd spend some time with one and then the other . . . like I was still no man's land . . . you know. . . ."

"What were they fighting about?"

"You name it. He'd say the sky was blue, she'd say you're a God-damned liar, and they'd be off . . . just like that. . . ."

"What was the matter with them?"

"Damned if I know. That's the way they were. Different strokes for different folks I guess. They woulda made it good, I guess, if it hadn't been for havin' a kid. . . . See, every time I'd run away they'd fight like hell about which one of them was responsible for me runnin' away. Then they'd have to go down to the police station to get me . . . or they'd have to go to school on accounta my hookey playin'. That'd start another battle. . . . They was incompatible I guess . . . they wasn't ever happy though, after they separated. They couldn't stand being away from each other."

"They must have had real problems. . . ."

"Everybody's got problems," Trace said, shrugging his shoulders. He lighted a cigarette and puffed nervously. "Hear that wind whistlin' outside . . . that goes on all the time. This place is like a concentration camp . . . they're tryin' to break me down . . . make me think I got problems . . . kinda mental torture. And they're so polite, too. . . . That's part of the treatment . . . torture treatment. . . ."

"Anybody who shoots dope must have a problem. . . ."

"Sure, he's got a problem, but not like what these loonies want you to think. . . . Jesus, they want you to think it was some deep down reason that you went to the stuff."

"Wasn't it?"

"Lemme tell you, just like it happened. I'm livin' in this furnished room. . . ."

"How old were you at this time?"

My interruption irritated him. "How old? I was . . . er . . . fifteen."

"Fifteen . . . and you were on your own?"

"Sure . . . I was hidin' out. See, I'd broken my probation and I had to hide out."

"This was one of your juvenile offenses. . . ."

"Yeah, at fifteen I ain't no grownup. So I've got this furnished room, and a buddy of mine he comes to me and he asks me if I'll let him take off in my room. Now, I know what he means because I found out all about dope in the juvenile lockup. So I says sure . . . and he drags in another guy with him on accounta they both had chipped in for the bag. So they cook it and split it but it don't split out right. And they start to hassle over it. Now I don't want no hasslin' . . . I got my belly full of that . . . so I tell them to give it to me. Then they ain't got nothin' to fight over. So they fix me. That was my first time."

"Did you enjoy it?"

"I'm very vague over that, on accounta I can't really remember. . . ."

"How were you living all this time? You were in a furnished room . . . fifteen years of age . . . weren't there questions by the landlord?"

"See, when you use your head, when you're quiet, when you present a nice, serious appearance, you ain't got no trouble. I didn't have no trouble. I was workin' in a grocery store. I was doin' real good. . . ."

"And your mother and father, they didn't attempt to find you?"

"How should I know . . . all I know is that they never did." Trace lighted another cigarette and listened. The wind really seemed to disturb him. "It'll blow like that all day . . . the snow'll hit the windows . . . this place gives me the crawls. . . ."

"When did you try your next shot?"

"Oh, must've been about three months later. I run into the

same two guys. Now, they're dealin' . . . dealin' so they can
support their habit. They was fifteen or so, so you can see they
ain't no big wheels. They're sellin' to other kids . . . so I asks
them about it. You know, I'm tryin' to figure what it is . . . how
much money can be made . . . and underneath I think I'm really
itchy to try the stuff again . . . because I was drinkin' at that time
pretty hard, too. . . ."

"At fifteen?"

"Yeah . . . but again, I do it in my room. No noise, no com-
motion . . . I'm always one for walkin' quietly and mindin' my
own business. . . ."

"But you weren't walking, Trace. . . ."

"What'dya mean I wasn't walkin'?" It was said waspishly.

"You were running . . . and pretty hard I should say at that.
You'd run away from home, you were a "loner," you were
drinking, and you had an itch to try another shot of heroin. I
should say you were running plenty hard. . . ."

"Hey, you ain't one of these loonies from here, are you? Because I ain't buyin' one of those problem bags. . . ."

I assured him that I had no connection with the staff or the
organization that operated the facility. "I'm not trying to sell
you anything, Trace. I'm commenting on what your actions
seemed to indicate. Is it possible that you were trying to
escape?"

"Nah. . . . In any case I got fixed again . . . I liked it . . .
and that was the beginning. Now can you see anythin' like some
deep, involved reason behind that? Just straight-forward likin'
the stuff."

"But how straight-forward was your life after that?"

"Oh, that's somethin' else again. My life got pretty involved
because, you know, stuff costs money, and the more you come
to use it the more money you got to have. So in that sense you
are right . . . my life wasn't straight-forward no more."

"And could you still walk quietly and mind your own
business?"

He went back to biting his nails. "I just told you my life wasn't straight-forward no more . . . you can't shoot stuff and not change your ways some. You gotta be on your toes . . . everybody's out to beat you. . . ."

That doesn't seem so different from what your life was before, Trace."

"It was, though. The stuff helped me . . . you know, I felt better . . . I could talk better . . . I could figger better. Like I didn't get so jumpy . . . I could like take things . . . noise and havin' people around. . . . You see, when I was high . . . I usta have such beautiful thoughts . . . I could see things. . . ."

"What could you see that you didn't see when you were not on dope?"

"I could see Trace. I could see Trace. And people looked at him like he was somebody. He didn't have to stand up in front of them, make an ass-hole out of himself on accounta he couldn't read or nothin' . . . or because his old lady was half crocked. . . . I could see Trace. . . ."

I offered him a cigarette. "You were pushing to keep yourself . . . ?"

"Yeah, I was pushin', but then I was doin' some boostin', too."

"Boosting is shoplifting?"

"Yeah . . . about then I started to use maybe five bags a day . . . some days six or seven . . . I was gettin' greedy. So my connection he was gettin' beat on his price. . . ."

"You mean you were shooting stuff that you should have been selling and beating your supplier out of money . . . is that it?"

"Kind of like that. So one day I go to him and he freezes me out . . . he just freezes me out. Now, I'm hooked. Like I ain't got no bargainin' room . . . I'm gonna get sick if I don't get stuff. And he ain't gonna give it to me . . . and I got no money to get it from no other supplier . . . so I hauled off and beat the hell outa him and I take my stuff. . . ."

"You beat him up and he just took it? Was he so much smaller than you?"

Trace shook his head as he scratched out his butt. "No, he wasn't, and that's what surprised him I think. Funny thing, even though I was comin' on with sickness, beatin' that guy up broke like a knot in my throat . . . like it was the first time I felt free. . . ."

"Did you have a grudge against him? Did you dislike him?"

"Well, he'd take me for everythin' he could get, but he was like every other supplier. . . . No, I wasn't really beatin' him up for himself. It was like somethin' I discovered, you know. Like Trace was gettin' out. . . ."

"What happened?"

"I split. I knew what would happen . . . I dropped the neighborhood fast. But now I'm like loose . . . beatin' him up made me loose and I realize that boostin' and pushin' ain't for me . . . I'm not cut out for that . . . robbin' is my thing. There's somethin' about it. . . ."

"You talking about armed robbery?"

"I had a gun. . . ."

"You know, Trace, you're one of the few heroin users I've ever talked with who used a gun."

"I been tellin' you I'm different . . . most other hype's are pretty screwed up people. Like they're soft and squishy types who couldn't make it if you wiped their asses for them. That's not me. I always could make it on my own . . . nothin' squishy in me . . . I just happened to use dope. That's why this place gives me the crawls, because I can't sit down and look at these other fiends in these group sessions they hold. They sit around laughin' and cryin' and shoutin' 'I'm concerned . . . I'm concerned . . . I'm relatin' . . . I'm relatin'. Help me . . . help me.' And you know all while they're lyin' . . . they're puttin' on a show for everybody, tryin' to impress the staff so that they'll get out sooner. They're a bunch of loonies. Not one of them has got enough balls to be himself . . . bunch of lyin', low-down bastards, who can't do nothin' for themselves. . . ."

"But you're one of them, aren't you?"

"Not me, Mister. Don't put me in with that bunch of phonies . . . only thing we got in common is my usin' dope. That's all . . . but I ain't like them. Nobody ever did nothin' for me . . . I did it for myself." He had worked himself up into a rage.

I asked quietly: "But didn't you associate with junkies? Wasn't that a necessary part of obtaining your supply?"

"I never hung around with them. I went in, got my stuff, and then cut out . . . I never hung around with them cruddy bastards who ain't got no backbone and no balls to do nothin'."

"You're a very angry man. . . ."

"And so would you be . . . if you go in for a bust . . . imagine . . . I walked into the police station with the works . . . the cooker, everythin' in my hands. I put 'em on the desk . . . I say to the cop on the desk 'I'm a junkie . . . here's my works . . . here's a bag of junk. . . . Book me.' And what happens to me? They send me here to Siberia to this looney bin . . . looney bin. . . . Just a straight honest confession I make . . . I give 'em the evidence . . . I'm lookin' for a straight honest bust . . . and what do I get . . .?"

"Maybe you've gotten what you've needed all along . . . a situation where you can be treated not as a criminal but as a man who has problems, who is in a sense sick. . . ."

Trace looked at the floor and shook his head and muttered with exasperation: "You're another one of them creepin' Jesuses. . . . I ain't sick . . . I ain't got no problems. . . . I used dope because I liked it . . . I stopped by walkin' into the police station on accounta my wife was gettin' sick . . . and I had to clean up . . . and I told her what I was gonna do. . . . I was gonna clean up. . . . I'm gettin' sick here though, that's for damn sure. What with them God-damned birds that keep screamin' in those trees all night or that wind that keeps howlin' or that snow that don't

ever stop fallin'. . . . If you're trying to make me get sick . . .
and you're one of these loonies. . . ."

"You're mistaken. This place is a new, special treatment
approach and I was invited here to observe it. I'm not part of
this program, I assure you."

"Do you think it's right to take a guy like me who in the best
faith goes in to be busted, who is genuinely lookin' to go to the
joint for a nice year or two so he can clean himself up . . . do
you think it's right to send him to a concentration camp? How
would you feel . . .? How would you feel . . .?" I wasn't sure
whether he wanted a response from me or not. "See, that's what
I'm faced with. I write to the wife . . . I can't tell her I got sixteen months . . . I got twenty-four months . . . I ain't got that
security . . . I don't know when I'm gonna get outa here. . . .
On accounta they round on you, they say: "Only you know, Mr.
Wycliffe . . . only you can answer that." You ever hear such
bullshit in your life . . .? They is tryin' to break me down into
some kinda dingo-dingo . . . a dingo-dingo starin' at my belly
button all day. . . ."

Trace was not like other heroin addicts I had known. His
options seemed so physical. He wasn't "running the game." He
used his fists, a gun, armed robbery. He was not typical. He
reminded me of a bantam fighting cock I had once seen in
Mexico. "I wonder how you happened to get married? Your
experience with your parents always fighting couldn't have been
much of a recommendation?"

"Circumstances alter cases. I come out after a three-year bust
for assaultin' a cop. I'm clean and for me I'm all torn up inside.
When you come out, you feel like you come back to life like Rip
Van Winkle. I go back to the neighborhood where I was raised
. . . my God, it's all changed . . . all changed. . . . The Irish
they ain't there no more . . . the Italians they're gone . . . the
handful of Polacks, they're gone, too. . . . All Spicks now. . . .
My old man is dead . . . my mother is God knows where. I go to

this church I went to when I was a kid . . . even the priest is not Irish anymore . . . they even got different saints on the altar. Like I'm really feelin' a foreigner. Then I run into this girl. She remembers me . . . we went to school together. We was never close. But she remembers me and my family. She ain't no beauty . . . but she remembers me . . . and everythin' melts inside of me. I lose my control . . . one thing leads to another . . . she gets pregnant . . . so we get married. . . ."

"It wasn't love?"

"Circumstances. I wasn't gonna split . . . I'm not that kinda guy. So I face into my responsibilities . . . we got married."

"Did she know about heroin and your prison experience?"

"I told her everythin'. . . ."

"What did it do to her to learn about your past?"

He snapped: "She wasn't marryin' my past . . . she married me."

"Did she think she could keep you off heroin?"

"We never talked about it. I didn't think about it . . . don't let things like that hang on your mind. . . . But Shirley was a good girl . . . she was a good wife . . . turned into a good mother. . . . She was a telephone operator . . . I fell in love with her voice. . . . She was no beauty, but like I fell in love with her voice, and after a while I fell in love with her. . . ."

"Did you get a job?"

"I worked on a truck for a while. And then I shot one bag on payday. Then I shot two bags . . . and then I was back on the stuff . . . and I blew it. . . ."

"Your wife couldn't make you see . . . ?"

"Sure she could make me see . . . she made me see that the gun was out . . . I didn't use a gun. She made me see that I'd only lose with the gun . . . because I had one gun and every cop had one . . . the percentages were all wrong. . . ."

Trace was biting his nails again, or rather he was biting what used to be nails. "You couldn't make yourself give up heroin?"

"I get so sick . . . Jesus I get so sick when I stop. . . . It's agony . . . it goes on for days. Shirley, she could see I was tryin' but she couldn't stand seein' me suffer. . . ."

"How were you living?"

"Until the second kid come along she was workin' and I was boostin'. . . ." Trace was frowning. "When she said we was gonna have another kid . . . I told her I wanna stop . . . can't have a family . . . can't go on like this . . . I'm gonna stop. I kicked right there. . . . I tried to use my head this time . . . I got some pills . . . sleepin' pills. . . . It took weeks . . . and I was always just about sick but them pills was murder . . . they was murder. So I had to do somethin'. I have a very low tolerance for pain . . . I guess . . . so I went back on the stuff. I told Shirley the way it was. I told her she shouldn't worry . . . I'd take care of everythin'. She should just have the baby . . . and I did. . . ."

"What do you mean you did?"

"I kept myself down to six bags a day and I went to work."

"How could you work when you were on heroin?"

"You can do anythin' when you have to, unless you're like one of these squishy dope fiends around here. I had responsibilities. I also had a habit . . . but I had determination."

"What kind of a job did you have?"

"I become a pickpocket. . . ."

"A pickpocket?"

"Shirley she didn't want me to use no gun . . . and boostin' is too uncertain. Picking pockets came easy . . . I was good at it. . . . I could get me a hundred a day like this . . . that was what I did."

"And you never got caught?"

"Never. I'd start like any businessman . . . I'd be at the midtown railroad station like a commuter. Then I'd switch over to the airline terminal, and after the night rush hour I'd go home."

"And you lived like this for how long?"

"About eighteen months. After the baby was born and my wife got back on her feet we bought a car, we got some furniture . . . but I was buildin' up my bags. See before, a hundred a day would take care of everythin' but then it got up to my needin' a hundred and fifty and then a hundred and eighty. It was gettin' outrageous . . . so one night I said to Shirley . . . she could go back to the telephone company and I'd have to take a bust. . . ."

"The prospect of your going into prison couldn't have. . . ."

"I wore the pants in the house. Shirley, she knew that I was givin' it to her straight . . . I was a good husband . . . I never lied to her."

"But you could have gone to a hospital. . . ."

"What good would that do?"

"They would have detoxified you. . . ."

"I learned only a bust can help me. There's somethin' about a prison . . . you can't get out, they let you alone, they handle you. . . ."

"So you walked into a police station. . . ."

"No, not right away. I only did that when everythin' else didn't work. I tried assaultin' a guy one night . . . thinkin' I'd be picked up, but the guy for some kooky reason claimed that it was an accident . . . so I got off. Then I tried breakin' a plate-glass window one night durin' a storm . . . and that turned out to be an accident. It was like I couldn't get arrested. So I told Shirley I'd walk in with the works. . . ."

"And what happened? They surely booked you then. . . ."

"They booked me all right. But the God-damned woman judge . . . soon as she started on this Mister Wycliffe stuff I knew my luck run out. She had my record . . . I confessed to things I never did . . . anythin' to get a bust. . . . She starts her lingo . . . I'm a sick man . . . how long can I be enslaved to heroin? The struggle I put my family through. . . . The best ends of justice is gonna be served by not puttin' me in the joint . . . but in some kind of treatment. Like the judge is makin' me out to be a victim of some kind . . . Jesus Christ . . . I was framed for sure. Nothin' I could say . . . nothin' . . . and here I am with all these squishy, bastardly dope fiends. . . ."

"I'm astonished, Trace!"

"You're astonished? What about me? What about me?" He gestured with his cigarette. "This is agony for me . . . this is really agony. . . . I got this heroin thing beat . . . with me it's just physical . . . I get sick when I don't get it . . . I get busted and then it's all over. . . ."

"But it's not all over, you always go back to it. Isn't that what's happened each time? Why do you go back to it?"

"Because I enjoy it . . . I enjoy it. . . ."

"But what about your wife and children? Do they enjoy it, too?"

He sighed. "Yeah, that's the point . . . that's the point . . . that's why I gotta cut it . . . because of Shirley and the two girls. And I'm ready. . . . I won't use it no more. But I gotta get outa here, away from these bugs. These are real scum, these junkies . . . lyin' bunch of bastards . . . gaming everybody. Soon as you see one he starts to tell you about his problems, how he come to use junk . . . and it's all lies. . . . A junkie, these junkies is all liars, makin' up problems. . . ."

The western horizon cooled to a dusky red, the trees were bare, and the road crackled with frost; a marsh bird fished in the twilight; I watched the seamed face, the bewildered expression in the eyes, as Trace said in those hard, staccato tones: "I ain't got no problems. I ain't a looney. I liked heroin. They can keep me here in this Siberia forever, but they ain't gonna make me say what I don't believe. I ain't got no problems. . . . See, I ain't got no problems . . . I'm clean . . . I ain't gonna use no more. . . . I shoot dope because I like it . . . and now I'm through with it. They can talk until they're blue in the face . . . I ain't got no problems . . . none." The wind was shifting; it would probably snow.

11 *One doesn't often meet elderly addicts; heroin doesn't promote longevity. However, they do exist, and of all the alienated people of our world they must be the most alienated. They are aliens in the drug world, they have lost their energy, their beauty, their ability to get the money to support their habits. They can't pimp, or prostitute, or mug, or snatch purses, or boost. They are even alienated from the square world's contempt, for the latter insists that drugs are a problem of the young. The old addict is the loneliest of the lonely, he feels totally desolate. This Old-Timer realizes, as some do, that a lifetime of habituation to a hard drug substance cannot be broken. He has no choice but to switch from one addictive substance to another, such as methadone, in order to function and survive and so salvage what remains of his life.*

The Old-Timer

The sunlight, the pine needles underfoot, the sparkle of the water on that ocean that spread out to infinity, all enameled on a perfect spring day. We sat in his garden. He was saying: "Every generation is a mystery to the one that precedes it. The young people always seem confused and rebellious, reckless and disrespectful. It's their energy, their constant movement that disturbs us. We want to have the pace regular, the questions familiar, the solutions to be along lines that we can recognize."

"This is what the kids refer to as the establishment."

He nodded his head and smiled. "Yes, that's what they say . . . but not how they say it. It has bite when they utter it."

His voice was deep and resonant, his face serene, his hair

139

white, yet I knew that he had been a heroin-user for many years, and this knowledge made me question his calm acceptance. "The establishment lumps together drugs and youth, Bennett."

"Yes, I know. Not only the establishment but the kids themselves. . . . When they see an old-timer like me they can't believe it . . . they simply can't believe it. They have their limitations, too. After all, they are the generation in transit, as it were. In a few years they will be occupying the seats in the establishment. But my credentials are unimpeachable. Those they can't scoff at. I used heroin when it wasn't associated with youth, when quite respectable people were users, when it was considered not an aspect of rebellion."

"And when you look at the drug scene today?"

He passed me a glass of iced tea and stirred some sugar into his own. "It's different. But then so are the times different, so vastly different that it's unproductive to make comparisons. I shot heroin for almost forty years."

"Forty years?"

"Yes, and there are others who have used for as long. Not many, but there are some. Usually the addict doesn't live too long. He dies not from the drug but from what I call drug-related causes—blood-poisoning, hepatitis, malnutrition, stab wounds, beatings, incorrect dosage, adulterated heroin." He put down his glass. "The addict is a pathetic creature. He's so inconsistent. He knows about body tolerance, he knows about manipulation, he knows the penal code, he knows a street chemistry for the overdose, but he doesn't have the simple intelligence to sterilize his needle." He shook his head. "So much gets worn down through usage. It becomes something in and for itself. It really becomes a world."

"How did you enter that world?"

"I'm sure that our friend the doctor told you about me, otherwise you'd hardly have come all this distance to see me."

"He told me that yours was a different slant."

He looked out toward the ocean. "That's just because of my age, I think. You see, addiction has got to be because of something missing in your make-up. It's got to be. Some component has been misplaced or mislaid or misconstrued. Drugs are not the problem . . . they become the problem after you use them. . . ."

"Why did you use them?" I watched the sunlight on his hair. His appearance was deceptively youthful. He reached for my emptied glass.

"Do you know how many times I have been asked that?"

"Plenty, I'm sure."

"And do you know I've hardly ever given the same reason twice in a row? Let me be very honest. The question has importance only because it makes me think. It puts me through changes as an addict would say. Answers by themselves mean damned little . . . but the questions you run to get answers are extremely important. It's the questions that are raised that make you reach, extend yourself. At different stages I've made up reasons for my using heroin. Just made them up, to try on, to kind of get a jumping-off place. But really deep down inside I'm not sure. . . . I can say this not as a cop-out, as a young addict might, but as a man who has not all those days left to him . . . not all that many."

"How many times have you entered hospitals or programs . . .?"

He interrupted: "To take a cure, as we used to unstylishly refer to it." He sighed. "At least twenty times. A young man has a problem. He's never used drugs. How does he know that going to drugs will ease that problem . . . not solve it . . . not open it up . . . just ease it or conceal it momentarily? Obviously, through introduction. In my day, I was introduced by my aunt. I adored her . . . I simply adored her. She was the most beautiful woman I'd ever seen, but she was a heroin user. Today the kids are introduced in a hundred ways because there is a climate of drugs. I don't have to go through the so-called pleasure society, the age of palliation for you. Turn on your television set or radio or open a paper. It's all there. Everybody inviting you to question whether your blood is what it should be or whether you're not really suffering from some malady for which you can buy this product. It's a climate. . . ."

"But surely not everybody is going to go to heroin because of this climate."

"Of course not, but many will become dependent on other palliatives. We've got it so spooked up now that there seem to be only two choices: law and order or legalization of certain things like marijuana. Ridiculous, isn't it? When I was young none of this was true, although one was still introduced to the drug culture. This aunt of mine . . . the lovely Angie . . . she had no family. She bought me my first suit of grown-up clothes. In those days your first pair of long pants was something you looked forward to like a male rite of coming of age. Well, it was Angie who bought that for me, Angie who bought my shoes and hat and coat. . . . It was Angie's money that started me in college. If Angie had said to me that up was down and Heaven was Hell I would have taken it as incontrovertible . . . because she was Angie, and I loved her. I adored her. She taught me table manners, how to enter a room, how to sit in a chair, how you hold a teacup . . . all of this was Angie. . . ."

"She was a user."

"She was a user. She'd been medically addicted. In those days doctors didn't realize what they do today. Angie had become addicted after a painful accident. So she was a user. How could I feel it was bad when this wonderful woman used it?"

"And because she used it, you used it?"

"I was made curious about it, I wanted to be with her . . . and she introduced me to it."

"It almost sounds sexual."

His voice was lowered. "I shouldn't be at all surprised. My own mother was a strong, determined woman. A day's work for a day's pay. . . . My father was a drinker. I was the baby of the family. There was never any fun there at home. My mother was also strictly religious . . . and Angie . . . even now, to say her name . . . after all these years . . . brings a glow. . . ."

"Did your mother know that she was a user?"

"I don't know . . . perhaps. My mother really didn't approve of her sister. She thought she should be married and settled." Bennett got some more iced tea for us. "You see, my grandfather had been a doctor in this small southern town. He'd invested his money wisely, and Angie was his favorite child. She'd been the only one in the family to go to college. She had good looks. And then she had this accident. . . . He left all his money to her. The house, the investments . . . and my mother was left with just her energy and her managing ability. My mother was successful, too. She had this restaurant. But Angie for me was life. I'd stay at my grandfather's house with her. . . ."

"I'll bet you never mentioned to your mother about this introduction to heroin?"

"Of course not . . . but not for the reason you're thinking of, I'll say. It wasn't any wrong or right about it . . . it's just that I didn't tell my mother much of anything. I might have told my father but not my mother. My father I felt sorry for because he was kind and gentle and never could do anything right . . . or so my mother taught us to think. . . . So you see, it wasn't middle-class attitudinizing at all."

"Angie gave you your first fix?"

"It wasn't in the vein . . . it was in the soft fleshy part of my arm."

"Did you get sick?"

"No, I didn't get sick . . . certainly I've been sick dozens and dozens of times, but then I just felt a kind of euphoria . . . at that time."

"How old were you?"

"Sixteen or so."

"Have you ever thought back on that time with reproach toward Angie?"

He smiled. "No, never . . . I wish I could persuade you to believe that you are looking back with present-day eyes on a different world . . . a world where heroin use was different . . . where heroin could be gotten in drugstores. . . ."

"After that initial experience did you begin using it regularly?"

"Oh, no. It must have been half a year later. . . ."

"With your aunt again?"

"I used her stuff but she didn't know it . . . it was the first time I did something furtive with Angie . . . and I've wondered about that these many years. . . . I wanted to have that feeling of euphoria again, but I think there was a twinge of shame attached to it."

"What was life like for you then, Bennett?"

"Life was pleasant. I was in school. I loved horses and sports. I had friends . . . I was in my senior year in high school. . . ."

"So if it hadn't been for your aunt . . . you might not have ever used heroin. Is that what you imply?"

He laughed. "Ever is a long time and I'm not a prophet. Perhaps not . . . perhaps. . . ." He shaded his eyes with his hand and looked toward a gull wheeling above us. "I used to wonder and maybe worry about Angie getting married. . . . She was about thirty-eight. . . . You see, I had this kind of dreamy cow-eyed feeling about her . . . I didn't know enough about heroin in those days. Angie had no need for a man; she was an addict. Sex didn't have any meaning for her. I think maybe I fulfilled all of her family urges . . . you know, her providing for me . . . her stroking my hair . . . or kissing me on the cheek. Kind of tame stuff after what you read today or see in the movies. But it was like that . . . really dreamy, another time. . . . But Angie wanted me to go to college. She told my mother about it. Now mother wanted me to come into the restaurant, but Angie said she wanted me to be like their father, a doctor. My mother pursed her lips, she stared at Angie . . . and she turned away. She was furious, but a good Christian didn't rage . . . so I went to college."

"And your father?"

"I remember sitting with him on the back porch. He was saying that my mother was 'a good woman' who didn't really have 'no letting off valves.' She drove herself too hard. He said that he was 'fixing' to take hold of things and then my mother would be better. She wouldn't have to feel so almighty responsible for everything. He said it was pretty much his fault that she was the way she was. . . . I don't think any of that was true, but I've been an addict so I know what kind of curious rationalizations one makes to make a world."

"Were you using then, at that time?"

"I was just dabbling."

"How did you do in college?"

"Well, I did very well. I majored in English. I did well until my junior year when I had an accident. I told you before I loved horses. I was thrown one day and I was seriously injured. I was in considerable pain for months . . . pain that was assuaged with drugs. Angie brought me home to her house and I developed a habit . . . I was about twenty years old. Curious things happened to me then. I retarded my recovery, I think . . . just to justify my use of heroin. I limped heavier, I grimaced in pain, I suffered . . . you see, I had become devious . . . as an addict will. . . . I felt guilty. I used to look at Angie who never showed anything like guilt or furtiveness. I remember asking her once what she felt about using. She handled it very simply. She said she had been using for too many years to be aware of anything wrong about it."

"How long did this go on?"

"It went on for about five years . . . about five years. . . . And then I had my first brush with the police."

"Because of heroin?"

He paused and considered. "Yes, though not because of possession or anything like that. You see, I had learned that I couldn't have the same friends once I had become addicted. I wasn't interested in their things, their activities . . . so I drifted into a group that was gambling, doing things that five years before would have appalled me. One night I got picked up in a raid on a disorderly house. Angie was furious with me. The first time she ever criticized me . . . she was really furious. She wasn't like my mother in a rage. My mother would fume and then turn away struggling with her feelings, wrestling with them as if they were tools of the devil. Angie just let fly. She broke dishes and vases . . . she was furious. I couldn't figure it out then. Now, I know . . . I know why. . . . It was all mixed up with her having used dope and having somehow sublimated all of her womanly feelings into me. It got dangerously like one of those Spanish plays, those dark blood plays. . . . For some reason—some feelings in the town about wanting to get back at my mother or something, or maybe people really get some satisfaction at throwing mud—I got a very harsh sentence. I got two years. Let me tell you, that was eye-opening for me . . . I never imagined how brutalizing prison could be. In the first place I had to take cold turkey. I really had a bad time. . . . It wasn't only coming off drugs, it was everything . . . the shame, the unreality of it all . . . the expression of suffering in my father's eyes as if this were another of his sins come to haunt him . . . the silent condemnation of my mother . . . her laconic "Angie is the one." You know, all of her pent-up feeling about Angie having gotten all of their father's money, Angie living as she did, my living with Angie . . . all of this along with coming off heroin was torment. Then the prison . . . the homosexuals there, the fact that I was a drug user. . . . For the first time I learned that the drug addict was at the bottom of the barrel . . . the lowest man in the prison class system. . . . Yes, it was the 'Ballad of Reading Gaol' for me." Bennett's face was drained of color and his hand shook. He looked at it and said huskily: "That was more than forty years ago . . . could you believe that memories could be so strong?"

"You served the full time."

"Yes, I did . . . I never got a parole . . . I put in the full time."

"And when you got out . . . did you go back with Angie?"

"No, I had changed . . . I was frightened . . . I felt no confidence . . . I felt a disgrace . . . I couldn't face the town . . .
I felt I'd been passed over. I went up north . . . I went to New
York . . . I thought I'd go back to school. You know, get a job
and go back to school. . . . I thought perhaps one day I'd get
into medical school and then go back to Angie . . . I was going
to prove to her and my people that I really had made something
of myself. . . ."

"Did you go back to school?"

"No. It was depression time. I was like everybody else . . . no
job, no future. . . . But you see I had been using heroin for years
regularly, and even though I had been clean for two years in
prison I could remember the high. So when things got unbearable for me . . . or what I felt to be unbearable, which is the
same thing, I went only for one thing . . . the juice. Now in the
thirties in New York there was no drug problem, really. . . ."

"But there were addicts. . . ."

"Yes, but they were very different from the addict of today . . .
very different. . . ."

"But heroin cost money. How did you get your money?"

"You mightn't believe it now, but I was good looking then.
Women provided me with money. I lived with one woman for
almost eight years until she died. I lived with another one for
more than five years. She found I was using heroin and threw
me out. . . . I signed myself into the hospital in Kentucky. You
know, the twenty-nine day cure . . . like a revolving door. . . .
I went in and cleaned up and came out . . . only to go back in
again and come out again."

"How were you living?"

"Off women. . . . They're such foolish creatures . . . if you'll
pet them and caress them . . . if you whisper to them and are
kindly to them, they'll go through hell for you. But I kept getting
a little lower each time. . . . I was finally living off a pair of
prostitutes . . . a pimp. . . ."

"And your family?"

"They didn't know where I was. And I tried to keep it that way. You see, it was painful for me to think about them, because that made me think about myself . . . I could see so clearly that I was spineless, passive, unmotivated, pleasure-loving . . . spoiled if you will. I sound just the way my father used to sound when he was hung over . . . a kind of weeping figure. No, I didn't want any part of my family. . . ."

"What about Angie?"

"Angie was something else . . . I skirted around that. Because it was something I didn't understand . . . my feelings for her. Every woman I'd ever had seemed somehow less than Angie. . . . But I'd been frightened by her fury that time . . . frightened and guilty . . . because there was something almost bordering on . . . as my mother would say . . . sin in her outburst. No, Angie . . . I 'rounded' on that as an addict would say . . . I rounded. . . ." He got up and faced the sun. "Life was changing, the drug scene was changing. I got picked up on a possession charge . . . and I was put away again for a year. The same old brutalizing. . . . I came out, the second World War had been fought . . . and there were drugs all over . . . the pace had stepped up. Before the war drugs were rare . . . the League of Nations had really cracked down on the drug traffic. But after the war they came back. Now heroin was adulterated, the user was in the ghetto and slum, the user was younger . . . and Bennett, he saw his first grey hairs . . . for the first time . . . somebody called me 'Pop.' Let me tell you, that comes as a devastating revelation . . . 'Pop.' I really hit the skids after that. I was in and out of hospitals . . . more jails. . . . My mother and father had both died . . . Angie was paralyzed and in a nursing home . . . my brothers had turned the one restaurant into a nationwide chain . . . one of my sisters had become a missionary in Africa . . . and Bennett, he was a junkie. . . . In my pride I had always referred to myself as a user. Then one day looking in the mirror . . . my whiskers grey and gritty, my face grey, my eyes red . . . I spat out: 'You junkie . . . you junkie.' I'd wake up in the morning and think Oh, God, another day . . . another day. And I was so tired . . . tired to my very marrow. . . . It's a flaying life . . . you're dirty outside and in, outside and in . . . and yet you hang on. You see the young junkies mumbling in their high, sitting on the park benches like so many unsteady birds, all clustered together for kinship. They don't trust one another but they cluster together because of their common need—heroin. But me, I didn't belong anymore . . . I was old. I wouldn't have belonged if I wasn't a user because I was old. . . . The drug crowd was now young. I even tried to O.D. myself, but the stuff was so poor it didn't work. The heroin was cut so it hardly had any juice to it. And then one night on the West Side I tripped over a metal drum. I landed on my stomach and ruptured something. I was bleeding and lying in the gutter . . . I could just imagine my mother saying that I'd finally made it to my right place after all . . . the gutter. A man came along walking his dog. He was too scared of me to want to do anything. The neighborhood was psyched out because of drug addicts . . . each of whom was a fiend. . . . The dog didn't growl at me . . . that was my salvation, the fact that the dog didn't growl. The guy saw how old I was and finally called an ambulance. From then on, things happened. I met our friend the doctor, who looked upon me as a rare bird . . . a dope fiend of sixty-five. He put me on methadone."

"And you came out here to California with him."

"Yes, I came out here . . . and I'm working for him . . . not with him . . . for him. He saved my life. . . ."

"Are you still on methadone?"

"I couldn't function without it. You see, heroin isn't just a habit, it's a way of life. Everything you do is conditioned by it . . . everything. . . . I'm too old for group therapy and confrontation to change. As I said before, I can give all kinds of reasons for using dope but I don't really know why and I can't stop. . . . Methadone stops the craving. It's addictive, and I want people to know that I am addicted to it . . . I'm a man who needs a crutch. I need this specialized environment . . . God knows why. . . . But our friend, the doctor, understood. So I take my orange juice with the methadone in it and I can work. I've got my small place here. I go to the narcotics center and speak to the young addicts . . . or I go to the schools and talk. My life has been shot through with drugs, they are all I know . . . so why shouldn't the end of my life be like the rest of it? I talk addiction all the time. . . . But all the same we don't know much about it . . . other than it alters, it destroys lives."

"Do the young users listen to you, Bennett?"

"No addict likes to listen, Mr. Cortina. I always tell them they've got six or seven more times to kick before it's too late . . . I always tell them they have a few years left to waste. Not to be in any hurry."

"Wow. That must be different for them."

"A junkie can talk to a junkie . . . and though I'm a grand-fatherly junkie, I'm still a junkie. . . ."

"Maybe methadone is the answer we've been looking for all these years, Bennett."

He smiled wryly. "Wouldn't it be nice to think so? Like having part of our society walking around on crutches all the time. . . . Methadone is only one part of it . . . one part of it. It helps certain users . . . but it shouldn't be used as a total panacea because it's not. It's an addictive substance . . . it's a substitute. It can be used on people like me whose whole orientation and function has been heroin, people who are incapable of getting by without it. But it's a cop-out when you think of using it for everybody. People use drugs for a variety of reasons . . . reasons that are signs of neglect and omission . . . people problems . . . things that happen at home, in school, in the neighborhood, funny little human things like lack of confidence, inability to read, or to talk easily . . . hangups . . . hangups. . . . No, methadone is one method of treatment. We've got to try to find others, particular ones for particular people. There's no easy way out, Mr. Cortina . . . no easy way . . . because if there had been I would have found it . . . because Bennett took every easy way he could," he said sadly, watching the sunlight dapple his hands.

12 *Innocence is hardly a quality one expects to discover in a drug addict. But I've encountered a recurring type of addict that reveals a simple innocence. The Mother is the best illustration of the group. Hope was natural and innocent, and I suspect that it was her realization that naturalness and innocence were woefully inadequate in our world that led her to heroin. The Hopes I've talked to had only themselves to give, and they gave without stint. This was their "thing," and in doing it they found debasement and self-violation. However, I must add that I have followed up some Hopes, and those who have been able to free themselves of their addiction have become towers of strength, refuges for all types of people in need of help.*

The Mother

A sweetness to the air, recalling the purity and promise of a virgin spring, pervaded the room. It hardly seemed a hospital, with its bright, airy, large rooms, the absence of disinfectant odor, the atmosphere of privacy.

Hope was saying: "You know, they may not like the alcoholic, or the murderer, or rapists, but the public can accept them like they were human. Now the narcotic addict . . . oh, brother . . . you can't get them close enough so that they can see an addict smells of sweat, gets hungry, can bleed . . . can have children, can do everything else any other human being does . . . but the public they don't give us the benefit of our humanity. They can jump on all the accusations like they was eager to call us thief, whore, robber, pusher, rapist . . . like by their calling us these things they somehow could sleep easier with their own conscience. We don't need for the public to call us anything . . . because no matter what they call us it can't be anything to match what we call ourselves . . . they can't punish us one half as hard as we punish ourselves . . . they can't do nothing to us that's anything near like what we do to ourselves."

Hope sat there, her back to the light, a squat figure, looking a little like a grandmother from a Russian novel, a grandmother whose life had been spent close to the soil, close to the springs of existence. Her forehead was lined, her eyes small and dark, her face intense. Her hair had been carefully set and curled, as if she were asking for it to be considered, rather than the rest of her, as the sum of her appearance.

"Why does the public hate us so, Mr. Cortina? Why does the public want its pound of flesh only from us?" For all that flat deadness of inflection there was something childlike in her voice.

"Well, the public, of which I am a part, Hope, is just plain scared . . . scared . . . the heroin addict is a terrifying figure, a figure of a creature who has, to them, abandoned his humanity. . . ."

"But why can't they understand that what we do, we do because we have a habit to support? We're addicted to something we've got to have . . . it ain't as if we can stop it by ourselves. . . . We never think like I'm a sick person . . . we never say this is a sickness. You can laugh if you want, but until I come in here I never thought of my shooting dope as a sickness."

"That never crossed your mind?"

"Not really so it meant anything. I knew I must have problems, but I didn't know what they were. The big problem wasn't junk . . . junk becomes a problem after you use it, but what sent you to junk is the real problem."

"Then hangup is a good word to describe it?"

She smiled. "A junkie word that's been sent to the dry-cleaner so it can be used by everybody. You know, because of something you can't handle, something that's chewed you up inside, you seek an escape. Don't let me sound too smart, it's just what I learned about it in here . . . but it's true. . . ."

"We all have our escapes: alcohol or gambling or hobbies or sadism . . . why didn't you use alcohol for example?"

She shifted in her chair. "First of all, my father was an alcoholic, so whiskey wasn't my thing. I tried it . . . I used to get so sick . . . sick all out of proportion to what I drank. . . . It was in my mind, you see, this whole thing connected with whiskey. I couldn't touch a drop without seeing my father there in the kitchen, his chest moving up and down, that smell around him, the film over his eyes, pounding the table, scaring my mother and us kids half out of our senses. . . . And then knowing that everybody in the whole house was hearing what was going on . . . knowing that a cop would come to pound on the door . . . knowing that the next day you'd walk down the stairs and all the doors would open and the people watch you . . . knowing that all the kids on the block would know, the school would know. . . . Yeah, whiskey made me sick. We had no home. My mother had no life. Poor soul . . . she died in a hospital in the charity ward of cancer . . . a thin, little thing. And I couldn't figure it out. How come? You know, was that why you was born? She was such a good slob. Nelly would do anything for you . . . she never had anything but she would give what she had. No, whiskey made me sick."

"How many children were there in your family?"

"Four brothers and three sisters . . . eight of us in all. I was the oldest . . . I kept them together . . . until the girls grew up. See, my sisters took after my mother, they were pretty . . . nice hair and noses, their faces attracted you . . . and I took good care of them, too, like they was my children. . . ."

"What happened to your father?"

"I took care of him, too, until he fell down the hold of a freighter one night. . . ."

"Did any of the other children go to heroin?"

"One of my brothers, he was the only one. He was lost from

the day he was born. . . . He was the last one. . . . He was like a kid who never knew anything but war . . . and when peace came he was still at war. . . . A cop shot him one night, breaking into a drugstore."

"How long did you take care of the family?"

"From the time I was fourteen until I was almost thirty."

"Then what happened?"

She paused, massaged her fingers, and then said shyly: "I had my first child. . . ."

Tentatively I asked: "You'd gotten married?"

"No . . . oh, no. Look at me," she said without self pity. "But I loved that baby, my first son. . . ."

"What did you do then?"

"Went right on . . . stayed right in the same apartment . . . like the whole cycle was starting over again."

"And the father of your child?"

"He was married. . . . He had a family of his own. But even if he hadn't been . . . he wouldn't have married me . . . I know that . . . I think I knew it then. I knew a lot of things. I realize now . . . I knew a lot of things. . . . I knew that baby and the other babies I had through other men kept me living . . . otherwise I would have killed myself."

"But why, Hope . . . why?"

"Look at me . . . look at me. . . . They used to call me the monster. . . ." She puffed away at her cigarette. "Except my children. I loved kids."

"How did you live?"

"On welfare. . . . Sometimes the different men would send money. And I worked. . . . When I was about thirty-five there was some money given to the city for people to work in neighborhood projects, and I got a part-time job working with underprivileged kids." She laughed suddenly. "Underprivileged kids . . . see, I lived in what we used to call a slum area, what they call now a ghetto. You know, three quarters of the families were on relief, underprivileged, poverty stricken. The kids couldn't

read right . . . I'd help them. Believe it or not they helped me
to learn how to read. Then there were dope addicts in the
neighborhood . . . trying to get them into hospitals. Tell you
a funny thing, Mr. Cortina, like I rebelled against working with
them at first. . . ." She smiled with a kind of dawning surprise.
"I guess I was like the general public, on account of I thought
they were dirty and worthless animals. . . . But I learned
that the average addict isn't dumb, they're smart, maybe smarter
than average. Sometimes they're artistic . . . in general I'd say
they got a lot on the cap."

"I've discovered them to be fairly perceptive people."

"And somehow I got it in mind that if I tried the stuff I might
learn how to help them . . . but that was a quick and easy reason,
I think now. That wasn't really it . . . I wasn't thinking of that,
I watched them . . . they seemed different, like they were
happy. . . ."

"Is it possible you felt comfortable with them?"

She glanced at me as she put out the cigarette. "You're right
. . . I felt I belonged with them. . . . But I honest to God didn't
know that you couldn't take or leave heroin . . . that I didn't
know. I was too ignorant . . . heroin won't let you go until you
look for outside help. Actually, I was gonna prove to these fellas
that you could quit it. Then one morning I woke up like I had
a cold. You know, my nose was running and my eyes burned
and I had pains in my back and legs . . . I didn't know where
I picked it up. Then one of the fellas came in from the block and
he laughed at my cold and told me I had a Jones. I asked him
who the hell was Jones. He said I was feeling withdrawal, that
I had a habit . . . a heroin habit. I was floored . . . I was floored.
But I was hooked. Me with four kids and this younger man who
was living with me who was an addict and who I called my
husband."

"How old were you, Hope?"

"Thirty-six."

"And you're how old now?"

"Forty-four."

"So you've been on stuff for eight years?" I offered her a cigarette. "Strange. You started late. . . ."

"You want to hear something even stranger? Do you know why I'm here in the South? Do you want to know why I looked for help to kick the habit? Because of my son . . . my first son. . . ." She paused and turned toward the window, whispering: "My son named Joel became addicted . . . my own son. . . . I guess it happened when he was about fifteen. You see what kind of a mother I must have been. . . . Everybody told me he was playing around. Finally it got to the point where I got off with my son . . . we got money and we copped together." Hope's shoulders trembled. "One morning I woke up . . . it was Christmas day . . . I saw my son laying on the bed . . . a kid, just a kid, my first born . . . he needed a haircut, his clothes were sloppy, his face was dirty." Hope sobbed. "It's hard . . . it's hard when it strikes home." Her body shook.

As gently as I could, I said: "It must be."

"See, I was on probation . . . I'd never been locked up, but I had passed some checks and I was picked up for it. That's when they put me on probation . . . that's when they came in and took away all my children except Joel. . . . So this Christmas day when I saw my boy there, he looked so young, like a rabbit . . . I run out and tried to find my probation officer. I found her . . . I told her 'I'm hooked, I'm hooked, I need help . . . my son is hooked, that's the worst part of it . . . I can't let you put me away unless you can help my son.' She told me that she couldn't help Joel because I was her problem. But she was a good skate, really, and finally she said she'd see what she could do. So when I went to court Joel came with me. The judge said he'd never had a case like that before him, a mother and a son . . . I swear I didn't really know what was going on around me I was so upset. . . ."

"It must have been something."

"But see, junkies are strong . . . they ain't weak . . . they're strong because they come out of a life in the jungle, Mr. Cortina. That's what's so crazy about junk. They say you go to junk because you're weak, and yet to get your stuff and live in the world of the junkie you gotta be stronger than ten people. See how mixed up it is?"

"What happened to your son?"

"He was placed in a special program, and the judge sent me here instead of to prison . . . he could have sent me to prison to serve my term for passing bum checks but he didn't. . . ."

"You've been here how long, Hope?"

"Seven months . . . seven months and four days," she said wiping her eyes. "My boy, he got 'indefinite,' but no more than twenty-seven months. Like it depends on his own progress."

"Without giving you pain, Hope . . . what has your son to go back to?"

She cocked her head. "That is the question isn't it? See, heroin makes you so selfish when you're using it, and when you come off of it . . . you got so much that you've got to straighten out for yourself. . . . I used to cry myself half sick when I first came in here thinking of the other three kids, thinking that I had done to them the very same thing my father had done to my mother and the kids . . . the very same thing. I used to fall on my knees and cry: 'Oh God, Oh God, Oh God, what have I done . . .? What have I done . . .?' I ached inside. . ." Tears streamed down her face. "I've had to look inside myself, Mr. Cortina . . . I have to every day and it kills me to find what I am. . . . I die just a little bit every day . . . I'm no mother . . . I'm some kind of slob . . . just the very thing I used to think people felt about me . . . I'm some kind of slob. . . ."

"But surely, since your son is in a rehabilitation program, they'll provide some kind of after-care for him."

"That's true, that's true. He will get that kind of help. . . ."

"You said you die a little bit every day . . . so do we all. . . . But perhaps you also are reborn and grow a little bit each day."

"I've never been a religious woman, Mr. Cortina, though I

ain't not religious, but I always believed in God. I do believe in God . . . I believe in His Will . . . and if I believe in God, then somehow I can't be nothing. I've got to be something because I'm alive . . . to believe in God makes me something."

"Hope, when do you think you'll be released from here?"

"Well, like they don't really say, right out . . . but it depends on me, most of it. Like I don't think I'm ready to go back yet. . . . Oh, when I first come in I thought I had to get out on account of this was the first time I didn't have my freedom, but now I know I've got to get down with myself right to the bottom of it all. . . . I've got to see right down to the bottom of all the ugliness that's me. I can't help my kids like this . . . I just got to accept that. For me to feel guilt, to feel the feelings they must about me having rejected them, having forced them into foster homes . . . all this is necessary. . . . There's no junk here to take away what pain I've got to have. I ain't ready to go out."

"That's certainly no cop-out."

She smiled. "You sound like one of us . . . but you're right. You've got to examine everything about yourself and then decide if you're really being honest or are you splitting honesty with yourself just a little. You know, you learn how to alibi and game yourself so completely you don't even know you're doing it."

"Have you gotten to the place yet where you have any idea of what made you go to heroin?"

"Like to put my finger on it and say this is it? No . . . no. . . ."

"You know some users, because they've been asked that question so much, shrug it off. Some will say that they didn't use for a particular reason, or it was curiosity, or I sometimes think that they make up something just to make me happy."

"Look, Mr. Cortina, nobody sticks a needle in his arm five times a day without a reason. There's a reason . . . sometimes even when you know the reason, it's that that keeps you fixing. But see, the junkie he's got layer after layer built over him like so many shawls that don't really fit too good but they cover him. . . . If you started early in the morning and begun to pull off my covers, if I didn't want that you should find out about me, you could pull them off until you was blue in the face and never uncover me. . . . We got this awful gift of 'rounding' . . . but it's not you or somebody else we're rounding on . . . it's ourselves. . . ." I passed her a cigarette. "Like I'm not young . . . and I ain't the first object you could warm up to when you see me, but that don't mean that maybe my wanting a man's arms around me ain't just as strong as the prettiest chick. . . . My want could be stronger on account of it ain't gonna be satisfied . . . so right here you got this thing called reality. . . . Reality and acceptance . . . having some bunch you can hang around with without having the jim-jams . . . see, Hope was always getting jammed. Now I told you before I was trying to help the addict before I was a user. That was true, but not one hundred percent. . . . Why . . . why did I have to go to the addict? Because that was the bottom of the barrel and that's where Hope placed herself . . . that's where Hope didn't worry about people pulling back from her. . . . How come Hope had to live with a junkie, to put the junkie's arms around her, to move his body next to hers? Because Hope couldn't believe that any man wanted her. . . . Even the men who went to bed with me . . . they joked about Hope, formed a kinda club. . . . I heard them one night. . . . You want it straight out, Mr. Cortina . . . you want it with all the acid? They screwed Hope with a flag over her face, they screwed her for old Glory . . . they said. . . ." Her face twisted and a laugh, harsh, scraping, came from her throat. "I picked up this young junkie and took him home . . . like you'd pick up a puppy. I took him home . . . I bought his stuff for him . . . I provided him with junk . . . to keep him . . . to keep him . . . so he could lay there next to me warm and breathing . . . so I could lift his arms and put them around my neck. Why, Mr. Cortina . . . why?" She coughed as she stamped out the cigarette. "You see how you hang yourself up . . . it's like you're in a spider's web, one you spin yourself. Somewhere along the way, at one point, you begin spinning and you don't stop. . . . Like, sure there are

other women—and I've met them—who had rougher times than
me, whose family situation was worse than mine, who came outa
neighborhoods that made mine seem like Nob Hill, and who
never used junk, who never became slobs, who never destroyed
four kids' lives. . . . But that wasn't Hope. Hope, she destroyed
four little kids, drove her own son to the stuff because of something in Hope. Look at it this way, Hope was the way she was
because of her father and mother and something inside of Hope.
Now Hope's son, he done the same thing, but in his case I can
see it like there was a blinding light on it. My Joel he never had
a chance. . . . He didn't know who his father was, his mother was
a slob junkie . . . how could Joel make any kinda world? If I'da
crippled him, I would have given him a better chance than I
did . . . at least then he would have had something on the outside
he could have pointed to and people could have recognized as
a handicap. How could Joel go to school, or have friends, or just
play and talk to others like kids do normally . . .?"

"Aren't you loading things on yourself, Hope? By your own
argument, aren't you wiping out your son's freedom of choice?"

"If I hadn't been what I was, if I hadn't been on junk, then
my Joel wouldn't have gone to it. . . . How would it have been
if your mother had a younger man in her home, keeping him,
using junk to hold him . . . lying and cheating and doing every
ugly thing . . .? Would you be here now, well-dressed, able to
ask questions . . . or would you be like me . . .? Excuse me Mr.
Cortina, I didn't mean to insult you. . . ."

"I can't answer your question, Hope. Not because I don't want
to . . . I don't know how."

"See, that's it, because in a way I can't answer it either. . . .
See, I think in my heart that my Joel used junk because he
wanted to help me. My son used because he wanted to help me,
Mr. Cortina. . . . That's just a feeling I got . . . I can't come
right out and say this is a fact. My boy couldn't answer it as a
fact, but I'm sure that I'm right . . . I know him like I know
myself. . . . I was always trying to give a piece of myself away . . .

anything so that you'd like me. . . . I was trying to buy your liking me, always trying the same thing . . . I was trying to buy the world with the only thing I had, myself. . . . Maybe that's why I love kids so much . . . because they never thought twice, they just took what I offered and were happy." She got up and walked to the window. She looked older than her years as she rested her head against the pane. "Ain't no point in complaining . . . in spinning another web . . . because I could now. I could spin it out and say Hope, she never had a chance, or Hope's troubles were so tremendous that they brought her down. No, that ain't it . . . but it's a temptation any dope fiend could use . . . and one I've used to play the game. . . . Inside of me now, as I stay in this place day after day, I have a wake. There are the coffins of my life, and I'm a mourner . . . I get so cold and paralyzed I can't feel nothing. In one casket is the Hope who was going to have a man who would love her all her life. In another casket is Hope who was going to work on the streets with the poor, the underprivileged. In another casket is Hope who was going to be the mother of her children. In another casket is Hope who did everything ugly and dirty, selfish and mean. . . . It's a wake, Mr. Cortina. . . ."

"But you're at the wake, Hope. You're an observer, so that means you are alive . . . you are alive."

She turned and stared at me. "Yes, I am. . . . The one casket I never told you about . . . the one you musta guessed, was the closed one . . . the one that showed Hope as beautiful. . . . That casket is covered . . . that Hope never was . . . never . . . never. . . . I was born this way. I'm not sorry for myself anymore. I'm ugly, Mr. Cortina . . . I don't know where you could find words to make me believe my full ugliness."

"Could it be that it's in your own mind, that ugliness?"

She came and sat down. "No, that's a cop-out you're offering me. I won't take it . . . I've got to take myself for my own value now. See my hair, how long it's growing . . . that will be the only crutch I'll use, because it is mine . . . it is all mine and so it ain't a lie or a front or a trick . . . it is mine. And if it can grow long enough I can bring it up around my face so you won't notice too much . . . I'm embarrassing you . . . but you asked why I went to heroin. Do you see why . . .? Do you see why . . .?"

No words of mine could soften the harsh reality she had to live with, no palliating phrase could alter the stern disfavor of her face. Her hair, however, was beautiful, and the expression on her face was beautiful.

13 *Practically all narcotic addicts live by their wits, by gaming, or rounding, addict jargon for flim-flam, for bilking the public. The hard drug user possesses an unerring gift for sizing up a victim and exploiting his weakness. The variety and skill of these swindles is limited only by the resourcefulness of the particular addict and the degree of his desperation for a fix. The public is the user's prey, his pigeon.*

The Gamester is an example of one of the most brilliant practitioners of the art. With style, adroitness, and a love of the ornate, this man could spin a dazzling web. And yet, like the web of the spider, it came from within himself, and so he too was in its toils. I often wonder how an individual with such imagination, energy, eloquence, and the power to spell-bind can be quickened into the exercise of these gifts only because of his need for heroin. When that need is satisfied, you see the other side, the dark side, a man mumbling, nodding, picking his nose.

The Gamester

"That's not to say that I'm a solid citizen, that I pay pew rent, that I attend the Rotary weekly, that I vote along party lines . . . but I can't be cut off from the society, cut off from the era, cut off from the country . . . like man I *am*."

He certainly was! Slender and energetic, possessing a voice with the range of a powerful instrument, sensitive, expressive hands, and a mobile face, "Fancy Phil the Flier" had granted me an audience. He removed his dark glasses, or "shades," and gestured with them. "You know, Doc, it's the loss of the frontier that's a major factor for some of us."

"The last time I saw you, Phil, you said you were done with stuff forever . . . or is it indelicate of me to bring that up . . . or perhaps I misunderstood you?"

Phil smiled, and with him it was a superb tool. That smile had deceived more people over the years, broken more hearts, lifted more jewelry. . . . "You have me at a disadvantage, Doc . . . I did say that. You know me, I'm always frank even if it costs me."

"Well, you're back here in the joint, so it must have cost you."

"I hesitated . . . I hesitated, and that was my downfall."

"What do you mean, you hesitated?"

"I paused, I considered things, I tinkered with myself, I stretched to make the square connection . . . I panicked . . . I got picked up for simple gamesmanship . . . me, Fancy Phil the Flier."

"Was that the charge?"

"You're squarer than you used to be, too, Doc. . . . I got picked up under this new law about addiction. They saw the tracks and here I am. . . . This is different than the joint. This is a program . . . get the nuance, a program. . . . I'm being treated, not custodialized."

I laughed at Phil's pleased grin. "Have you taken over the place yet?"

"Let's say, I'm observing . . . I'm observing."

"You took me in completely the last time we talked, Phil. You ran the game and I fell for it, I really fell for it. You charmed me into a suspension of my own perceptions. When I wrote up the interview, I used it to persuade a commission on crime to change their views about the drug problem. I really forgot a cardinal rule of this work—never trust a junkie, on the stuff or off the stuff. That *is* a working rule, isn't it?"

"No, question about it, Doc. Only one slight inclusion . . . the junkie himself suffers the same hazard."

"You mean self deception . . .? Is this the start of a new game for my benefit, Phil?"

"Sounds as if you took my faltering personally, as if I had betrayed you, Doc. . . ."

"I've got to be honest with you, Phil. I really thought that if ever a guy would make it, you were the one. You were the one."

He adjusted his position in the chair. He did it, as he did everything, gracefully. "You know, it is just possible that I had a small loss myself . . . like, man, I had some investment, too . . . like I ain't all that pleased to have a failure . . . on account of I read your carefully disguised article about me and I was taken in, too. How's that grab you? I was taken in, too . . . maybe, I ought to hold you responsible for tampering with my natural instincts, for warping my essential tendencies, my equipment for survival." He put on his glasses and his teeth gleamed as his lips parted in a smile. "You know, Doc, I was much impressed by that line you ran for me . . . that business about me being the squarest of the square. See, I personalize everything. You said that all junkies are supreme conformists because they can't do anything without heroin, they got to have it at regular intervals in order to live. Man, that was money for me . . . money . . . but you did screw me up, Doc. You for damn sure screwed me up."

Phil was the only heroin user I had ever known who could affect my professional attitude, principally because he could lift up the mantle and poke away at the man beneath. Worse than that he showed me how square I really was, or at least he made me feel that I was. This would be the third time we had talked together over a six-year period, I wondered how old Phil was. He looked the same as he had when I had seen him the first time, though I had since become grey. "How did I screw you up?"

"You had me go out and accept the world as if its values had some kind of meaning, its attitudes had some kind of validity whereas the junkie's world didn't. Man, I regret to say this in plain English . . . but that is shit . . . shit. . . . That nice civilized world with them nice values and attitudes is more savage and

selfish than the junkie's world. . . . As a matter of fact, Doc . . .
I think the world ought to be put in some kind of program to
learn the junkie values. . . ."

I leaned back in my chair and laughed. "Phil, you are marvellous . . . you are. . . ."

He grinned. "I'm serious, man. They are like strung out . . .
they're running all kinds of changes. That world's got to be using
something, they just can't be for real. . . . Just take this Vietnam
war . . . man, that's unreal. . . . Have you ever heard a hype lie
and cop-out and round on his reasons for shooting heroin any
worse than that happy square society is lying and copping out
and rounding about that Vietnam thing. Jesus Christ, man, that
solid White, Christian, ethical world is slaughtering and singing
hymns at the same time. The friendly police forces are up tight,
the happy colleges are up tight, the entertaining Congress is up
tight . . . man, that world you sent me out to is strung out. . . .
Like, man, they are all fucked up. No junkie, no matter how low
a bum he is, could ever do any more terrible things than your
happy White world. You better change your focus, Doc . . .
better forget us junkies and start working with that square
world. . . ." His face broke into a smile as he watched me. "You
can't decide whether this is a new cop-out or not, huh, Doc."

"It's different, Phil. How much were you using a day to survive
in that terrible world you glimpsed out there?"

"Oh, I was using some . . . some . . . I started slow but I
slipped into twelve or fourteen bags in no time at all. Yeah,
I was right back on full-time . . . like I had no tomorrow."

"And the family?"

"Gone . . . scattered like seed."

"How many children did you have?"

"Well, all the current statistics are not in, but I guess about
sixteen. With all due respect to Mr. Moynihan, I guess I'm the
absent Black father. I went to the girls' mothers and I explained
to each and every one of them that I really was irresponsible,
that I regretted that I had impregnated their daughters but they

could see I was no proper material for being a parent. . . .
Actually I was hardly worthy to offer my hand to any one of
them. . . ."

"That must have gone over big with them."

"In one case it led to further complications . . . that's why
I can't be sure about the number of children I've fathered."

"Do you mean that you went to bed with one of the mothers?"

"How coarse you make it sound, Doc . . . how coarse . . . it
was a moment of rapport, a tender moment welling up from a
bond. . . ."

"Phil, you're amazing. . . ."

"Yes, I am. . . . But you're going to have to change that world
out there, Doc, if you want me to do anything in it . . . and don't
you bring out one of those virtuous, White, Protestant ethics
now about my trying . . . don't you do that. . . ."

"That's a new note for you, Phil. . . . I don't remember your
emphasizing your race in our last interview . . . your being a
Negro."

"Black, Doc . . . Black, please, remember I'm hoping this
interview will get into The Amsterdam News, too."

"Were you interested in the Black movement when you were
out there?"

"Certainly, I was. I was one of the prime movers. I organized
a war fund . . . a kind of true casualty budget. . . ."

"What happened?"

"I shot up that money, too. . . . They kicked me out. They
beat me up for betraying the cause. They accused me of being
worse than Whitey, they run it like I was Judas the Iscariot. . . ."

I was puzzled. "Phil, are you running the game with me?"

He grinned. "Man, I told you I tried when I was out there.
I really tried to use all of them fine values. You didn't tell me,
though, that them fine values they ain't for real . . . you gotta
say 'em but you just don't believe them. . . . You loused me
up. . . ."

"How long were you out?"

"Almost two years."

"And how long were you off stuff?"

"Nine months."

"So you were in the joint for four years and you were out without heroin for nine months. . . . You were off for almost five years . . . five years. . . ."

"That's right, Doc . . . almost five years. . . ."

"How could you slip back?"

"Real easy." His teeth gleamed. "Doc, I'm sorry, but you just don't accept certain things, certain realities about us. We enjoy what heroin does to us . . . we enjoy it."

"Why don't you go to England?"

"They won't let me in because I've got a record as a user . . . and don't turn around now and tell me that I should try methadone maintenance because I don't like it but I do like stuff."

"Phil, how can such an astonishingly perceptive guy be so obtuse?"

"Why don't I ask you the same question, Doc, huh?"

"But I'm not in here, I'm not using heroin."

"But given your circumstances, your White beginnings, I might not be here either. Your blithe assumption that shooting dope is bad for me is cock-eyed. It's bad for your White society is what you're really saying, bad for your White institutions . . . not bad for me. Now, you know that heroin ain't bad for you . . . it ain't like LSD or speed or the pills . . . it don't affect your tissue or brain. So let's get really down with it . . . drugs and the Black man is really a White man's problem because it affects a White America. . . ."

"But Phil, look what it's done to you?"

"What's it done to me?"

"You'll have spent about ten years of your life in prisons or institutions, you'll have denied all of your talents. What about your music or your poetry or your acting?"

"What about them?"

"You were going to do so much . . . you had so much potential. If you insist on thinking Black . . . that Black movement can't afford to lose your gifts. . . ."

"By God, Doc, if we could darken your skin a little I believe we could find you some prophet robes. Damn but you can run it." Phil grinned.

"Is it that you really are crippled inside, Phil?"

"I'm not crippled, Doc . . . I'm maneuvering. I've got to buy myself space to turn around in. I didn't do that when I was out . . . I stretched too far and I fell . . . I stretched too far and that world, no matter what you say about my potential, it wasn't waiting with outstretched hands clutching greenbacks. I tinkered with myself and those values . . . they weren't mine . . . they're Whitey's. And the Black man, he ain't ready for them. The Black man he's trying real hard to get as much as the White man. He wants to sink his fists into that fat, that fat, so he can get just as screwed up as Whitey. Screwed up on cars and clothes and broads and parties and color television and suburbs. Yes, sir, Doc, you guys have done a good job . . . you've infected all of us Blacks with your White virus of gain. Make the money, run the game, run it, man, run it. Make the Black man forget that he's got soul, he's got emotion, he's got endurance . . . that's why so many of us Blacks use junk, to escape the trap you Whites have baited for us . . . to remain free."

"You were never free, Phil . . . never, and it's not because of your race. You weren't free because you used heroin. There's something inside of you that stands between you and freedom."

Phil slapped his hands together, shook his head and almost crooned as he said: "Baby, see that's what I mean. Baby, I love you because you run the game, just like us junkies. . . . You talk about freedom, big, fresh-air-blowing-through-your-kinky-hair freedom. . . . Man, you don't get me to rise for that fly of freedom. That's one of them White myths, one of them blown values, that freedom you talk about. Ain't nobody out in that world who is free, ain't nobody out there who can talk so easy as me right now . . . they gotta choke it up, stuff it down or squash it . . . and then they got to take a pill or a martini or another broad to live with it. Like, Doc, this is what I been saying, you throw out these concepts like they were for real. Man, they ain't . . . they ain't. Try that on the young junkie. Talk to him about freedom and motivation and maturity, don't tell old Fancy Phil the Flier. I see through it. . . . Maybe these young dudes'll buy it but not old Phil."

"You delight me, Phil. Your words flash and sparkle like jewels. . . . It's a type of auto-intoxication. That rhythm mesmerizes the listener so that he loses consciousness of what you say . . . and then you go to work and lift his valuables. . . . If it's a woman you lift her reserve or a man you lift his wallet . . . and race doesn't mean anything to you because you prey on Black and White indiscriminately . . . you just prey. Phil, you're a predator. . . . How were you getting your money to buy stuff when you were out there, huh, except through preying?"

"See, man, like I said, the frontier is gone, the unknown has vanished. Man is the last thing left to conquer and I'm forced to work on him. . . ."

"How were you getting your money for heroin?"

"Well, like I said . . . I was one of the big men in this movement and I organized this war chest. I really enjoyed that going around making appeals for support . . . allowing that this was a fight to the death, that the soldiers in this battle had to risk life, somehow we had to have insurance in case the worst happened. I was really good at it, Doc. I had the women cryin' and the men ready to storm the Alamo. God, they'd pull their money out so fast and fill up the hat so full . . . they just couldn't wait for it to come to them. . . . Oh, yes, I was somethin' to see. . . ."

"And were you so pleased that you could play on their emotions and take their hard-earned money from them? Were you so pleased to be like the lowest White scoundrel during the carpet-bagger days . . . were you so pleased to exploit your own people?"

Phil shook his head and wagged a finger. "No, sir, Doc, it don't work that way. You ain't gonna sting me onto the defensive. . . ."

I lighted a cigarette and offered it to him. "You don't have to go on the defensive; you told me before that the movement kicked you out because you stole the money . . . your own kicked you out and called you Judas . . . that's what you told me. . . ."

"That's because they were all screwed up reaching for power."

"You mean, they didn't understand how come Phil would steal money from his own. . . ."

"But, man, they didn't raise that money, I did. . . . It was me who got them quarters and halves. I wasn't planning on stealing that money, I was investing it. . . ."

"Investing it in Phil."

He paused for a moment and took off his sunglasses. His grin was unnatural. "Now, wait, you're pushing me now, Doc . . . I was investing that money. . . . I could see that banks and insurance companies did the same thing . . . money earns money. . . ."

"What did you invest it in?"

"Things that would bring a return."

"Things like call girls and heroin?"

"Well, the Mafia's in banks, ain't they?"

"So, that's your competition, the Mafia?"

Phil crushed out the cigarette. "Doc, you're too middle class. . . ."

"Like your Black movement that kicked you out and called you Judas . . . they're too middle class, too?"

"No, they was just stupid. They're so used to being cheated that they're all suspicion. They couldn't see that I was building up their money for them. . . ."

"Through addicting their children and women and husbands and fathers and brothers . . . how short-sighted of them."

Phil reached for my cigarettes. He watched my face, his brow wrinkled. "This is more of your middle-class sensibility, Doc. . . . Where's the Black man gonna put his money out so it shows a quick return?"

"That wasn't it, Phil. That wasn't it at all. It was simply that Fancy Phil didn't know any other way. Fancy Phil is a product of his own junkie world where everything is done in terms of short cuts and cop-outs. That's what it was . . . and your own people could see it and they kicked you out and then you turned to the one thing that allows you to live with yourself, heroin. You couldn't face it . . . the truth . . . so you turned back to junk. . . . Isn't that so, Phil?"

"You know, you'd make a fella fall on his knees, like one of those old preachers, Doc."

"It's true, Phil. You left school after the eighth grade because you wanted to take a short cut . . . not because of any great disagreement about school program . . . because you were an operator and you had to get out there . . . because you lacked the discipline to hang on and take the knocks we all have to take. You took to running women, to being a pimp, because they could keep you in the fat cat class without your having to do anything other than to feed them heroin. You took to the confidence games because you lacked the guts to use a gun and really be a pirate. . . . No, Phil, on every turn you took the short cut, the easy way, the typical wet pants junkie way. You're a junkie, Phil, through and through. You just know the game . . . you just know the game. . . . You'd really better think of methadone maintenance, or getting smuggled into England or Sweden, because you're going to spend the rest of your life in the joint or in an institution of some kind because you can't live outside. . . . You're dangerous . . . you're the most dangerous kind of individual. . . ."

Suddenly I heard my own voice. It was low and I was speak-

ing in almost a hiss. I was appalled at my own fury. I had played
right into his hands. Phil was the supreme manipulator, the
master gamesman. He grinned with triumph as he said, quietly,
kindly, magnanimously: "My Lord, how up tight you are. I'm
earning my money this morning, Doc. I'm wringing you through
a kind of private therapy. . . . I hope now that when you write
up this interview you're going to put it down like it is . . . we'll
allow you to disguise it a little bit . . . but I hope you will let the
hate shine through . . . because that's what you reveal . . . hate."
Phil spelled the word for me in measured letters. "You hate me
and all junkies with all the fury of your soul. You're supposed
to be our friend and interpreter to the square world . . . but at
bottom you're like all the rest: we got to find salvation your
way, otherwise we are damned. You just hate me, don't you,
Doc? You hate me as you hate all junkies . . . hate."

It was his adroitness, his sheer adroitness that gave me back
my control. Phil's strength was also his weakness. He had said
too much. I lighted a cigarette, I let him see my hand shake. I
wiped my head and said: "It's true, Phil . . . it's true. It must
be true that I hate you."

It was the one thing in the world that Fancy Phil hadn't an-
ticipated from me. He was caught off guard. With a serious expression on his face he considered his position. If I would add
something further, Phil with his incredible swiftness could make
use of it, but I was silent. I just sat and smoked, watching him.
At last he said: "Since I been in here, Doc, I've been studying
music. . . . You know, how you really read and put it down on
music paper." He paused, waiting for my reply. He removed his
sunglasses and polished them very elaborately, but I continued
to smoke and watch him. "I figure I'll put my feelings into music.
I don't make out too good with people. They just don't understand my type, you know. So I figure I'll get up real tight with
my music and poetry and get over my message that way . . . my
message, Doc. . . . You know, so I'll be really pouring out just
what it is I have inside of me." Again he waited for my re-

sponse, then he continued: "It was like you said in that interview you wrote up the last time . . . 'Phil is an alien even in the world of the junkie. . . . Phil is an incomplete man. And only when Phil can find some fragment that will serve to complete him, only then will Phil be able to face himself and then the world.' That was true, Doc. You really were on the cap when you wrote that, and I tell you I thought about it for days. You really put it to me right on the mustard. So now, I figure with my music, which I am really getting somewhere with, my music and my poetry, I've found that fragment that'll put me together . . . because leave us face it, Doc . . . Fancy Phil he is now thirty-seven, he ain't getting no younger, and when you use junk all the years I have the years don't get no easier." Again he waited expectantly. "Can I have one of your smokes?" I passed him the pack and lighted the cigarette for him and then leaned back in my chair. His voice changed subtlely, a note of wistfulness in it. "You know when I was outside, I did try, Doc . . . I did try. . . . Lemme tell you how come I went back on the horse. . . . Like I was telling you before . . . I did belong to this Black movement. It caught me up. I studied some Black history, but man it was slow. It didn't move fast enough for Phil. I liked the going out to the people and telling them about what we had to do to bring Whitey to his feet . . . even though the people I talked to knew more about Black history and injustice than I did. . . . I was able to move them, make them dig up their money . . . I could rap to them like they never been rapped to before. I had them in the palm of my hand; it did something for them, but for me it did nothing, Doc. I was naked and cold inside. Honest to God I was. I didn't feel at home with them activists . . . you were right, I couldn't feel at home with anybody, I was an alien. I wasn't a Black man or a White man . . . I was a guy who shot stuff for nineteen years. That's who I was, a heroinist . . . I wasn't caught up in nothing, I was running the game. And each time I roused them was each time I failed me. . . . I took the money, not for money but to run another

game . . . to run another game. . . . I got me a stable of
chicks. . . . I got a kilo of stuff with the money . . . I got it cut
and packaged and out on the street. I was turning better than
fifteen hundred dollars a day. I was going to put that money
back in the fund. They was so stupid they didn't even know I
took, that's how clever I was. I brought back twenty-seven thousand dollars to the brothers. . . . I'd only taken ten thousand.
I showed them how I'd made the money almost triple itself. . . ."
Phil stared at me. "They beat me up . . . they beat me up and
stomped my ribs, and tore my face. . . . They called the money
shit money because of the way I'd made it. See, they really believed in the movement . . . they really wanted dope out of
Harlem . . . they.really believed I was Judas the Iscariot. You
know me, Doc, I ain't much when it comes to fists . . . I'm real
scared of being cut up. . . . I never went in for that kind of stuff.
No guns, no knives, no blood . . . that's not for Fancy Phil.
Girls, running the game, some high-class selling . . . but most
of all talking, that's Phil. So when the brothers they broke me
up and then called the cops . . . I was busted, really busted inside. . . . I was this here alien . . . I was a junkie. Them brothers
as they belted me around kept spittin' at me: 'Junkie, junkie,
junkie, junkie. . . .' So you see, Doc, you were right . . . auto-
intoxication, that's what you said. . . ."

I studied his face, the hunched shoulders, the image of the
deflated man. At last I snorted: "Phil, you are a marvel. You'll
game the undertaker when he comes to lay you out."

"You're reading me wrong, baby. You're reading me wrong.
. . . These are cold days for Phil. Them mornings are cold, and
that cold spreads all the way through. What am I going to do,
Doc?"

"Talk, Phil, just talk and game your way right through
life. . . ."

"Do you really hate me, Doc? Do you really think I'm a
dangerous man? Do you really think I've got to stay in an institution all my life?"

"What do you think, Phil?"

He put his hand over his lips, cocked his head, his face appeared young and frightened. He whispered: "It's not true is it, Doc . . .?"

"I'm sorry for you, Phil . . . I'm sorry for you."

"You'll come back and see me . . . you'll come back . . . I'll change . . . you'll see, Doc . . . you'll see . . . I'll change. . . ."

"Sure, Phil . . . sure."

As I left I wondered, had I been gamed again or had I witnessed a beginning?

14 *An ex-drug addict finds acceptance in the community as an ex-addict, using his experience to educate others. There is no more radiant human being than the former hard drug user. This is a person of infinite patience, compassion, truth, understanding, tolerance, love. His capacity to help others is unlimited. Mrs. Sutter is like this, a dedicated woman, still working to help others, never taking her freedom from drugs for granted. She is a real force in drug prevention and rehabilitation. Here is no charismatic hocus-pocus, no self-aggrandizement, no mystique, no cult. For the real work in the field of drug prevention the former addict is invaluable. He has got to be straight; if he isn't he knows that he is setting himself up, all over again, for heroin.*

An Old Tale

Out of place and out of time, the house was huge, rambling, and structurally a mongrel. Its place should have been the New England seacoast, its time the turn of the century; instead it was perched on the flat midlands of a wheat state, and the hot sunlight of the present day shimmered from its cupolas. It was a private narcotics treatment center.

"There are plenty of places for the young drug abuser, because, Mr. Cortina, drugs are considered to be a problem of the young today. So those of us who are middle-aged or older don't find those surroundings helpful. Since the problem of drug abuse is partly one of alienation, anything that further alienates can be done without."

Mrs. Sutter, was a lady in her fifties, trim with grey hair

178

smartly arranged and a marvellous voice. It was dark and rich
in tone. I asked: "How come you came here?"

"The house was made available to us and most importantly
the town allowed us to come in. I think in all honesty they didn't
realize what drug abusers were for a long time, and by then we
were part of the landscape."

"You've been here nineteen years?"

"Yes, it'll be twenty years this fall."

"How come you became involved? Were you a social worker
or a psychologist?"

"No, I have even better qualifications; I was a heroin user."

"I see."

"You know, it's very hard for any kind of individual who's
been out of society for any length of time to find an opening, to
crawl back in. One of the biggest problems is to fill in the gaps
in any kind of application. Suddenly you find yourself trying
to explain a four-year interruption in your history. If you're
honest about it and say 'I was in prison or in a hospital or in a
treatment program,' chances are you won't succeed in getting
the job or the apartment or what have you. If you're dishonest
you're leaving yourself wide open for exposure. And if you're
like so many ex-users you're tentative anyway, accustomed to
alibiing, susceptible to failure, and you go right back to your
old ways. . . . I'd had this experience, and finally I thought that
the one safe way for me to join the establishment was to capital-
ize on what I was, an ex-drug addict. Society would accept me
as that, and it was in being exactly that where I could make a
contribution and still help myself to stay off heroin."

"You mean talking about drug abuse and working with people using drugs helps you to stay clean?"

"Reinforces you. Believe me, drugs are what I know best.
Drug attitudes, values, patterns have conditioned me. In a
moment of real stress, even today, I find myself thinking of the
old drug ways. . . . But, you understand, here the town has
helped us enormously. They use us. We have a regular program

in the schools for young people. We go to the churches, to the
P.T.A., to the service clubs. We're making our contribution in
our way." She passed me a cigarette box. "You know, we've
gotten up so tight about drugs we begin to see them as the problem. They're not. You go to drugs to handle problems. The
problems really are those casualties of living that we all go
through, though not all of us handle them well, or allow for a
range of choice. But you didn't come here to hear me lecture. I'm
sure in your work you know most of the stories . . . I'll get your
first interviewee for you."

I smiled and put down my cigarette. "I thought I had started
with my first interview, Mrs. Sutter."

"Mine is an old tale, Mr. Cortina. An old tale."

"Would you mind sharing it?"

She looked at me for a moment thoughtfully. "You ask yourself, 'does the drug user start from a confused point of view or
does drug usage make him confused?' In the beginning I never
thought of myself as being confused. It seemed all the confusion
commenced with the drugs. The question the world asks over
and over, 'Why did you start,' is the question the addict asks,
too. It's very hard to penetrate to that center, because it's not
where the addict comes from, although it's where he has to get
to. I can't blame anybody. I spent years blaming everybody and
everything for what had happened to me. At last I realized it
was something I wanted to do."

"You didn't know that at the time, though?"

"Of course not. I married an addict. . . . Loving him, living
with him, observing him, I knew the consequences. You'd have
to be blind, deaf, and unconscious not to."

"Many times I have heard a woman say that she married an
addict thinking that her love would make him break the habit."

"That's common . . . but mine was a little different. I thought
that if I used he would see what it was doing to me and stop. . . .
It succeeded . . . he did stop, but I didn't. . . ." Mrs. Sutter's

voice was like a splendid cello. "I'd met this young man in my Freshman year at college. He was nineteen and I was a year younger. It was one of those things, instant attraction. But even in those days he was using benzedrine . . . pot wasn't so common then. He was having a hard time in school. College wasn't for him, but he had a family that insisted. He was an only child, from a religiously mixed background, and he was pretty mixed up. I'd listen to him; he'd pour out his woes. As for me I was in the clouds. It never occurred to me that I wasn't helping him by agreeing with him, holding his hand, soothing him, justifying him . . . I wasn't helping him at all. I was in love, Mr. Cortina. . . ." She paused. "Before, I said it was an old tale . . . but you know, even as I talk to you now, I can remember . . . that time . . . remember what it was like to see him come across the campus. . . ." She paused and lighted a cigarette. "His father was Jewish and his mother a Catholic, and somehow he got jammed (there's an addict word for you) in a kind of emotional revolving door. I don't think his people had money. I think both had had to struggle very hard for what they had . . . perhaps that's why they wanted so badly for Sid to become a doctor. He really loved automobile engines. In any case, his grades were bad, and he was put on probation. There were some letters back and forth with his parents, and the upshot was that he left college and got drafted into the army . . . and he asked me to marry him. I did. He was stationed not too far away and he'd come back some weekends. As I said before, I knew he was using benzedrine and somehow I knew he was using pills when he got in the army. I knew he was fooling around, but I was young and in love and I thought in time he would give it up . . . you know, 'if he loves me, he'll give it all up'."

"What about your people, Mrs. Sutter?"

"I came from Michigan, a farm. My father never made it as a farmer so he had to work as a mill hand . . . my mother was a dressmaker with a lot of children. There were five girls and four boys . . . I suppose today that kind of life would be looked on as terribly marginal . . . and it was in a certain sense, in an emotional sense. . . . When Sid came along, I was ready, Mr. Cortina, I was ready. I was primed to fall in love . . . I needed somebody to love so badly. That's where it wasn't quite fair to Sid. I needed him desperately. I really wasn't at college for an education; I was at college so I wouldn't have to be home. I was on scholarship. . . ." She rubbed out her cigarette and looked at me. "I must sound pretty practiced to you in this recounting— what a young addict calls 'running a story.' "

"Well, I imagine, Mrs. Sutter, that you're always using your own experience in your kind of work. Isn't that why it's right on your finger tips, as it were?"

"Yes, and that's why I'm grateful that you wanted to interview me, because you'll force me to re-examine things that I've perhaps scanted or rounded on a little. Nobody would believe how powerful the heroin culture is . . . nobody. You have to have been in it to understand its sheer magnitude. It's there for the user more meaningfully than sex or food or aspiration." She studied her hands. "It's very difficult most times to make people understand that . . . you're not just taking dope, you're joining a culture with its special jargon, outlook, behavior . . . it's a vast net. And only when you get some inkling of this can you glimpse how difficult it is for anybody to rid himself of the hard drug habit."

"The physical rejection is really not that hard, I've learned from addicts."

"Three days or four days or longer, but whatever the time involved the physical dependence is broken. I've kicked without anything, I suppose, twenty-five times, Mr. Cortina. Twenty-five times. And some of those times were pretty awful . . . I was real sick . . . real sick. . . . One time I was kicking and pregnant as well." She appeared surprised. "That's something I haven't told before, for all the times I've related my life's history. It's a pretty sordid topic for a teachers' tea. One has got to be remorselessly honest." Her voice trailed off, as if she had been interrupted. She said quietly: "One uses heroin to avoid pain, to avoid personal investment, to conceal incompleteness. To renounce drugs, each of these reasons is exposed with a magnification that leaves you without a shred of personal worth. You reach the worst of your imagined fears—those that drove you to heroin in the first place—when you begin that slow walk out of addiction. I say to these people: 'don't criticize the addict for his faltering, he is being asked to exert a degree of strength required of a St. Francis or a St. Sebastian. Every addict who kicks, who returns to society, is an individual of incredible strength, for he has emerged from the ordure of his own life.' "

Mrs. Sutter's face was grave. Suddenly she looked up and smiled. "I'm sorry, I seemed to have strayed. . . . It won't help the order of your interview. . . ."

"There's no formal order to these interviews, Mrs. Sutter. It's not often that I find someone who can talk so eloquently about addiction."

"I was telling you about my family, wasn't I?"

"You said that you went to college to get away from home. . . ."

"Yes. To escape the meagerness, the aridity. It was the post-Depression years. Things were terribly harsh . . . but what dug at me was the realization that my people would have been as they were without a Depression. I felt that they had no vision, they were grubbers, and I had no idea how they had become that way other than the life they lived had chamfered them down. I was afraid of that, Mr. Cortina . . . I didn't want to get that way. I was the oldest girl. I should have stayed at home, gotten a job, helped with the family. I'll never forget my father standing in the kitchen, gaunt, his short-cropped grey hair, his Adam's apple bobbing, his fingers plaiting his overalls leg. He was trying to understand why his daughter was going a thousand miles away. He was trapped by his own mixed feelings. You see, Mr. Cortina, he didn't know how to talk to me. You know what his words were, when he finally forced them out? I'll never forget them: 'Expect you won't need heavy clothes out there.' I was escaping. . . ."

"How about your husband in the army . . . didn't they discover that he was using stimulants?"

"It took them six months and they broke him. He smashed up a jeep and injured the officer he was chauffering. I was just finishing my freshman year when Sid came back. He was bitter. He felt the army had wronged him. . . . If you closed your eyes and listened to Sid, you would imagine from his complaints a kind of chained Prometheus, but then, open-eyed, you'd see him for a skinny, nice-looking twenty-year-old . . . and a very young twenty-year-old at that. But I didn't care. I loved him. I quit college and got a job. Sid went to work as well. We had an apartment. Sid had a hard time holding jobs for very long. He found it difficult to stick anything out. He was out a lot running around with a fairly rough bunch. And then I began to find money missing from my pocketbook, or I'd find if I didn't get Sid's pay on payday it would be all gone. The toaster would disappear, the radio . . . my wristwatch . . . I had some spoons from my grandmother, they went. . . . I'd ask him to bring his friends home . . . 'bring them home, Sid. They're your friends . . . this is your home . . . have them bring their wives and sweethearts . . . I'd like to meet them. . . .' You know, I had a sick feeling in my stomach that he was running around with somebody else. Oh, the times that I wished that it had been another woman, Mr. Cortina. I would have welcomed her . . . I could have fought her, I would have had a chance. . . . But it wasn't a woman, it was heroin . . . heroin. That's where the furnishings were going, the jewelry, the money. He brought these friends home. . . . They were his age . . . they all had one thing in common, it seemed to me: a kind of silence . . . a silence among themselves until after they visited the bathroom . . . then talk would break out like so many bursts of gunfire. . . ."

"They were using your bathroom to take off?"

"Yes, Sid invited them in to cop. Poor Sid had had to get down to the very lowest rung. . . ."

"Did you learn from him that he was hooked?"

"Oh, yes. I had this feeling inside that something was very wrong. I began to get very careful about the money and having things lie around that could be pawned or fenced. Inevitably, short of stealing, Sid would not have money to buy his fix . . . that's when he confessed. I remember he begged me for two dollars . . . that's what it was for a bag in those days. . . . He cried and promised that he would change but he was so sick that he had to score. So I gave him the money . . . I couldn't see him suffer. . . ."

"But was he really suffering, Mrs. Sutter?"

"No . . . but I thought he was and I loved him. Just to have him come to me meant something. You see, he had become a stranger to me . . . never a passing touch of my body. . . . I was young . . . and then sometimes when I happened to look at him I'd catch an expression of hate on his face . . . hate . . . as if I had done him some terrible injury. . . . I got the feeling that I was responsible for driving him to heroin."

"I'm sure he was aware of this and turned it to his advantage. Did you support his habit?"

"You do know the addict, don't you, Mr. Cortina? That's exactly what happened. I found myself working two jobs to support Sid's addiction. . . . You see, I'd see them on the streets now. They'd always been there, but now having an addict in my own home opened my eyes. . . . To see them nod and mumble, in their half-speed way . . . yes, I saw them all around me in the street. One night I was home and he brought his friends in . . . I know he was providing some of their stuff for them . . . I had this sense that I'd reached the end. Sid was looking at me with such an expression of loathing . . . I knew once he went into the bathroom and came out that expression would change. . . . I said to one of his cronies: 'Do that to me . . . hit me . . .

hit me. . . .' I held out my arm. . . . He stared at me. That jarred
him all right. 'Hit me or I'll scream out and have the cops in.' I
turned away, I couldn't watch that needle. . . . It took a second.
A second, Mr. Cortina. Sid came out of the bathroom . . . I
brushed by him . . . I was sick, retching. . . . I heard him say:
'What did you do to her?' He came into the bathroom while I
was vomiting and snarled at me: 'You stupid cunt, you stupid
cunt. . . .' The language he used would have ordinarily made
me writhe, but now a kind of incredible rapture flooded me, like
a sexual orgasm . . . I'd gotten my wings, as the addict phrases
it. . . . That was the beginning, Mr. Cortina . . . I was going to
make Sid realize what he had done to me. What a naive fool I
was. . . . How I gamed myself. . . . I had heroin. I used to fantasize that I was doing what I was to bring Sid to his senses . . .
fantasize, Mr. Cortina . . . because I loved the high. It was the
ultimate answer for every casualty of Thelma Sutter's life."

"I imagine there were major changes in your life."

"Oh, such changes . . . such changes. . . . I'll tell you one thing,
I got down to Sid's level . . . I read him as I had never read
him before. I saw him as if every covering had been stripped
from him: an immature, aggrieved, stunted little child . . . dependent, scared, devious, lazy, vicious, totally selfish. . . . But
still there was something of the old love left. . . ." She shuddered.
"When I think back . . . a nightmare . . . a nightmare, Mr.
Cortina. . . . You don't lose sight of yourself . . . your self
parades before you as you are, but the heroin allows you to
entertain what you are with a degree of objectivity . . . it deadens
your disgust with yourself, it permits you to view each flaw with
a sense of distance, always with the sly suggestion that you
could really do something about this if you wanted to, you really
had this recourse if you wanted to use it. . . . Heroin showed me
a Thelma I never knew existed . . . narrow, selfish, grasping, immature, unmotivated, cunning. . . . Why had I run away from
home? Why had I left college? Why had I put up with Sid? Oh,
yes, Mr. Cortina, heroin gives you a high, but there is a lowdown

on it, too." She grimaced. "The addict doesn't lose sight of his incredible failures—he merely views them from the projection room."

"What happened?"

She lighted a cigarette. "First thing, the inevitable thing, I lost first one job and then the second job. You can't be much of a stenographer when you're on the nod . . . or cashier in a restaurant. . . ."

"Did your addiction do anything to your husband at all?"

"Yes, it did. He tried to get me to stop. I remember his trying to get me to go to one of the very early drug clinics. I remember him saying: 'Go, even if you don't do anything but sit there . . . go, Thelma. . . .' "

"But he was still on stuff?"

"Oh, yes . . . I said 'nightmare' before . . . believe me, there were times when there was no money and we'd both kick cold turkey in that apartment. Do you know what the outline of hell is, Mr. Cortina? It's a man and wife, both addicts, both kicking at the same time in the same room. . . ."

I looked at her face, it had become grey with the memory.

"How long did this go on?"

"About two years, and then I was picked up for passing a bum check. That was the first of my brushes with the law. . . ."

"And Sid, did he never get picked up?"

"He got picked up for shoplifting . . . that was his thing. He really was terribly afraid of violence. As a matter of fact, I often think his army experience had bothered him terribly because he was the kind who would run a mile from a fight. . . . Sid got a year in the state prison . . . I was put on probation. . . ."

"Did you stop using?"

"I cut down . . . I got a job . . . I began to get letters from Sid. . . . He conned me into thinking he had changed. He'd gotten into contact with his people. He told me he was coming back and we'd start all over again . . . but I was shooting two or three times a week. . . ."

"Did he come back?"

"Oh, yes. . . . When he came in the door, out of prison for six hours, he was high . . . I knew it as he walked in." She lighted a cigarette. "It wasn't long before I was shooting as much as before . . . along with Sid. . . ."

"You were still on probation?"

"Yes. . . . I was leery about trying any more bad-check passing. There was only one way I could go, Mr. Cortina . . . I became a whore."

If she had shot off a gun, I couldn't have been more stunned by her simple, unemotional statement. I had heard countless women tell me that they had supported their drug habit through prostitution, but to see this elegant lady . . . confess to hustling. . . .

"And Sid?"

"I was supporting him through my hustling. We had a place which served as our business establishment. Oh, yes, Mr. Cortina, Sid and I were bound together by a common bond, heroin, as we had never been bound together by love. . . ."

"The drug scene must have been different in those years from today."

"Very different. The users were older . . . you didn't see the kids that you see today. . . . There was a lot of paragoric used and dilaudid . . . you'd ask your acquaintances if they were on or off. . . . If you could ever say there was a touch of gentility in drug use, it might be said about those times."

"How old were you at this time?"

"I was twenty-four and Sid a year older. He got hit one night by a car and was taken to the hospital. I was hustling, and I'll never forget how scared I was when a cop knocked at the door. I panicked and ran down the fire escape. . . . Another cop down below on the street caught me . . . he told me my husband was injured. . . ."

"Was it serious?"

"Yes, very serious . . . broken back. He was in the hospital more than a year. I had to tell the doctor that he was an addict. He was a good man, that doctor. He helped Sid through the worst of his torment. His folks came on after a few months . . . and when he was released from the hospital he went back East to them. . . ."

"And all this while you were on the street?"

"Yes . . . I wouldn't see his people. I ducked them and I ducked Sid because he was always after me to stop using. I couldn't stop using. . . . You know, lots of times a user will say to you that you have to reach a place where you want to stop. That on the surface may sound like a cop-out, but it really isn't."

"This kind of life on the street must have been a fantastic experience for you?"

"Once you accept your addiction nothing after that is fantastic. You know, they say you can't make a hypnotized person do anything he wouldn't do in his regular state. The same can't be said when a person is addicted to heroin. Oh, you're conscious of the degradation, but again from a distance, from an insulation. . . . You know, you wake up in the morning . . . or late afternoon . . . you don't have your shot in the house . . . no coffee, no food . . . you just got to get that first shot. . . . You're so bone weary . . . so tired, Mr. Cortina. You think, 'Oh God, another day,' but all the while you're pulling yourself together, searching in your purse for the money to pay for that shot. . . ."

"How long did this go on, Mrs. Sutter?"

She shook her head: "I guess I was twenty-seven when I got picked up for soliciting, or as they said, 'loitering'. I was put into a detention center. That's when I kicked cold turkey and discovered I was pregnant at the same time." There was a pause. She glanced at me, her face composed, almost serene, and said: "Thank you for not asking about the father . . . I had no idea . . . I was a whore who had an accident. But something did come out of that pregnancy that had a great effect on me. . . . I didn't get a sentence. I was released, but the medical examiner said to me that my baby would be addicted unless I stopped. You know, you hear so much about the cruelty and brutalizing in prisons and detention centers . . . and it's true. . . . You can't begin to realize how coarse, how debasing, how dehumanizing, how disorienting a jail experience can be, but there are also examples of simple and unexpected human kindnesses. That medical examiner was one of those unexpectedly kind people. I never knew his name or anything about him, but I can hear him saying softly: 'That baby is entitled to its life, Miss.' "

"Did you get in touch with your husband?"

"Oh, no, that was dead. . . . I couldn't get in touch with anyone. All those steps would have meant too much pain . . . and incidentally, they would have been the right steps for my rehabilitation. I hadn't gotten to that place yet. . . . But the baby marks a real break in my history. I had to stay off heroin . . . I had to stay off because of the baby . . . and I did. I stayed off for eight months. . . . The baby was born dead. . . . They didn't know about RH factor in those days. The baby was dead and whatever I had been banking on was also dead. Still a junkie way of looking at things, you see, Mr. Cortina. The baby was going to do something . . . not Thelma, the baby."

"You went back on heroin?"

"Right away. I no sooner got out of the hospital than I scored. But I was weak and run down. I was only out a little while before I had an O.D. and wound up in the hospital again. While I was there I got a letter from Sid . . . it had been forwarded half a dozen times. It was the same old Sid . . . running down his people, how hard life was . . . the same old querulous boy. . . . I knew he had by now returned to stuff . . . but you know, lying there in the hospital, I couldn't help but remember how I had loved him. . . ."

"How long had you been on heroin by this time?"

"Ten years."

"Had it changed you greatly . . . I mean physically?"

"Oh, yes. I was skin and bone, my teeth were bad . . . I was always breaking out with sores. . . . You know, the addict is an amateur chemist . . . but he's so naive he'll use an unsterile needle . . . that's somehow in the nature of his total mixup. . . . Physically, I was in poor condition . . . I certainly wasn't eager to look at myself in the mirror. When I did it showed a hard, coarse, grained face. . . . I don't think I was like that inside . . . but looking at the face frightened me. . . ."

"Why?"

"Because I saw what I think I had always run away from . . . a self grubby and crabbed, niggardly in outlook, a kind of soil-gritty farm woman. . . . At this time, Mr. Cortina, I was at the bottom . . . I was broken in body and spirit. I think I was as close to giving up as I ever came. . . ."

"What about the prospect of a shot of heroin?"

She looked at me keenly. "That's very shrewd insight. I didn't want a shot . . . I didn't want a shot. . . . And I had had opportunities there in the hospital to have gotten a shot. . . . But I had reached that place . . . I was done. Oh, I fell back three times after that, but each time I quickly went to a clinic. I haven't used heroin in twenty-three years. I have a profound respect for its power, though."

"What is the answer, Mrs. Sutter? What do we do to keep the young person away from drugs?"

"There's no all-embracing answer. I'm never sure about searching for answers . . . answers by themselves are not helpful. As the addict would say, 'run the questions, man, run the questions.' It's in the questions that we can seek out those half-impulses, those half-strengths. Relationships, functions, emotions, understanding. . . . Honesty, honesty. . . . These simple, simple bread and butter staples of family life, school life, community life . . . this is the food that either satisfies or turns off a kid so he has to look for something that will help him support his non-function. Let's face it, if drugs were wiped from the face of the earth, Mr. Cortina . . . the dissatisfied, the alienated, the crippled would find some other manner to cop-out. . . . Not drugs . . . people . . . relationships. Do you know after all these years . . . with everything that's happened . . . when I go to the front door here, I nearly always hold my breath. . . . Always thinking that perhaps it will be Sid arriving at last."

15 *A twelve-year-old boy died in Harlem. They say that heroin killed him. Last week I walked the streets in the Buffalo ghettos, the week before in Rochester, and before that the streets of Baltimore and New York and New Orleans and Chicago and San Francisco. And in every place it was the same, the young people nodding and muttering in their doped twilight, their slum streets barren of everything but rats and garbage, filth and degradation, indignity and debasement, hopelessness and despair, ostracism and indifference. Heroin will kill these children. They will say that it is drugs that menace them. They will say once we have stamped out the pusher we will have the problem licked. They will say these things. My Fourteen-Year-Old whom I interviewed five years ago will say nothing: he is dead.*

The Fourteen-Year-Old

When I recall Cyril, my memory is peppered with sights and sounds of the city, for this was his world. Outside, the sounds swelled and receded, punctuated by sirens, trucks and buses shifting gears, garbage cans being thrown to the sidewalk— and the endless throb of soul music riding now above and now below the dominant noise that was Harlem. These were the sounds. As for the sights, I remember a dark, small room, with several votive candles guttering before sacred pictures, and a large crucifix on one wall, the corpus of this Christ seeming more emaciated and broken than others I had seen.

I had been invited by a clergyman to conduct interviews with drug users in his neighborhood. I had just finished with my first when the priest introduced Cyril, saying: "Mr. Cortina, I'd like

193

to introduce you to Cyril. He's not on your list of people to interview, he just dropped by . . . but I think you'll find you have a lot to talk about."

Cyril was a slight, dark figure with a scar on his temple, full lips, and eyes curiously shaded. He appeared to be drowsy. He waited for me to put out my hand, following the gesture and then responding to it slowly.

"How old are you, Cyril?"

"Fourteen."

His was a muffled speech. I smiled at him. "That's the age when a fella begins to pull away from his parents a little bit, when he begins keeping certain things to himself. Does that happen with you?"

"Yeah, you could say that, man."

"There are certain things you just shy away from telling your parents about. . . ."

"No . . . sometimes, you know, I got some disagreements, but I talk to her."

"So, you will talk to your parents. You'll tell them anything?"

"Well, like when I do somethin' wrong, somethin' bad . . . that she shouldn't know."

"What would happen do you think if you told them?"

"It's only my mother anyway. . . . She'd sit down and talk with me . . . she's soft hearted. . . ."

"That means you can get away with a lot if she's soft hearted."

"All kinds of things. . . ."

His speech was slow, muffled, soft, sleepy. I had to strain to catch some of his words. "Does that have drawbacks? Being able to get away with a lot of things . . .?"

"Yeah . . . yeah . . . it do. . . . I can take a chance to do somethin' on accounta my mother is soft hearted. . . ."

"What about your father?"

"Oh, he doesn't live with the family . . . I see him once or twice a week or so."

"Your mother and father are separated?"

"Yeah . . . yeah, they've been apart for some time."

"Are there other children in the family, Cyril?"

"Four . . . my sister she's got two children, she's the oldest."

"This sister, she lives with your mother too?"

"No, she just moved out . . . she ain't but eighteen . . . but there's three other boys in the bunch. . . . I'm the middle boy."

"We hear so much about neighborhoods today, Cyril . . . what kind of a neighborhood do you live in?"

"Well, it's the way people say, it's a slum." Cyril's voice revealed no emotion, it was colorless, the pace uniformly slow. He offered: "Yeah, you know, we don't have no hot water. . . ."

"A cold-water flat?" I said with a curious feeling of nostalgia, for that was a term I had known in the late 1920s and '30s.

"We have to heat the water on the stove . . . heat it on the stove."

"Do you have a bathtub?"

"Yeah . . . but we gotta fill the basin and heat it on the stove and then dump it in the tub, you know?"

"So your mother has to heat water for doing dishes or washing clothes or anything else? She must have to work hard."

"She do . . . but we helps her . . . she asks us to help."

"How long have you lived there?"

"Fourteen years."

"You were born there?" He nodded his head. "How many rooms in this apartment?"

"Four . . . me and my brothers we has the same room. Now that my sister and her kids done left . . . it'll be fewer."

"How is your apartment heated?"

"Stoves and steam heat . . . but the steam heat it ain't dependable. The super we complain to him but he don't do nothin'."

"Does he live in the same building, this superintendent?"

"No, he lives two blocks down."

"If you get no satisfaction from the super, do you complain to the landlord?"

"Don't ever see him. . . . He sends the agent . . . and him he's always soft mouthin'. My moms says you gotta yell for a week and a half before somethin' gets done . . . you know, like if a pipe busts or the winda busts . . . you jest gotta yell. . . . My moms wants to move. . . ."

"What about vermin . . . do you know what I mean by vermin?"

"We got them . . . we got a whole lot of them. But it's not so much of a problem on accounta we got traps all over the rooms. Like I like to watch TV at night because the rats are movin' around. They keep movin' around, you know. We tried killin' 'em with stuff, but it's too dangerous, that poison, my moms says."

"These conditions, Cyril, that you live in, are they different from the other people in your neighborhood?"

He seemed to be focusing his eyes at me. "No, man, they's all the same . . . all them houses . . . got rats and mices and cock-roaches. . . ."

"Is it a quiet block you live on?"

"No, it ain't quiet . . . they's the police cars . . . they makes a lot of noise . . . they's the ambulances, and the people yellin' . . . people fightin' . . . especially on the third floor they's always fightin' and cuttin' themselves up . . . no, it ain't quiet. . . ."

"It must be very disturbing."

"No, it ain't disturbin', cause I'm used to it."

"Is home a place you like to be, Cyril?"

"I like to be home. . . ."

"Even though you're cold and the rats run around. . . ?"

"Ruther be home . . . we got heaters and we traps the rats . . . ruther be home."

Cyril never changed his position in the chair, he seemed to be a part of it. "Does your mother go out to work?"

"She works every day. . . ."

"And she makes enough to buy food and clothes and pay all the bills?"

"Yeah, and my father, he sends money, sometimes . . . buys

me shoes or a pair of pants sometimes . . . used to some-times. . . ."

"Are you in school, Cyril?"

"I'm in the ninth grade."

"Well, that's just about right for your age, the ninth grade, isn't it?" He nodded his head. "Are you a good student . . .? Do you like school?"

"It's all right . . . I guesses I likes it . . . I wants to graduate, like the way them people talks about it . . . you needs an edjica-tion. . . ."

"What about the subjects . . . do you think they'll help you when you get out in the world?"

"They're teachin' all-right things. Like what they're teachin' you understand it but . . . but it's all okay I expects. . . ."

"What's your favorite subject, Cyril?"

"Math . . . math . . . like I'm all right with math. I ain't no capper but I'm . . . I ain't never failed math. . . ."

"Have you failed other subjects?"

"Yeah . . . whole lots . . . English . . . mostly and science . . . they ain't. . . ." Cyril seemed to be losing the thread of his own responses. His voice was deep down in his throat.

I suited my volume to his and practically whispered. "Do you have a great many friends?" Sleepily he nodded. "And they are your own age? What's the school like, Cyril? Is it like your neighborhood: noisy, kids yelling and fighting?"

"I go to school way out . . . way out. . . ."

I hazarded a guess as to his meaning. "You mean, you go to school in a different part of the city?"

"Lower Manhattan, I got transferred. . . ."

"You were transferred?"

"The school transferred me on accounta I had a fight with a teacher. . . . He started pushin' me to the back of the room . . . he was a substitute and he kept a pushin' me. He coulda tol' me to go back there like a gentleman but he kept pushin' me. You know, when the bell wuz ringin', we wuz goin' outside . . .

he told me 'Git to the back of the room. . . .' There wuz a line
an' I wuzn't in the line. 'Git to the back of the room and git in
that line.' I said, the bell it had rung and I could go out . . . so he
pushed me real hard and I hit him . . . I punched him . . . I
started to run out and he yelled: 'Don't worry, I'll get you.'
The next day I got suspended. My moms she went to the principal . . . she told me I wuz wrong to hit the dude . . . but she
took the school side when she wuz talkin' to the principal. . . ."

"Didn't you tell her about the pushing?"

"I told her but she said I wuz wrong . . . I shouldn't of done
it. I wuzn't mad at my moms . . . she wuz right. . . . I wish I'da
not done it. . . ."

"There was a good deal of this in your school? Kids fighting
with teachers and suspensions?"

"Lot of it, all the time. The kids don't like the teachers. . . .
Substitutes come in and they don't know how things is . . . the
kids take advantage of that . . . dare the substitute and then
when the substitute can't take it no more they'd be a fight. Lots
of fights in that school in the halls and bathrooms. . . ."

"What about this new school that you were transferred to?
Is there much fighting there?"

"Sure . . . alway's fightin'. Not me, though."

"Why is that?"

"I told my moms I wouldn't hit no more teachers. . . ."

"Do you have grass in your school . . . weed . . .?"

"You mean reefer?"

"Yes, marijuana."

"Sure . . . and heroin . . . all over the school. . . ."

"Do the kids buy it outside the school?"

"Outside the school? No, man, right in the school . . . the
kids themselves is pushin' stuff . . . like the students is pushin'
the stuff . . . the kids. . . ."

"Do you smoke reefers, Cyril . . .?"

"I smokes 'em. . . ."

"How did you happen to start?"

"I believe, follow the crowd 'cause everybody else start smokin'. They tol' me how it is, you know. . . ."

"What else was your crowd doing that you followed?"

"Then I started sniffin' glue . . . then I started snortin'."

"Snorting heroin?"

"Yeah, snortin' heroin . . . bothered my nose . . . got it sore so's it usta bleed, then I went for G. shots. . . ."

"Skin popping, is that what you mean?"

"For a little while, then I mained . . . I mained. . . ."

"Mainlined, shooting it into your vein . . .?"

He looked at me from beneath his drooping lids and said slowly: "I mainlined . . . man. . . ."

"Where did you get the money to pay for you heroin, Cyril?"

"I wuz sellin' dope . . . I wuz sellin' stuff, man."

"Is it easy to get a job pushing heroin?"

"If they knows you and they trusts you . . . it ain't hard. . . . They watches you for a little bit and then they knows you is a good kid. . . . They gives you a package like . . . they wuz like ten bags in it. I sell seven bags for them and I got three myself . . . and I kin sell that or shoot it. . . ."

"How long were you using before you started to push, Cyril?"

"Jest so long as I needed money to shoot . . . I couldn't git no more money . . . so I got to sell."

"How long before you became addicted . . .?"

"Two months . . . I got a Jones. . . ."

"How much were you using a day?"

"Ten or eleven bags a day. . . ."

"How much is that in money?"

"Them's two-dollar bags so I wuz using about twenty dollars a day . . . I didn't have no big habit. . . ."

"This was seven days a week you had to use?"

"Whatcha mean, man, seven days a week?"

"You had to have stuff every day . . . Saturday, Sunday. . . ."

"Sure . . . sure. . . ."

"So you had to have a hundred and forty dollars worth of

heroin a week. A hundred and forty dollars a week for a guy
your age is a lot of money. . . ."

"That's true . . . that's true. . . ."

"How old were you when you first started with heroin?"

"'Bout . . . twelve and a half. . . ."

"Are you still pushing, Cyril?"

"Sure. . . ."

"To whom do you sell? Do you have special customers?"

"Sell to anybody . . . anybody. . . ."

"You'd sell to a ten-year-old kid?"

"Sell to anybody who's got the money, man . . . anybody . . .
Mostly kids though. Grownups don't like to buy from a kid. . . ."

"Have you ever been arrested by the police for pushing?"

"Uh uh . . . never . . . never!"

"How come, Cyril?"

"I live in a block where there's a whole lot of pushers there,
you know. . . ."

"Does that mean the cops turn their backs on the sales?"

"Whatcha mean, man?"

"The cops don't care?"

"Oh, they cares but they can't keep up with it. They arrests
some guys sometimes. . . . Like once in a while they's a panic
on and they cleans up the street, but it ain't much that that
happens . . . ain't much. . . ."

"Cyril, are you on heroin right now?"

"Yes, sir. . . ."

"When did you take off last?"

"'Bout four hours ago."

"When are you going to need your next fix?"

"Jest soon's I quits you. . . ."

"Do you feel uncomfortable?"

"I ain't bothered yet none. . . ."

"Do you object to talking with me about yourself?"

"It don't bother me none, man. . . ."

"You realize what I do . . . did the Father tell you?"

"Yeah . . . he tol' me. . . . I believes in that . . . keep kids off junk. . . ."

"You do believe in that . . .?" I watched his half-speed responses. "How do you manage to continue your schooling now that you're addicted, Cyril?"

"I don't hardly go anyway. I'm kinda stoppin' . . . kinda stoppin'. See, I can't go but for three, four hours before I gotta take off. . . . See, I'm droppin' out. . . ."

"Do you like heroin, Cyril?"

"Not, not no more."

"Why not?"

"Costs too much money."

"Suppose you could get it free?"

"Whatcha mean free?"

"Suppose you didn't have to pay for it. Would you use it then?"

"Yeah . . . oh, yeah . . . I'd like it then. . . ."

"What is it you like about heroin, Cyril?"

"It's the high, man, the high. . . . You is way up there . . . way up."

Even with a youngster, the response to that question had become almost routine. "What is it that the high does for you, Cyril?"

He studied my face and frowned. "What the high does to me? Makes me feel good."

I felt that I had to back off because I couldn't devise a follow-up question. I asked: "Does your mother know that you're addicted?"

"Yeah, she know now . . . she come in onct and see'd me with a set of works. . . . She's tryin' to git me to go to a hospital . . . to git offa junk."

"Cyril, do you see yourself as being different than other kids now that you're a heroin addict?"

"No, not much . . . I ain't no different . . . most the kids around here is on stuff. . . ."

"But doesn't the need to get heroin . . . doesn't it make you more inclined to break the law, make you tougher, more crafty. You know, you have to steal . . . snatch purses. . . ."

"You steals, that's true . . . but I don't snatch purses. . . . I couldn't do that 'cause it would remind me of my mother . . . like them women they's got their welfare money in their pocketbooks and some junkie snatches it and runs and then that poor woman she'll jest sit there and cry on accounta how she gonna feed them kids. . . . No, I don't steal no pocketbooks, man . . . though I does steal. . . . But it's on accounta your habit . . . but mostly I pushes the stuff."

"And your friends, they have to steal and snatch purses in order to buy the stuff from you?"

"I don't ask 'em how they gits their money."

"In other words, it's just a business for you?"

He looked at me and asked: "Business? Ain't no business for me. . . . Some of 'em runs it as a business . . . always can git a job as a pusher, if they knows you and trusts you. . . . Ain't no business for me . . . I gotta feed my habit."

"How come you went on the stuff, Cyril?"

"Well, I got hooked up with the wrong crowd, I guesses . . . wanted to be like them."

"But why? Did they twist your arm, did they force you to take your first shot?"

"Wasn't nothin' like that. . . ."

"Then how come a kid can stick a needle in his veins?"

For the first time in our exchange, Cyril gave a rueful smile. "I wuz scared of needles . . . at first. . . . Then you want the high. You don't think no more about the needle."

"So you say you used because you were just following the crowd?" He nodded his head in agreement. "But you won't follow the crowd when it snatches purses."

"I'm no dude to do everythin' they does. . . ."

"Are you saying that you wanted to use heroin?"

"Yeah, must be that. . . ." He pondered his reply. "Must be

that . . . that's why I come here to Father Ralph. My moms she wants me to come . . . she wants me to go away. . . . Father Ralph he says you shoot stuff on accounta you got a problem. . . . Maybe I does but seems like to me I ain't . . . I jest was followin' the crowd. . . ."

"But does the crowd come in here to talk with Father Ralph about going into a treatment program?"

"Oh, no, man . . . they's out there in the sun on them benches. . . ."

"So, you see, Cyril doesn't follow the crowd blindly. Perhaps Father Ralph is right . . . maybe Cyril uses heroin as an escape, maybe Cyril does have a problem, maybe Cyril is going to have to ask himself that question and struggle to find an answer."

"I ain't decided yet. . . . I come here on accounta my moms . . . jest for my moms."

Cyril seemed to be a little less drowsy, something had changed in his manner. I asked him: "Aren't you scared of being picked up by the police for being a pusher?"

"Yeah . . . yeah, every time I picks up a bundle I's scared that they is gonna grab me. . . ."

"You're not suspicious that I'm a cop?"

He looked at me calmly and said: "If you wuz a cop you wouldn't all be talkin' to me so long. . . . You ain't no cop . . . man, you ain't no cop. . . . I knows that!"

"How many kids do you sell to, Cyril?"

"Whole lot . . . hundred at least. . . ."

"Do you give them a bag to get them started?"

"Give 'em a bag for nothin'? You'd be broke. . . . I don't give 'em nothin' for nothin'. . . ."

"There's no shortage of customers, then . . . paying customers?"

"I kin sell all the time . . . but I has my habit. Some of the connections who don't use they got money in their pockets, El Dorados, women, and nice clothes . . . they's big men, but they ain't got no habit to feed neither . . . but they's big men."

"You see the older addicts in your block all the time, Cyril, men and women who have been hooked for a long time? Usually they're shabby and on the nod, mumbling to themselves, soiling themselves in some cases. . . . Does it ever worry you that you might become like them?"

"I got a idea it's gonna happen if I goes on messin' with the stuff . . . but I likes the high." He fumbled in his pocket for a cigarette. I lighted it for him and asked: "Are you beginning to feel restless, Cyril?"

"Restless? No, I ain't. . . ."

"I asked because you're not as relaxed as you were before. How long will it be before you begin to feel discomfort?"

"Begin to feel tight soon . . . maybe thirty minutes . . . or so."

"Have you ever tried to stop . . . to kick, Cyril?"

"Lots of times. . . ."

"Why? You like the high you say . . . why?"

"On accounta my moms. . . . I kicked . . . git sick . . . you know, throws up real dry . . . you heaves . . . and your eyes they run and you git them cramps. Man, them pains you git. . . . Then somebody'll come along and see you is got a Jones and they'll straighten you. . . . Once you git your shot them pains they goes away like magic. I's kicked cold for moms . . . it don't work."

He was leaning forward now, his elbows on his knees, his head in his hands. "Cyril, is there any way to prevent the young people in your neighborhood from using dope?"

"Not that I knows of 'cept they stop puttin' it in the neighborhood. . . . That's all I could say. . . ."

"The people who give you your supply that you sell, do you know them?"

"Some of them. . . ."

"Do they live in the neighborhood?"

"Most of them don't live here. . . ."

"Are they Whites . . .?"

He looked at me with amazement. "Not here, they's all

Blacks." He took a drag from the cigarette. "Maybe they gits it from Whites, but not around here, man."

"They must have suppliers, too. . . ."

"I guesses so . . . I guesses so . . . but I don't know 'bout that."

"Somebody must be making an awful lot of money from dope. What's the stuff like that you're handling, Cyril?"

"Whatcha mean?"

"I mean the quality of the heroin?"

"It's all right for the money . . . it's all right for the money, you know."

"How can you tell if you've got good stuff or not?"

"You can't tell 'ceptin' when you uses it."

"Is that why kids die?"

"They gits greedy or they gits a bad dose or sometimes the dose is too good . . . too good."

"Does it scare you?" I watched him consider. He shrugged. "Does that scare you?"

"Hospital's only two blocks over. . . ." Slowly he rose from his chair and stretched. He looked down at me; I'd almost forgotten as I listened to him talk that he was an undersized teenager.

"Time for you to go, Cyril . . .?"

"It's gittin' there."

"Where will you go to take off now?"

"Home."

"Where's your stuff?"

A swift expression of suspicion appeared on his face. He looked at me, hesitated and then said: "I got it stashed."

"After this shot that you're going to take, when will you have to take your next one?"

"'Bout six-thirty . . . depends on how much I uses now. . . ."

"How much will you use?"

"Three, four bags . . . three, four. . . ."

"That'll keep you all night . . . or it'll keep you until you go to bed?"

"I don't go to bed."

"You don't go to bed?"

"I sits up in the chair lookin' at TV . . . I dozes in the chair . . . kinda sleeps that way. . . . Then I wakes up and walks around the rooms . . . I looks out the window and down to the street. Sometimes I goes down on to the block and walks around and gossips. . . . I don't go to bed. . . ."

"What does your mother say, Cyril?"

"You mean about my not goin' to bed? I keeps real quiet so's I don't wake her 'cause she works hard all the day. . . ."

"Has your mother seen you take off?"

He was offended and horrified by my question. His voice became sharp. "What you think I is, takin' off in froñt of my moms? I got respect for her, man."

"I beg your pardon. I didn't mean to insult you. . . ."

"I wouldn't ever do that, man . . . not that. . . ."

"Your mother must worry about you, Cyril."

"She do. . . . She says lately I's gittin' real thin . . . but you don't eat like you should when you is on junk. . . . She tries to make me eat and I lifts the fork and chews, but I ain't hungry . . . not really hungry."

"So she's right, you are losing weight? Do you suppose that you're kidding yourself, Cyril?"

"Whatcha mean, kiddin' myself?"

"Do you suppose that heroin has taken over your life? That it is directing everything you do, that it's increasing its demand on you a little more each day?"

He knitted his brow. "I's usin' more'n I usta . . . that's true. . . ." He wandered over to the window and stared out.

"And you'll keep using more, won't you?"

"I'm gonna stop. . . ."

"What makes you think so?"

"I'm gonna stop when I gits around to it. . . ."

"Did you ever consider that you may not get that chance?"

With his back to me I couldn't tell if he understood my

remark. He turned around slowly and repeated: "Everybody stops when they gits around to it." Cyril had changed. He was irritable now. He shifted his weight from side to side, his eyes avoided my face.

"You said you were shooting about twenty dollars worth of dope a day. Do you realize that's about seven thousand dollars a year? Does your mother make that much in a year?"

"Whatcha mean seven thousand a year?"

"That's what you're spending on dope. . . ."

"That's a lot of money. . . ."

"Be a pretty good salary for a fourteen-year-old. . . ." My own feelings were beginning to get in the way as I looked at the youngster. I asked: "What does the future hold for you, Cyril?"

He looked out the window. "Like them other ones out there . . . nothin'." And in one swift, unexpected movement, he went out the door.

I went and stood on the rectory stoop. In that crowded street there was no sign of Cyril.

16 *This Younger Brother was at odds not only with his family but with a culture; not a unique phenomenon. Why didn't he just break away? Why did he go to heroin? Increasingly, I have been finding young users like the Younger Brother. They share one common characteristic: they all seem to be incomplete eccentrics. Drug users are alienated people, but rarely are they eccentrics. It seems almost that total eccentricity implies great strength of character and purpose, a kind of individual affirmation of a life role. The Younger Brother and his kind lack this audacity, and yet curiously they hang just on the brink. They are like the chick inside the egg; they cannot strike that one blow that will shatter the shell.*

The Younger-Brother Syndrome

Peat pots, potting soil, black, organic fertilizer, and stacks upon stacks of empty planting flats. Silvio emerged from this background like a slender new growth. His face was lean and brown, seamed by wind and sun. He had agreed to the interview readily, seemingly indifferent to my assurances about protecting his identity.

"When I was on stuff everybody saw me and knew what I was, so now that I'm clean I should worry about who knows I was a dope fiend?" He sat on a wooden bench and lighted a cigarette. "Do you mind sitting out here and talking? We can go in the house if you like, but I enjoy this time of day . . . you know, the twilight first starting, the way those poplars shimmer, the sound of that wind in the corner of the shed."

I didn't have to be convinced about the setting. I sat down on a crate and asked: "You live here alone, Silvio?"

"Alone?" He shook his head. "I never think of it that way. I have three cats, two dogs, a de-scented skunk, a coon, and about three million starting plants." He puffed thoughtfully on his cigarette. "I'm surrounded by living things, things I work with and on, things that I have to put myself into in order for them to survive . . . and in their survival, I survive. . . . Sound pretty cloudy to you, like a watered down Thoreau?"

"Our friend, the doctor, had given me a little of your background, so I knew about your nursery."

"He should know. He was the one who finally put me straight on Silvio. Without him I'd be right back there floating."

"How long did you use heroin, Silvio?"

"I used it for the better part of twelve years . . . sometimes I was using tremendous amounts. . . ."

"How did you happen to start? Or will that bring back memories you'd sooner forget?"

He carefully put out his cigarette. "How do you think I fill my days, Mr. Cortina? I'm handling soil and living things, but my mind is forever sifting the past—my brother Gino, my father, my mother, my sisters, my two wives. Let's talk." He leaned back staring at the dusk. "How did I start? Very simply. I was running with the wrong crowd. I smoked pot; the crowd switched to pills and then to heroin. That's the simple progression. I don't buy the pussy-footing about marijuana being safer than alcohol . . . I don't buy the nonconnection with hard drugs. You get the right guy started on pot and sooner or later he'll end up on the spike . . . just like Silvio. Let's face it, it's not pot or hashish or coke or horse that's the problem . . . it's why you use any kind of chemical in the first place. So I'm not trying to be slick when I tell you how I started. . . ."

"I gather that you know why you used stuff? Many users and ex-users insist that they don't know why. . . ."

"Five years ago I would have told you the same thing . . . the same thing. . . . You know us, Mr. Cortina. How does that simple description of the addict go? Unmotivated, passive, and emotionally immature! Hundred percent correct!" Silvio sounded dogmatic. He struck me as trying to direct the interview, which was perfectly acceptable to me, but I wondered about him coming on so strong—this was not a frequent attribute of the ex-user.

"See, I'm a perfect example of the second son, the younger-brother syndrome."

I couldn't conceal a smile but Silvio's face was grave. He obviously felt my smile was out of place, for he said: "You know, even though words lose their meanings through the wrong use, sometimes, just sometimes they can be absolutely accurate. Because I'm telling you just where Silvio was coming from, exactly what bag . . . the younger-brother syndrome. . . . You'll catch it in me right now . . . pushy, competitive, needing to dominate, to impress, to gain attention. . . ."

I felt guilty about that smile, for there was a ring of enormous conviction in Silvio's voice—and perhaps a note of appeal to me. "What was your home life like, Silvio?"

"There were five children, my mother and father, and you know how most Italian families are, dozens of relatives. I had three sisters younger than I was and my big brother Gino. And believe me, Gino was my BIG brother in every way . . . you know what I mean."

"He was a distinct factor in the family?"

"Right . . . exactly. If I wanted to go to a dance or if I wanted to go and do anything I'd first clear it with Gino and then my father if I really wanted to go . . . if I didn't and went to my father first without consulting Gino there was no chance. My father was a milkman . . . do you know what I mean . . . I think they call them route salesmen. He'd go around in this truck and deliver milk to these apartments and stores. Now, with this kind of a job he had screwy hours. Like he'd leave the house at two o'clock in the morning and not get back until maybe three in the afternoon and then he'd have to go to bed. He made good money, on account of he was a good, hard-working guy . . . but you can see how Gino became so important. Besides, Gino was good in everything." Silvio flung his arms out as if he were including everything in the world as his brother's conquest. "He was physically big . . . make two out of me. He lifted weights, he boxed, he played football, baseball, he was an altar boy, he was an A student . . . Gino . . . what can I say? He was my brother. When he walked into the apartment, everything stopped. . . . It was a Gino world."

"What about Silvio?"

The thin, brown face creased into a smile. "If you use a grapefruit to symbolize Gino, you'd have to use a carrot seed—do you know how small they are?—for Silvio. He was no good at anything but he tried everything. He got a rupture trying to prove that he could heft weights like Gino. He got a broken nose trying to prove he could play football like Gino. He got his jawbone broken trying to box like Gino. He got suspended four times in school because he couldn't be the class leader like Gino so he became the class cut-up. And believe me, every step of the way of this pilgrimage, Gino was my Father Confessor . . . I couldn't do anything without big brother being right there with advice, direction, correction, criticism, complaint. . . ." He turned around and faced me, his voice suddenly hard. "The only thing that Silvio did that Gino couldn't was to stick a needle in his veins."

"Didn't your parents see how hard Gino was pushing you?"

"For them that was good . . . Gino was living up to the tradition. He was next in line . . . it's a dynasty. The oldest son, Gino, Jr. It was a good thing . . . it was his role."

"Did he have as much say to your sisters?"

"Sure. He knew every guy they ran around with. He'd talk to them. He let them know there was no funny business with my sisters, otherwise. . . ." As Silvio talked a slow smile spread across his face. "I'll tell you a funny thing. I had one sister,

Philomena. She wasn't pretty, and she was crazy for the boys
. . . what kids used to whisper about in corners, you know, certain
girls being hot stuff? Well, that was my middle sister Philomena.
. . . She had most of the family sex, I think. Anyway, she had
gotten hold of this little mild guy who was studying at night to
be an accountant. Nice little scared-of-his-life never-open-his-
mouth momma's boy. No doubt in my mind at all that Philomena
seduced him. . . . Gino found out and he went after Walter.
Walter joined the marines and got shipped to Korea to escape
Gino." Silvio laughed. "That's the first time I've laughed at a
memory, Mr. Cortina. I'm sure Philomena knew everything that
could be known about contraception."

"Your father seems conspicuously absent, Silvio."

"But he wasn't. . . . You see, Gino, he reported regularly to
my father. He worshipped my father. The better he did his job
as big brother the greater his emotional reward from my father."
Silvio lighted another cigarette. "You know, when you been in
and out of hospitals like I have you pick up a lot of knowledge
about the way people work. Family and blood is really a kind of
dynamite . . . it was for me. . . ."

"But didn't you ever talk to your father yourself?"

"Oh, sure, but not really talking . . . I never stuttered, you
know, but when I was with my father I stuttered. Figure that
out. He was a hard-working man. Six days a week he'd be out in
that milk truck. Sunday he'd have his bottle of wine. He'd play
his bocce ball. The relatives would come to the house. The priest
he'd come in. You'd smell the onions and the sweet basil, the
oil . . . and Gino would sit down at the table with the rest of the
male relatives, bigger than all of them, scholar and athlete . . .
and Silvio he'd nibble around the edges."

"And your mother?"

"God rest her soul, she was a saint. She knew that something
was wrong, but she belonged to the tradition, too. She'd cry when
I was in trouble in school. She'd tell me in Italian, 'why don't
you try to be like Gino . . .?' "

"Did you get into trouble with the police as a kid?"

"Never any real trouble. Oh, you know, the snotty wiseguy routine, mouth off at a cop and then duck over a back fence. Or shooting craps under a street light and then run away like hell. . . . But I never stole or shiplifted or anything like that."

"But you were having trouble in school, so I take it that you did play hookey."

"Yeah, I tried until Gino put the kibosh on that, too. . . . He talked to me about the disrespect I was bringing down on the family. He told me how hard my father worked and how hard my mother worked and what a good name our family had, and on and on like a sausage-grinder. Inside I was tighter than a cork forced into a small bottle. . . . Gino he took care of it, all right. He went to my father and told him that I was running with the wrong crowd, that the neighborhood was going to the dogs, and that we'd better move."

"And that was enough for your father to move?"

"Mr. Cortina, you don't understand the strength of family among Italians. Sure, my father talked to me. . . . He demanded to know what I was doing. . . . I can remember my face burning . . . and the words stuttering in my throat like I had hard beans rattling there. . . . Finally I burst out crying. He never put a hand on me. . . . I burst out crying. . . . He said: 'Go tell Gino, you sorry . . . be good now.' Two months later we moved out to a new neighborhood."

"Had the old neighborhood been so bad?"

Silvio moved his hands in dismissal. "I tell you one thing, there was no dope in that neighborhood . . . I never saw a junkie in all the fourteen years I lived there. . . . But in the new neighborhood . . . no apartments, one family and two family houses . . . more of a mixed neighborhood; people had some money . . . the school was different, too."

"But there you didn't have that example of Gino. He wasn't known there. It was a fresh beginning for him, too."

"Funny you put your finger on that," said Silvio, scraping

some soil from the table. "In some subconscious way I must've realized the same thing. I honest to God tried . . . but it must have been the pressure I put on myself. . . . I got so I couldn't read out loud . . . I really began to stutter badly. I couldn't keep up with the grades. Things began to go from bad to worse. No matter what Gino did now I began to really play hookey, to run around with a pretty wild bunch. They were smoking pot and I started . . . Tell you something, I didn't like pot . . . it made me dizzy, but it also made me laugh a lot . . . that was something I didn't do much of . . . laugh, that is. And another thing, I found that pot helped me to talk . . . I could get out to girls . . . what a junkie calls rapping. There was one girl in the bunch, a real pothead . . . her old man was a lawyer. She was crazy. Did the damndest things on a dare. Trying to get attention, you know. . . . You know how we rapped together? I'd run down my brother Gino and she'd run down her father."

"Well, somewhere along the line, Gino or your father must have gotten into the picture."

"Oh, sure . . . they were called down to the school. It got so bad I ran away from home . . . never very far . . . ran to an uncle or an aunt and then Gino would come and get me. He'd stand shaking his head . . . that was worse than if he took a swipe at me . . . worse. . . . Finally I was on pills, and they . . . the 'downs,' sleeping pills . . . became my thing. I was away, really away. God, it was like seeing everything through gauze. Gino, my father, my mother, the girls, home . . . all of it like seeing through gauze."

"Had you ever heard anything about how dangerous the barbiturates were?"

"Who cared? There's no thinking intellectually about danger or risk or consequences at those times. Jesus, I seen the time when I would have shot anything into my arm if it was white and would cook up. . . . That's a line of shit for a kid on the run, Mr. Cortina . . . you couldn't get near me that way. That's what Gino did. He got books and phamphlets on the dangers of

drugs. He lectured me. . . . I remember one night, late, very late
it must have been because my father was in the kitchen in his
heavy woolen shirt . . . in those days milkmen used to wear a
kind of leather vest to protect their chest in the cold . . . that
leather vest hanging on the chair, my mother crying her eyes
out, my sisters in the other room sitting around in a group . . .
see, they were women and had to be separated . . . and Gino
standing above me. It was a family council. I was high on pills
and I must have been pretty dopey, but I can remember this . . .
my father stood up and grabbed this vest and threw it at me. He
yelled, 'You're not my son . . . you're not my son. I cut you
away . . . I cut you away like you never lived. . . .' "

Silvio's hands were trembling. "How old were you then?"

"About sixteen . . . just sixteen. . . ."

"What happened?"

"I remember Gino picking up the vest and saying something
to my father in Italian . . . I can't imagine what it was because
my mother was sobbing so hard. My father grabbed the vest,
shouted at my sisters in the other room to go to bed, told my
mother to go to bed, and he went out, slamming the door so hard
the dishes rattled. There was just Gino and me left. And he
began to talk to me. . . . I can't remember what he said . . . I
can't. Sometime after that, maybe the next day for all I know,
Gino had me taken out of school and took me to the doctor. Now
I guess I must have been hooked on those pills because I was
in misery . . . I was in so much misery that the doctor gave me
something. Junk is bad when you come off of it but pills are
murder . . . at least they were murder for me. I had at least two
months of hell . . . sick inside and out . . . and all the time Gino
was there. . . . I was so ashamed, so guilty, and at the same time
I was trying to figure ways to get back at Gino. How do you like
that for screwed up psychology? The whole family watched me
now . . . I couldn't go down on the street without a bodyguard.
This went on, Mr. Cortina, for almost six months. And then one
day . . . I don't know, Gino was in college by this time, and my

mother was sick, I think . . . I got out of the house, went downtown and signed up for the army. I falsified my age and they
took me . . . they took me. I went home and faced Gino . . . I
was going to run him some kind of story at first about where I'd
been and finally I stuttered out what I'd done. His reaction was
completely different from what I expected. He thought it was a
good thing, and if he thought so, my father would think so . . .
so I became a soldier."

"Of course you didn't tell them you were a drug user?"

"I wasn't on the needle in those days, so how would they
know?"

"How long did you remain in the army?"

"I was in for one hitch."

"Army discipline bother you, Silvio?"

"At first it did. I guess I was discipline-shy all right. But it got
better for me as it went along. I got my equivalency diploma and
I learned about store keeping, and my stutter stopped."

By now the dusk had covered everything and Silvio switched
on a work lamp. "What about drug taking in the army?"

"Drugs were there if I wanted them, but somehow I didn't
go for them. I was drinking because I used to have my bad days
. . . real bad . . . you know . . . thinking about home. I was going
through all those changes. See, I never really went back home,
not because I couldn't but because I was ashamed to. Oh, I
could see things . . . you know I'd pick up a girl and sit telling
her about Gino and the family . . . after I was pretty well liquored
up. . . . See, Mr. Cortina, I knew I'd have to go back there. That
was my bag . . . I had somehow to go back there . . . I had to or
I was doomed . . . at least that's what I thought. . . . So in 1956
I came out of the army and I went home. So help me God, the
first thing I did when I got in the neighborhood was to smoke a
joint . . . and I didn't like pot . . . I smoked a joint so I'd be able
to talk. There was the family, like nothing had changed. My
father was a little distant at first, but the uniform and the fact
that I'd grown up a little . . . that bridged a few chasms . . . and

all the relatives, the whole bag . . . and I was stuttering. . . ."

"And Gino?"

"Gino was out of college and was a policeman. . . ."

"A policeman? Were you surprised at that?"

"In a way, I suppose I was. I had such crazy ideas about my brother, though . . . I thought he might become the Pope or something. . . . You know, he could have been anything he wanted, I thought. . . . But you know, even then, after so many years away and now being the center of all that attention, I felt uncomfortable and out of place. Then Gino walked into the room and all the attention shifted to him. Just like nothing had ever happened."

"Had you any plans for your future?"

"I thought in a vague way that I might open a store or something like that . . . a small business of my own. . . . Gino asked me the same thing right off the bat. Keep me 'occupied' he said. He offered me money to help me get started. So I opened a corner grocery store, specializing in Italian food. For about two years I tried this. . . . Then Gino made a terrific advance . . . he was made a lieutenant. That day was the day I took my first shot of heroin. . . ." Silvio sighed deeply, wearily. "It's getting pretty dark out here. Let's go inside before the mosquitoes eat us alive."

Inside was a simple, well-furnished bachelor set-up. "You said you had two wives."

"Yes, my first wife was a neighborhood girl, the girl who used to tell me about her lawyer father, the one I used to run down Gino to, remember? By now she was on junk, so we were birds of a feather. Thank God we never had any kids. . . ."

"After that first shot, you obviously continued. . . ."

"Oh, certainly . . . with all of the usual junkie rationale. It's never going to control me . . . I could handle it . . . all the crap. I'd take money out of the cash register for my shot and put a note inside saying I owed six bucks, because Gino would check the records. It was a farce. The man who worked for me used to watch me go out and then come back . . . he could see the alteration. . . ."

"And your wife?"

"Finally she got so bad, so outrageous, that it even made me stop . . . I think she even made my family get off my back. On account of she was whoring. My wife, their in-law! I thought Gino would go crazy because here was a case that he couldn't control. I enjoyed watching his frustration. There wasn't anything he could do, but it kept him so busy he couldn't spend time watching me use."

"Quite a situation. . . ."

Silvio brought out a couple of bottles of beer. "Oh, Christ, it was a mess . . . and I was enjoying it, Mr. Cortina . . . I was enjoying it . . . watching my family being dragged through the mud. What kind of a man could I be?"

"Were you using heavily?"

"Ten bags a day. I used to buy it at wholesale prices to be able to afford it. Because, you see, I kept on working."

"Why didn't you keep your wife supplied?"

"I would have. I did for a while. But she got very suspicious of me because of the family . . . Gino being a cop and her old man a lawyer. Pretty screwed up."

"What happened to her?"

Slowly he poured the beer into his glass. "She was found dead in a hallway one night, an overdose. Gino said she'd gotten some poison . . . I don't think so . . . I don't think so. . . . I think somebody gave her a bag of uncut stuff. It was pure. Too good. Her system couldn't take it and she O.D'd."

"Are you saying that it was deliberate . . .?"

"I've thought about it a lot . . . a lot . . . I think there was something fishy about her death."

"What happened then?"

"Same thing as always happens . . . Gino stepped in and I went to the U.S. Government hospital for the cure. . . ."

"How long were you there?"

He sipped his beer. "Four months. I came back by bus. Soon as that bus hit the turnpike I wanted a shot. It hadn't been in my mind, but when I saw the lights of the city . . . I knew I was going to cop . . . I scored and I was off all over again. . . ."

"How did you live?"

"I worked as long as I could. I always worked. You know, the average person doesn't realize that junkies do work as long as they can. I did everything, but I was shooting a lot and I couldn't keep up with my habit. . . . I started to push but the connection couldn't trust me . . . so they turned me off. . . . Then I met this woman . . . she was a school teacher . . . she was ten years older than me . . . we got married . . . she taught English. She was a good woman. . . ."

"Did you stop using after you met her?"

"No, I tried to keep what I was doing from her but it didn't work. She found out. But she loved me, so . . . she held on to me. . . . She even paid for my stuff. Dolly was like that, she wanted me. . . ."

"Couldn't have been much of a relationship for her, could it, Silvio?"

"When you come right down to it, you wouldn't think so, if you know anything about hypes, but she got something out of it. Then one night I was really high . . . I knew I shoulda stayed home, but the same thing was in my craw about the family and I went back to the house. My mother had been sick . . . one of my sisters had written to me. . . . Like I say, I was really floating. . . . There was Gino smoking out in the front . . . he'd gotten heavier . . . he never said a word to me . . . he let fly with two punches and he plastered me into that street. The blood was running down my face and all I could smell was sweet basil and olive oil. See, I didn't know but my mother had just died. Now I was loaded and I had a set of works in my pocket. That could have sent me to jail, but when I got to the hospital Gino had gotten rid of the works . . . after all, he was a cop. . . ."

"And your wife?"

"Gino got to her. They sent me away again. Dolly would come and visit me every week . . . send me money and clothes. She fussed over me . . . if I ever lacked attention in my life, she made up for it. I came out. She had bought a house up in the country. There was a vegetable stand and a small greenhouse. . . . I stayed off stuff for nineteen months. I was clean, clean as I'd never been, Mr. Cortina. . . ." He lowered his voice. "I found I liked that work. Working with plants, being outdoors alone all the time. To see my hands make something grow. . . ."

"And it must have been wonderful for your wife as well."

His thin face twisted in a wry smile. "It wasn't. . . . Silvio off stuff was a different man from Silvio on stuff . . . I was strong, had my own ideas, I was independent . . . I don't know how to explain." He hesitated and stammered for a moment. It was the first time he had done so in the exchange. "God help me, because she was a good woman, I didn't need her . . . I wasn't doing for her what she needed . . . she needed me to be helpless, to be looked after. . . . That sounds pretty ruthless, doesn't it . . .? We broke up . . . we broke up. Dolly went back to the city, went back to teaching, and I stayed there alone and worked. . . . I stayed there for another nine months and it got into my head that I was afraid to even visit the city. And I began to think I was staying off in the country just because I couldn't trust myself in the city, that Gino had been right all these years, Silvio really needed a keeper. I finally, like any junkie, gamed myself into thinking that I was going to prove to everybody, but most of all Gino, that I was man enough to go back to the city and take care of myself."

"But you said you enjoyed your work, the country, being alone. . . ."

"But I also told you about the younger-brother syndrome. You know, it all swirled up, strength, weakness, shame, guilt, all a God-damned stew. . . ."

"But, man, you had been dependent on King Heroin."

Silvio said sharply: "King Heroin, that's shit. Shit. . . . That's a popular phrase glamorizing heroin used by writers and soft mouths. Nothing kingly about heroin . . . sounds good but its still shit. . . . When you're hooked you're not thinking of phrases, you're just scheming for that next shot. . . ."

"You went back to dope?"

"Of course, of course. . . . For two more years I shot . . . a bum . . . a bum . . . Gino was right . . . he was right . . . he'd always been right. Every time I cooked a shot I'd mumble 'that son of a bitch Gino.' And every time I shot I put myself one step closer to my own suicide. . . ."

"Didn't you get picked up?"

"No, you learn to be clever. . . . I was dealing now . . . I was dealing, I was even making money . . . I was watching my habit. . . ."

"That was a real difference in your addiction pattern, wasn't it?"

"It really was, it was a new layer. Now, I used to get around to where they were cutting up the stuff. I made a good connection with another guy, a guy I had known when I was a kid in the old neighborhood. He had connections with the syndicate I guess. But we worked it up real good . . . until one night I went to his place. . . . It was no fancy place . . . the hallway stank . . . walls were wet . . . real crummy place. . . . I went up the stairs, and you learn to walk softly, you get so suspicious. . . . I heard a door open, somebody cleared his throat, and I ducked into a kind of small hall that led into a couple of flats . . . the light in the hallway wasn't too good . . . but I recognized him as he came along stuffing an envelope in his breast pocket . . . it was my brother Gino. Hhhe . . . hhhhe . . . hhhhad jjjjjjust cccccome outa mmmmy cccccconnection's fffflat." Silvio suddenly got up and walked to the screen door and stood looking into the darkness, trying to control himself. At last he came back to the table, offered me a cigarette, and lighted one for himself. "I left after Gino was gone . . . and I cooked myself up a terrific shot. I was loaded. I must've been out ten or twelve hours. . . . When I

come to, I couldn't figure whether I'd dreamed all of that or not
. . . I couldn't believe . . . and then in my overcoat I found the
roll of bills I had in the lining, the money I was carrying to
pay for the load of stuff . . . I hadn't been dreaming. It really
had happened. . . ."

"And then?"

"I went to a police station and turned myself in with a set of
works in one hand and a couple of bags. They booked me and
threw me in a cell. I took cold turkey. In a day or so Gino
showed up. The police have a terrific grapevine to protect their
own, you know. He came into the cell. He stood there looking
down at me, disgust on his face. He said: 'Poppa was right.
You're not his son. You're not part of this family. You killed
your mother . . . you'll always kill everything around you. You're
no good. You're a bum. You're not my brother. I cut you off, I
cut you off, Silvio.'

"I watched his face. He still had the power to make me
crumble inside. I started to say something about watching him
take a pay-off . . . I thought I'd start to stutter, and then, so help
me God, Mr. Cortina, I deliberately put on a stutter when I said:
'YYYYYYYYou're rrrrright, GGGGGGino.' "

There was a scratching at the screen door. Silvio went and
opened it and brought in a small, deformed skunk. "I was going
to say so much to Gino but. . . ." He fondled the animal. "I
know he tried to get the charge dropped, but I pleaded guilty.
I wanted to be put away. I got two years . . . and when I came
out, I went into our friend, the doctor's, program. . . . I really
owe my life to the doctor. For the first time I began to understand. . . . I'm not trying to cop-out and say it was Gino's fault
. . . it was my fault . . . my fault with surrounding circumstances.
. . . See this little beast . . . he's deformed . . . he got broken up
in a trap. I found him. With care and affection, he's come
around. . . . Can you say the same for a man, Mr. Cortina? Can
you say the same for a man?"

17 *Concern. It is a key word, concept, and abiding pre-occupation of the drug addict; it has an almost mystical connotation for him. One gathers that "concern" is something that must overtake the addict, overwhelm him. It is someone's concern for him that he feels will prove so powerful that he will be able to overcome his alienation, his chronic distrust, his suspiciousness, his everlasting sense of failure, his dependency. It is this need for concern that makes the addict receptive to treatment. The Prophet was one of many like this.*

The Prophet

Standing in the cold, I caught my first, fleeting glimpse of the prophet as he gracefully melted away with my suitcase. He had mingled with the passengers discharged from the airport bus, as we clustered together in the midnight storm, trying in the poor light to identify our baggage. I saw and lost my bag in the same instant; it hovered in front of me and then disappeared. But I recalled the long, long overcoat, the gaunt face, the reddish hair where the moisture trembled. He looked like a prophet.

Months and months later, after I had despaired of the airport bus management indemnifying me for my stolen luggage, the incident was brought freshly to my mind: for unless memory was playing me false, the prophet was seated in front of me. In the improved lighting, he appeared much as he had in that gloomy street, except he was younger, more emaciated, a sort of attenuated Greco-esque holy man. As a gesture to the fitness of my memory, I was interviewing Alan Curassos in a church-sponsored narcotics treatment facility. He ran his slender fingers

223

through his red hair. He was telling me about a user's day. I did not, at least not then, obtrude our previous meeting on him.

"It's a day or a night . . . or maybe a passage of time is the best way to put it . . . because you see, day and night get kind of mixed together for the dope addict. . . . So much depends on what you're doin' to get your money for the junk." He spoke carefully, softly, in a low key.

"What were you doing to get yours?" I asked as seriously as I could.

There must have been something revealed in my tone despite all of my care, for he looked at me critically. "What I had to."

"And what were some of the things you had to do?"

"Shopliftin', petty thefts, breakin' and enterin' . . . things like that. Again it depends. You need your stuff every day. Like your habit, it don't take a day off on Sunday. . . . Now this is maybe the Lord's day, but for the dope fiend it's the opposite. . . . Very few stores are open, the junkie gets up real tight, maybe strung out, and that's when he does somethin' stupid, somethin' that gets him into trouble." He clasped his arms together. "Drugstores, small grocery stores, maybe a doctor's office . . . a poor box in a church. . . . That's how I'm here, Mr. Cortina."

"What do you mean?"

"I tried to rifle a poor box in the church next door. . . ."

"And you were caught?"

"Yeah . . . but it was a trap. . . ." He smiled; his teeth, like those of many addicts, were bad. "Father Anselm uses it as bait . . . it rings an alarm inside . . . he comes out and you're caught."

"Isn't there a good bit of hazard for him? What happens if a guy is real strung out and he attacks him?"

In those soft, low-keyed tones, Alan Curassos said: "Most dope addicts ain't violent people . . . the newspapers and television and movies make you think so, but we ain't. . . . When he came up to me, I tried to game my way out . . . I had just had a quarter in my hand, like I was droppin' it in the box . . . but see, he had that box made so you had trouble openin' it, just enough trouble to give him time to catch you."

"What did he do then?"

"He invited me over here. I figgered he was holdin' me until a cop would come . . . but he just walked away ahead of me up the church aisle. . . . You know, you're suspicious anyway and when a guy, a guy in a robe, he turns his back on you then you're twice as suspicious . . . what kind of a game is he runnin'? So I looked around real good . . . plenty of places to spy on you in some churches . . . you know, confession boxes, niches where some statues are standin'. I couldn't figger it out. See, I'm gettin' sick, too. I'm gettin' real panicky inside. But this priest he keeps walkin' on . . . so I'm not really on the cap, so I quick ducks down the aisle toward the back . . . I look out on the street . . . there's a cop floatin' along . . . just happens to be floatin' along. So I goes back inside. There's the priest way up at the altar steps, just waitin' . . . so I'm trapped. I'm trapped. . . . And anyway, I ain't feelin' so hot . . . I'm real rundown . . . and by now I'm sick. If they blew at me I woulda crumpled anyway. So I goes up with him. He brings me over here. A doctor comes in and I get some methadone. . . . The whole thing is a special bag . . . you know what I mean, a special bag. . . ."

"A hoax, you mean . . .? This is Father Anselm's way of working with drug abusers . . .?"

"Yeah, this is the bag he comes from. . . ."

"How come you never heard about it? Addicts have a terrific grapevine. . . ."

"It ain't so terrific. . . . Addicts they cluster together but they ain't communicatin' all that good . . . it's always for a junkie, 'where's he comin' from?' See, he's so gosh-darn suspicious. . . ."

The "gosh-darn" made me grin. "So you had never heard about Father Anselm's special approach to the drug problem?"

"No, this ain't my neighborhood, but I used all of mine up . . . you know, you use up neighborhoods like anythin' else, like toothpastes, it runs out. Like you was askin' about my day. . . .

Well, there's only so many times I can beat out this department store or that one or this supermarket or that one . . . then they're layin' for you . . . so you gotta shift. After a while you're right back beatin' out the old places. That's how I didn't know about that loaded poor box. See, this is a junkie neighborhood . . . lotta strange, freaky kids floatin' around . . . maybe Hippies or Yippies or somethin' . . . like they ain't like me. . . . So in any case this neighborhood it slid way down. So Father Anselm he figgers he'll beat 'em at their own. The church people get together . . . they're bein' robbed blind anyway . . . this way they figger maybe, just maybe they got a chance. So this Anselm, oh, what a man with a phrase . . . he'll game you outa anythin'. Good thing he's a priest and not a hype . . . he'da been the best gamer ever lived. . . . He talks the local cops into cooperatin' . . . he talks a coupla doctors, and the local assemblyman . . . he gets some social workers to chip in their time . . . he's got a clinic. . . ."

"What about the neighborhood?"

"Look, everybody around here is so gosh-darn self conscious about drugs now it's a hard place for a hype to make out. See, like this priest," Alan stammered with excitement, "like this priest, he's made a therapeutic climate outa the neighborhood. How's that grab you? Ain't that a game if you ever heard one?"

"How long have you been on stuff, Alan?"

"Fourteen years . . . on and off. You know, you get busted and you're off for your bust but when you come out you go back. . . . I started on stuff when I was about sixteen. Before that I used pot and pills . . . but the pills they wasn't for me. . . . They make you too outrageous. Me anyway. Now pot was okay, but I got to be a pothead. Then one day I'm in a car . . . I think I am . . . you know, all in my head . . . and I'm gonna crash on accounta I see this truck comin' at me, so I busts into a store window . . . all in my head, you understand . . . everythin' except the forty-six stitches they took in my body from the glass carvin' me up. So like pot ain't for me no more and I go to junk.

When I'm first on junk, brother, like I know that's it for me. Like Romeo and Juliet, that's what stuff is for Alan Curassos. . . ."

"How many times have you been busted, Alan?"

He shook his head. "I can't recall for sure. . . . He muttered a rough count to himself. "Eighteen or twenty times at least."

"And how many times in the joint?"

"Three times . . . I can't go back no more . . . no more, otherwise I'm up for good. . . ."

"How old are you, Alan?"

"Twenty-nine."

"And how long have you been off heroin?"

"Eleven months and four days."

I quickly calculated. Our encounter, when he had stolen my suitcase, had occurred just about fourteen months before. I related the old score I had with him.

"Yeah, that musta been me, Mr. Cortina. . . . I'm sorry it happened to you . . . I don't remember one bag from another, you realize . . . I was down real low just about then and I usta hang around the airport terminal to see what was up . . . I was gettin' outrageous then. . . ."

"Just for my own curiosity, Alan, did you open these bags?"

"Sure. You'd be surprised what people has stashed away . . . you know, real respectable people with fancy bags with all kinds of stuff inside: pills, pot . . . they even had a racket on heroin comin' into the country this way. Sure, swipe a bag with heroin in it. . . ."

"You must have had a grand time with my bag; it contained my notes on heroin abuse."

"I don't remember. Maybe I never opened yours on accounta I was pretty crushed down about that time. I musta fenced it."

"I hope you got a decent price . . . it was a good bag," I said ruefully.

"Chances are I didn't. . . . Fence'll try and get everythin' for nothin'. In those days I took what I could get 'cause I was so down . . . other days I'd shop around for somebody else to buy it. You know, there's pretty much a goin' price for most things . . . like most times if you done business with a guy before you know pretty much what he's gonna give you. . . ."

"I'm sorry I interrupted you with that personal reference. You were telling me about this set-up of Father Anselm's. How come you stuck it out here? You've kicked lots of times, you've been in jail, you probably have taken hospital cures . . . how come?"

"He cares for me."

"He cares for you? Haven't others cared for you as well?"

That long face was grave with thought. "My mother did . . . in a way . . . and some others, too, I must be honest. But not like the Father. . . . He's got concern for me so that I want that concern. You know what I mean, Mr. Cortina? Like that concern he feels for me I don't have to earn it first, it's there, offered to me right off the bat. That's what's different. . . . Like he gives it to me without any kinda conditions. I was always a loner . . . I had my room, my TV set . . . I'd beat the streets from ten o'clock in the mornin' until maybe midnight . . . always hustlin'. Afterwards I'd come home, fix, and go to sleep. You don't eat . . . you just run yourself from bag to bag, until you gets so tired . . . so dead tired you don't care about nothin'. . . ."

"Concern, you say?"

"Nobody is ever gonna do anythin' about the dope fiend until they look out for his feelin's. Like drug addicts are very sensitive people. . . . And what with all the different situations and changes that a junkie goes through he gets even more sensitive. It gets pretty mixed up. . . . The addict he hides himself away behind junk and he does terrible things to get junk, which makes him hide himself away even more so he can't take in how terrible he is. . . . You can't believe anybody is concerned for you, 'cause you hate yourself so, you got no concern for yourself. You catch that? But this priest he had concern for me."

"And that made you give up heroin?"

"Give up heroin? Who knows . . . I'm tryin', Mr. Cortina. . . . After fourteen years what do you give up easy? Lots a things build up even around having a dog for fourteen years. You never open a door in the same way if you've had a dog for fourteen years. . . . So what about a guy like me on junk for fourteen years? Have I given up heroin?"

"Why did you start in the first place, Alan?"

He shook his head, his gaze inward. "I'm tryin' to find out myself. I'm not runnin' the game. I could say to you 'curiosity.' That's the regular answer for some hypes, or for the real gamester, he'll make up a real good story. . . . See, you gotta first get down with knowin' that you just don't use heroin unless you got a problem. . . . You gotta have time to get down with yourself, to look at yourself . . . and then not run away. Not run away. . . . An addict is always lookin' at himself but he's always doin' it through heroin . . . like he's got on shades. The big trick is to look at yourself for real. I don't know why, Mr. Cortina . . . but I'm lookin'. . . . There's little things . . . like I couldn't ever stand up in front of a bunch of kids and read right. . . . Now, who ever heard of that as bein' like a small reason for shootin' stuff? Now I was always tall and skinny, like I never could fight or play ball good. In my school you had to come out and face guys. . . . I was always scared . . . so I learns to put on a image . . . you know, I'm real impossible tough. . . . But I can't read. . . . Like a little bit gets added each day to everythin'. . . . You know, a little bit of sand driftin' each day covered up the Sphinx. . . . Now my family, my old man, he was a truckman . . . a drinker, a bull for broads. . . . I wasn't his kind of son . . . I couldn't measure up. . . . My mother, we had somethin' goin', but whether it was somethin' because my old man was like he was or because it was for real. . . . I was tall and skinny . . . I was really a loner. . . . Why did I use junk? First, why did I use pills, pot? And really, what was there, if there was anythin' that could have stopped me from usin' before I ever started. That's the question, Mr. Cortina . . . what was there that coulda stopped me before I started?"

That ascetic face had spots of red on the cheekbones, flush with excitement. "Why is that the question, Alan?"

"Because that's the only total cure for narcotic addiction . . . stop it before it starts. . . . Now for me I gotta round on it . . . I gotta come back the other way. See, I ain't really old yet but I'm gettin' there . . . and like Father Anselm says, we got to catch these kids around here. Whenever you can catch a kid and talk him out of usin' you realize yourself what maybe was your lack. . . ."

"You said before that there were a number of young people in this neighborhood. You said they were 'freaky'?"

"They are, believe me, they are. They been to college. . . . They take the clothes they come here in and swap for old jerky rags . . . like they gotta put on a image . . . they gotta taste life. Don't take no bath, don't take no rules . . . how do you talk to them . . .? They're runnin'. Now when they come from that bag they don't want no priest like Father Anselm rappin' with them. They had that, they thinks . . . no preachin', no advice. . . ." Alan smiled and said with admiration: "But get that gamester of a priest . . . he's got a guy like Alan Curassos . . . he never got through the tenth grade. . . . Nothin' these kids can talk about with junk that I ain't been through . . . and I let 'em know that they ain't so God-damned important that I'm gonna wipe their asses each time they scrape the cellar like their mothers and fathers would. . . . I get carried away, Mr. Cortina."

"It must be very different, this drug scene, from the one you came out of, Alan?"

"Different? Nah . . . the same thing . . . neglect, Mr. Cortina . . . neglect. . . . The junkie from my crowd is the same as these kids. He can't make it with the squares, and because he can't make it he's got a personal crusade. Like me, why didn't I come out and fight what was wrong in my life? I didn't, I hid away mumblin', 'Alan, he ain't gonna play that stupid game.' Same as these kids . . . they ain't gonna play on accounta the older generation they can't understand them, they loused up the world. . . . All true . . . but Jesus, do you prove it by going psycho yourself? It's a cop-out . . . a cop-out . . . like I'm gonna hold my breath until my face turns blue until you gives me my way. . . ." He looked up at me. "I sound like a parent, huh? They used to be very puzzlin' for me in the beginnin', these kids. Made me close up just like when I was in school . . . these kids, you know, so much younger than me. . . . Then I'd get up real tight, but that Father Anselm, he could see. . . . What a feel he's got. . . . Pretty soon, he'd be down there with me. That concern, like I said before. Then I'd pick myself up . . . I'd rap with them again . . . the war, philosophy . . . some French writers. . . . The war for me was Alan Curassos; philosophy, how do I get my next fix; and French writers was them dirty books I seen as a kid. But I listened to 'em. I got up real tight. . . . Only one place I could break through . . . dope. . . . There I was a graduate . . . dope . . . dope. . . ."

"Do they come back, do they listen?"

"Some do, when they feel you have concern . . . concern you just gives to them without strings like concern was given to me, Mr. Cortina. . . . They're kids like most junkies are really kids, and that world out there ain't so God-damned lovely . . . it's gamin' all the time. . . . But like Father Anselm says . . . somebody's got to try . . . why not you, Alan Curassos . . .? Sound crazy to you Mr. Cortina, huh?"

I recalled that drenching, cold rain, that lank figure stealing off with my property . . . my immediate description of him . . . prophet.